Liferay 6.x Portal Enterprise Intranets Cookbook

Over 60 hands-on recipes to help you efficiently create
complex and highly personalized enterprise intranet
solutions with Liferay Portal 6.x CE

Piotr Filipowicz

Katarzyna Ziółkowska

BIRMINGHAM - MUMBAI

Liferay 6.x Portal Enterprise Intranets Cookbook

First published: June 2015

Production reference: 1260515

Published by Packt Publishing Ltd.
Livery Place
35 Livery Street
Birmingham B3 2PB, UK.

ISBN 978-1-78216-428-9

www.packtpub.com

Credits

Authors

Piotr Filipowicz

Katarzyna Ziółkowska

Reviewers

Pierpaolo Cira

Zoltán Fiala

Giuseppe Urso

Acquisition Editor

Llewellyn Rozario

Content Development Editor

Merwyn D'souza

Technical Editor

Vijin Boricha

Copy Editors

Relin Hedly

Karuna Narayanan

Project Coordinator

Neha Bhatnagar

Proofreaders

Stephen Copestake

Safis Editing

Indexer

Mariammal Chettiyar

Graphic

Abhinash Sahu

Production Coordinator

Conidon Miranda

Cover Work

Conidon Miranda

About the Authors

Piotr Filipowicz is a Liferay architect and senior developer at eo Networks S.A., Poland. He is an expert in content management systems (CMS). Piotr currently holds the position of team leader in a group involved in developing Liferay-based software. His accomplishments in enhancing and creating various Liferay components are evident from his various successful implementations. His experience and knowledge are supported by certificates such as Liferay Portal Administrator, Sun Certified Web Component Developer for the Java Platform, and Sun Certified Programmer for the Java 2 platform. Piotr is also one of the founders of the www. liferay-guru.com blog, which contains a lot of information on Liferay and the CMS world.

Since 2002, he has created various kinds of IT systems, ranging from desktop applications to CMS applications, supporting large banking and financial systems. His main area of interest is web applications. Piotr uses Java and J2EE technologies on a daily basis, but he is open to learning other technologies and solutions. He holds a master's degree in software systems from Bialystok University of Technology, Poland.

I would like to thank my family for their patience and tolerance during all those hours that I spent in front of my laptop writing this book. Many thanks to my lovely wife, Eliza, for her patience and support towards her always busy husband. This book wouldn't have been possible without her help. I would also like to thank my parents and parents-in-law for their love, understanding, and encouragement.

Last but not least, I sincerely thank all my team members at work for the support and valuable information I got from them. Also, many thanks and appreciation to the entire Packt Publishing team and our reviewers, Giuseppe Urso, Pierpaolo Cira, and Zoltán Fiala, for their constructive criticism and help in enhancing my writing style. It was a great pleasure working with them.

Katarzyna Ziółkowska is employed at eo Networks S.A., Poland, as an IT analyst. She is designated as the head of the analysis section. Her work focuses on government websites and intranets, corporate business applications and websites. Katarzyna is a specialist in content management systems. She has been working with Liferay Portal since 2010 and has designed various products based on this technology using not only its default functionalities, but also expanding them and designing entirely new modules.

Since 2003, her main areas of interest revolved around business process modeling, managing business requirements, understanding user's needs, and designing usable systems. She is also one of the authors who writes on `www.liferay-guru.com`, where she shares her experience and knowledge on Liferay Portal CMS.

Katarzyna is certified in Prince 2 Foundation, Agile Project Management Foundation, and is a Professional Scrum Master. She is also a member of International Institute of Business Analysis. She holds a master's degree in arts in Russian philology from the University of Warsaw, Faculty of Applied Linguistics, Poland.

I would like to thank Krzyś for his unwavering support and understanding. I would also like to thank Szymon Gołębiewski; he is the reason my adventure with Liferay began.

About the Reviewers

Pierpaolo Cira is a Liferay Certified Professional Developer and has been working as a software developer, software architect, and system integrator since 2001.

He has been involved in many e-business, knowledge management, e-learning e-tourism, brand monitoring, and business intelligence research projects at the University of Salento in collaboration with companies such as Oracle and IBM on several research projects. He also collaborated on the design and development of the first implementation of the OMG SBVR editing tool. He reviewed *Android Apps with Eclipse, O. Cinar, Apress* 2012. He has been working on several enterprise web applications based on Liferay Portal and Alfresco ECM, such as web portals, intranets, and document management systems, for public administrations and big companies.

Currently, he is a consultant on Liferay Portal and Big Data technologies and solutions.

He can be found on Twitter at `@pierpaci`.

I would like to thank my family and my wife for their support and patience.

Zoltán Fiala leads a competence center for software development at adesso AG in Hamburg, Germany. He holds a PhD in web engineering from Dresden University of Technology and has worked as a SharePoint and Liferay architect and project manager for several IT consultancy firms in the past. Zoltán has significant experience in the design and development of web content management and portal solutions. For more information on Zoltán, refer to `http://www.z-fiala.net`.

Giuseppe Urso is a software engineer with 10 years of extensive working experience in the design and agile development of service-oriented applications and distributed systems based on Java SE and Java EE. He works in the IT industry as a senior systems architect and Java developer, handling responsibilities involving architecture design and the implementation of several large-scale projects based on Alfresco ECM and Liferay Portal. His major areas of expertise include Amazon Web Services (AWS), Elastic Compute Cloud (EC2) technologies, and Message-oriented Middleware. Giuseppe earned his master's degree in computer engineering at the University of Salento, Italy. He is a licensed engineer and member of the Professional Engineers Association called "Ordine degli Ingegneri della Provincia di Lecce". He is an Alfresco certified administrator and committer on the Alfresco-SDK project. As an open source enthusiast, he runs a personal blog at www.giuseppeurso.eu, where he writes articles and useful guidelines on Java, Alfresco, Liferay, and practices of GNU/Linux systems administration.

www.PacktPub.com

Support files, eBooks, discount offers, and more

For support files and downloads related to your book, please visit www.PacktPub.com.

Did you know that Packt offers eBook versions of every book published, with PDF and ePub files available? You can upgrade to the eBook version at www.PacktPub.com and as a print book customer, you are entitled to a discount on the eBook copy. Get in touch with us at service@packtpub.com for more details.

At www.PacktPub.com, you can also read a collection of free technical articles, sign up for a range of free newsletters and receive exclusive discounts and offers on Packt books and eBooks.

https://www2.packtpub.com/books/subscription/packtlib

Do you need instant solutions to your IT questions? PacktLib is Packt's online digital book library. Here, you can search, access, and read Packt's entire library of books.

Why Subscribe?

- ▶ Fully searchable across every book published by Packt
- ▶ Copy and paste, print, and bookmark content
- ▶ On demand and accessible via a web browser

Free Access for Packt account holders

If you have an account with Packt at www.PacktPub.com, you can use this to access PacktLib today and view 9 entirely free books. Simply use your login credentials for immediate access.

Table of Contents

Preface

Liferay Portal is one of the most popular portal frameworks on the market, offering many out-of-the-box features to build, install, configure, and customize portal or intranet solutions. The main purpose of this book is to help you successfully build the intranet system by providing step-by-step recipes. You will be taken on a tour that covers the most common issues when dealing with Liferay. In every recipe, you will find solutions to real-life problems with many explanations. The chapters are organized and ordered in such a way that they will help you go through the intranet configuration step by step.

What this book covers

Chapter 1, Installation and Basic Configuration, provides you with a basic knowledge on how to install and run Liferay on Apache Tomcat. It also teaches you how to create a new basic portlet.

Chapter 2, Authentication and Registration Process, describes several useful ways to correctly configure authentication. It helps you learn about integration with a popular single sign-on mechanism: CAS and communicate it with LDAP.

Chapter 3, Working with a Liferay User / User Group / Organization, introduces you to the concept of user, user group, and organization management in Liferay. It also explains how to use them together.

Chapter 4, Liferay Site Configuration, offers many useful recipes connected with site configuration, such as creating sites, their templates, and enabling staging and versioning.

Chapter 5, Roles and Permissions, discusses roles and permissions and the possibility to build a scalable grid of roles depending on the user's position in the company.

Chapter 6, Documents and Media in Liferay, introduces you to portlet, which provides media and document file storage. This chapter also offers you advice on how to correctly configure it. You will also learn how to integrate documents and media portlet with Amazon S3 storage.

Chapter 7, *Working with Content*, talks about the most common CMS feature, that is, web content management.

Chapter 8, *Search and Content Presentation Tools*, introduces various functionalities connected with the searching and content presentation tool. This chapter also talks about tagging and categorizing assets.

Chapter 9, *Liferay Workflow Capability*, teaches you how to apply workflow on assets and deploy the Kaleo Web portlet.

Chapter 10, *Collaboration Tools*, provides recipes in collaboration with Wiki, blogs, message boards, calendars, and so on.

Chapter 11, *Quick Tricks and Advanced Knowledge*, contains a set of various recipes, which help you to perform specific tasks for your intranet sites. There are many subjects, for example, enabling SMTP, configuring clustered environment, or using the Liferay service bus.

Chapter 12, *Basic Performance Tuning*, offers information on scalable infrastructure and discusses most common problems associated with performance.

What you need for this book

This book uses Liferay Portal version 6.2 with the following settings:

- MySQL database 5.5
- Java JRE and JDK 7
- Apache Ant with 1.7 version or later
- Apache Maven 3.0.5 or later
- Liferay Portal 6.2 bundled with Tomcat 7
- Eclipse IDE Indigo or later

All recipes are based on the Linux operating system, but all of them can be done (with only a little effort) on Windows or iOS.

Who this book is for

If you are a Java developer or administrator with a technical background and want to install and configure Liferay Portal as an enterprise intranet, this is the book for you. In short, reusable recipes help you realize business goals as working features in Liferay. This book will also give you useful hints on how to easily improve the default functionality of the system and its performance.

Sections

In this book, you will find several headings that appear frequently (Getting ready, How to do it, How it works, There's more, and See also).

To give clear instructions on how to complete a recipe, we use these sections as follows:

Getting ready

This section tells you what to expect in the recipe, and describes how to set up any software or any preliminary settings required for the recipe.

How to do it...

This section contains the steps required to follow the recipe.

How it works...

This section usually consists of a detailed explanation of what happened in the previous section.

There's more...

This section consists of additional information about the recipe in order to make the reader more knowledgeable about the recipe.

See also

This section provides helpful links to other useful information for the recipe.

Conventions

In this book, you will find a number of text styles that distinguish between different kinds of information. Here are some examples of these styles and an explanation of their meaning.

Code words in text, database table names, folder names, filenames, file extensions, pathnames, dummy URLs, user input, and Twitter handles are shown as follows: "We can include other contexts through the use of the `include` directive."

A block of code is set as follows:

```
<div>$curEntry.getTitle($locale)</div>
<div>$curEntry.getDescription($locale)</div>
<div>
  $taglibLiferay.assetTagsSummary(
    $curEntry.getClassName(), $curEntry.getClassPK(),
    null, null, $renderResponse.createRenderURL()
  )
</div>
```

When we wish to draw your attention to a particular part of a code block, the relevant lines or items are set in bold:

```
</timer-notification>
  <reassignments>
    <user>
      <email-address>
        test@liferay.com
      </email-address>
    </user>
  </reassignments>
</timer-actions>
```

Any command-line input or output is written as follows:

```
$ java -version
java version "1.7.0_45"
Java(TM) SE Runtime Environment (build 1.7.0_45-b18)
Java HotSpot(TM) 64-Bit Server VM (build 24.45-b08, mixed mode).
```

New terms and **important words** are shown in bold. Words that you see on the screen, for example, in menus or dialog boxes, appear in the text like this: "Click on the **Control Panel** link."

 Warnings or important notes appear in a box like this.

 Tips and tricks appear like this.

Reader feedback

Feedback from our readers is always welcome. Let us know what you think about this book—what you liked or disliked. Reader feedback is important for us as it helps us develop titles that you will really get the most out of.

To send us general feedback, simply e-mail `feedback@packtpub.com`, and mention the book's title in the subject of your message.

If there is a topic that you have expertise in and you are interested in either writing or contributing to a book, see our author guide at `www.packtpub.com/authors`.

Customer support

Now that you are the proud owner of a Packt book, we have a number of things to help you to get the most from your purchase.

Downloading the example code

You can download the example code files from your account at `http://www.packtpub.com` for all the Packt Publishing books you have purchased. If you purchased this book elsewhere, you can visit `http://www.packtpub.com/support` and register to have the files e-mailed directly to you.

Errata

Although we have taken every care to ensure the accuracy of our content, mistakes do happen. If you find a mistake in one of our books—maybe a mistake in the text or the code—we would be grateful if you could report this to us. By doing so, you can save other readers from frustration and help us improve subsequent versions of this book. If you find any errata, please report them by visiting `http://www.packtpub.com/submit-errata`, selecting your book, clicking on the **Errata Submission Form** link, and entering the details of your errata. Once your errata are verified, your submission will be accepted and the errata will be uploaded to our website or added to any list of existing errata under the Errata section of that title.

To view the previously submitted errata, go to `https://www.packtpub.com/books/content/support` and enter the name of the book in the search field. The required information will appear under the **Errata** section.

Piracy

Piracy of copyrighted material on the Internet is an ongoing problem across all media. At Packt, we take the protection of our copyright and licenses very seriously. If you come across any illegal copies of our works in any form on the Internet, please provide us with the location address or website name immediately so that we can pursue a remedy.

Please contact us at `copyright@packtpub.com` with a link to the suspected pirated material.

We appreciate your help in protecting our authors and our ability to bring you valuable content.

Questions

If you have a problem with any aspect of this book, you can contact us at `questions@packtpub.com`, and we will do our best to address the problem.

1
Installation and Basic Configuration

In this chapter, we will cover the following topics:

- ▸ Quick running Liferay on a Tomcat bundle
- ▸ The Liferay setup wizard and first login
- ▸ Setting up the developer's environment
- ▸ Creating a custom portlet

Introduction

Liferay is the market's leading provider of open source portal solutions. It provides a solid platform to serve our site to all clients. It is difficult to say what Liferay is. On the one hand, Liferay is a great content-management system, but on the other hand, it provides many tools for collaboration and communication between users. It can also be a social platform with many functionalities, such as wall, message board, chat, and many others. Furthermore, it is a portlet container that is JSR-168 and JSR-286 compliant. **Java Specification Requests (JSRs)** describes final specifications for the Java platform. A portlet is a small web application that produces fragments of HTML code that are aggregated into a portal. JSR-168 and JSR-286 specifications standardize how portlets interact with portlet containers. These specifications also describe a standard application programming interface for Java portlet development. In other words, Liferay is only responsible for aggregating the set of portlets that are to appear on any particular page. This approach gives users a great tool to organize and customize portlets in order to build whole portals, social platforms, or intranets. Within Liferay, a portal is composed of a number of portlets, which are self-contained interactive elements that are written to a particular standard. A number of publications describe Liferay's advantages. In this book, we will try to delve deeper into Liferay's architecture and its functionalities.

The primary purpose of this chapter is to give you an insight about Liferay's installation and management with basic configuration. We realize that there are many ways to download, compile, install, and run Liferay Portal. Our main purpose is to provide some clear and basic information about the starting package on which we will rely and work. This chapter explains the main processes that are performed on every compiling action or on every startup action.

Liferay Portal is distributed in two different editions:

> **Liferay Portal Community Edition (CE)**: This is a free and open source version of Liferay

> **Liferay Portal Enterprise Edition (EE)**: This is a commercial offering that has Liferay engineers, support, and services

This book is based on the Liferay Portal Community Edition (CE) version with the newest release, which is 6.2.

To start the journey with Liferay, there are a few starting points that contain a lot of useful information, which are as follows:

URL	Description
`http://www.liferay.com/`	Official Liferay site
`http://www.liferay.com/downloads/liferay-portal/available-releases`	Place with available releases
`http://www.liferay.com/documentation/liferay-portal/6.2/user-guide` and `https://dev.liferay.com/`	User guides and documentation
`http://svn.liferay.com/repos/public/portal`	Old-fashion repository of Liferay code. > **Login**: Enter guest in this field > **Password**: This field is to be left empty
`https://github.com/liferay/liferay-portal/tree/6.2.x`	[Recommended] GitHub repository

Liferay introduced 7.0 version, which will be released on September 2015. Do not check out Liferay sources from the trunk. There are many changes between 6.2 and the trunk version. In the 7.0 version, Liferay will provide OSGi integration and many new features. These new features help users and developers achieve a whole bunch of out-of-the-box functionalities (for instance, Elasticsearch as a search server based on the Lucene framework).

Quick running Liferay on a Tomcat bundle

The simplest way to run Liferay is to download a specific bundle from the Liferay official site. A Liferay bundle is just a compressed archive that contains all that is needed to host the Liferay Portal. A bundle consists of a Java-based application server and the deployed Liferay Portal core application. Liferay provides these bundle runtimes with different application servers (that is, Tomcat, JBoss, Geronimo, and so on) so that you can use any one based on your choice. This method is recommended for people who just want to run Liferay Portal, look at its functionalities, and configure their site using the GUI. In this recipe, you will learn the art of setting up Liferay on Tomcat and the MySQL database engine.

Getting ready

First, make sure that JRE or JDK is properly installed. Type the following command line:

```
$ java -version
```

The result should be similar to this:

```
$ java -version
java version "1.7.0_45"
Java(TM) SE Runtime Environment (build 1.7.0_45-b18)
Java HotSpot(TM) 64-Bit Server VM (build 24.45-b08, mixed mode).
```

Also, check out the Java SDK version. Liferay recommends Java 7 or later.

Moreover, determine whether the MySQL server installation is done:

```
$ mysql --version
```

As a result, the actual installed version should be displayed. Here is an example:

```
mysql  Ver 14.14 Distrib 5.5.34, for debian-linux-gnu (x86_64)
```

Also, check out the MySQL version. We recommend 5.5 version or later.

How to do it...

In order to run Liferay on a Tomcat bundle, follow these steps:

1. Create a database with the name `lportal`:

    ```
    CREATE DATABASE lportal CHARACTER SET utf8 COLLATE
    utf8_general_ci;
    grant all privileges on lportal.* to '{USERNAME}'@'%'
    identified by 'PASSWORD';
    ```

    Make sure that the MySQL user has permissions to create tables.

2. Download the correct Liferay version on the Tomcat bundle from `http://www.liferay.com/downloads/liferay-portal/available-releases`.

3. Unzip the downloaded archive.

4. Go to the extracted folder `liferay-portal-6.2-ce-ga2`. This path will be called `${liferay.home}` folder.

5. Go to the `${liferay.home}` folder and create a file called `portal-ext.properties`.

6. Edit `portal-ext.properties` and set the database properties:

   ```
   jdbc.default.driverClassName=com.mysql.jdbc.Driver
   jdbc.default.url=jdbc:mysql://localhost/lportal?useUnicode=true&ch
   aracterEncoding=UTF-8&useFastDateParsing=false
   jdbc.default.username={USERNAME}
   jdbc.default.password={PASSWORD}
   ```

7. Find the Tomcat folder and go to the `tomcat-7.0.42/bin/` location.

8. Run the `./startup.sh` script (`startup.bat` for Windows OS) and look into the `tomcat-7.0.42/logs/catalina.out` log.

9. In a browser, type `http://localhost:8080` location. By default, Tomcat listens on port 8080. It should render the Liferay setup wizard by default. This wizard will ask for basic information, such as, portal name, default language, and administrator user details.

How it works...

Running the Liferay Portal from a prepared bundle is quite an easy task to accomplish. However, it is worth knowing what exactly happens when Tomcat is being started. Take a brief look at the `catalina.out` log and try to examine it line by line.

Loading the configuration descriptor

The first thing is to deploy `ROOT.xml`. In our `catalina.out` file, there is a line present, which is shown as follows:

```
INFO: Deploying configuration descriptor /home/piotr/liferay-portal-
6.2-ce-ga2/tomcat-7.0.42/conf/Catalina/localhost/ROOT.xml
```

It means that the configuration file turns on the `crossContext` attribute in Tomcat 7. This setting is required because Liferay is a portlet container. Hence, it is an application that should have access to other applications called portlets. The Apache Tomcat documentation says:

> *"Set to true if you want calls within this application to ServletContext.getContext() to successfully return a request dispatcher for other web applications running on this virtual host."*

Loading system properties and portal properties

The next few lines of the logfile show portal properties and system properties that are loaded from specific locations:

```
Loading jar:file:/home/piotr/liferay-portal-6.2-ce-ga2/tomcat-7.0.42/
webapps/ROOT/WEB-INF/lib/portal-impl.jar!/system.properties
Loading jar:file:/home/piotr/liferay-portal-6.2-ce-ga2/tomcat-7.0.42/
webapps/ROOT/WEB-INF/lib/portal-impl.jar!/system.properties
Loading jar:file:/home/piotr/liferay-portal-6.2-ce-ga2/tomcat-7.0.42/
webapps/ROOT/WEB-INF/lib/portal-impl.jar!/portal.properties
Loading file:/home/piotr/liferay-portal-6.2-ce-ga2/portal-ext.
properties
```

The main configuration file for Liferay Portal is `portal.properties`, which contains a detailed explanation about the properties that it defines. There are at least three possible ways to override `portal.properties`. There is a functionality to put `portal-ext.properties` in the ext plugin, in the `${liferay.home}` directory, or in `portal-setup-wizard.properties`. But which file is the most important? The answer is placed in `portal.properties` file. The default read order is `portal.properties`, `portal-bundle.properties`, `portal-ext.properties`, and then `portal-setup-wizard.properties`:

```
include-and-override=portal-bundle.properties
include-and-override=${liferay.home}/portal-bundle.properties
include-and-override=portal-ext.properties
include-and-override=${liferay.home}/portal-ext.properties
include-and-override=portal-setup-wizard.properties
include-and-override=${liferay.home}/portal-setup-
wizard.properties
```

Detecting the database and database dialect

The next step is to recognize the database's dialect:

```
12:35:47,469 INFO   [localhost-startStop-1][DialectDetector:71]
Determine dialect for MySQL 5
12:35:47,504 INFO   [localhost-startStop-1][DialectDetector:136] Found
dialect org.hibernate.dialect.MySQLDialect
```

Liferay supports many database engines, such as DB2, Derby, Hypersonic, Ingres, MySQL, Oracle, P6Spy, PostgreSQL, and Sybase. The default database is Hypersonic, which stores all data in the `${liferay.home}/data/hsql/lportal` directory. This is a good option for developers who want to run JUnit tests, which modify data by testing the persistence layer or business process.

On every restart, Liferay tries to get the build number (Liferay version) from the `Release_` table. If this table doesn't exist, it calls `ReleaseLocalService.createTablesAndPopulate()`.

If it is not possible to get the build number, Liferay logs the following information:

```
WARN  [localhost-startStop-1] [ReleaseLocalServiceImpl:171] Table
'lportal.Release_' doesn't exist
```

The `createTablesAndPopulate` method runs following scripts:

- `liferay-portal/sql/portal-tables.sql`: This creates the required tables
- `liferay-portal/sql/portal-data-common.sql`: This adds the default data
- `liferay-portal/sql/portal-data-counter.sql`: This inits the unique key generator
- `liferay-portal/sql/portal-data-release.sql`: This sets the release date
- `liferay-portal/sql/indexes.sql`: This adds database indexes
- `liferay-portal/sql/sequences.sql`: By default, this file is empty.

Apart from creating tables and populating data, Liferay triggers the `VerifyProcess` mechanism. This process will run on every startup to verify and fix any integrity problems found in the database. This is the perfect place for developers to add custom code to check the integrity of specific cases.

Starting the autodeploy scanner and deploying plugins

The last step is initializing the autodeploy and the hotdeploy listeners. In general, these mechanisms install all the plugins into the Tomcat container and register them as portlets, hooks, themes, and so on. In particular, there are at least three deploying approaches: sandbox deploy, autodeploy, and hotdeploy.

 By default, Liferay uses the autodeploy and hotdeploy listeners. In fact, sandbox can currently deploy only themes and portlets.

The autodeploy mechanism is responsible for listening on a specific directory to install on-the-fly new plugins and copying them into the Tomcat hotdeploy process. A definition of that directory is placed in `portal.properties`, and by default, it is in the `deploy` folder:

```
auto.deploy.deploy.dir=${liferay.home}/deploy
```

Every type of plugin has its own autodeploy mechanism. This mechanism runs all the necessary steps to install it correctly in the Liferay container. In simple terms, the autodeploy mechanism generates the `web.xml` file and adds the required libraries to specific plugins. Definitions of these classes are placed in the `portal.properties` file with an `auto.deploy.*` prefix. Each class extends `BaseAutoDeployListener`.

The second process, hotdeploy, is responsible for registering plugins in Liferay. There are many steps, such as creating database tables, setting preferences, registering Spring application contexts, and so on. Of course, each step depends on the type of plugin. In `portal.properties`, there are definitions for each type of class:

```
hot.deploy.listeners=
com.liferay.portal.deploy.hot.PluginPackageHotDeployListener,
com.liferay.portal.deploy.hot.SpringHotDeployListener,
com.liferay.portal.deploy.hot.ServletContextListenerHotDeployListe
ner,
com.liferay.portal.deploy.hot.ExtHotDeployListener,
com.liferay.portal.deploy.hot.HookHotDeployListener,
com.liferay.portal.deploy.hot.JSONWebServiceHotDeployListener,
com.liferay.portal.deploy.hot.LayoutTemplateHotDeployListener,
com.liferay.portal.deploy.hot.PortletHotDeployListener,
com.liferay.portal.deploy.hot.SocialHotDeployListener,
com.liferay.portal.deploy.hot.ThemeHotDeployListener,
com.liferay.portal.deploy.hot.ThemeLoaderHotDeployListener,
com.liferay.portal.deploy.hot.MessagingHotDeployListener
```

 In the deployment process, the Liferay deployer modifies the `web.xml` file, adds specific dependencies, and packs it again. Ensure that you do not copy the WAR file directly to the Tomcat `webapps` folder. If you do so, the plugin will not work.

There's more...

Often, enterprises have an established Java EE infrastructure upon which they would like to install Liferay. You must consider also the enterprise's security policies. These policies sometimes prevent the download and installation of the Tomcat bundle into a location of your choice. In this situation, a bundle will not suffice, and you have to manually install Liferay from its WAR archive into an already existing Apache Tomcat application server.

There are six steps to achieve this goal. They are as follows:

1. Copy specific JAR files and dependencies to the Tomcat global `lib` folder, `$TOMCAT_HOME/lib/ext`.

2. Enable `crossContext` by adding the `ROOT.xml` file to the `$TOMCAT_HOME/conf/Catalina/localhost` folder.

3. Set custom `$JAVA_OPTS` parameters in the `$TOMCAT_HOME/bin/setenv.sh` file:

    ```
    JAVA_OPTS="$JAVA_OPTS -Dfile.encoding=UTF8 -Dorg.apache.catalina.
    loader.WebappClassLoader.ENABLE_CLEAR_REFERENCES=false -Duser.
    timezone=GMT -Xmx1024m -XX:MaxPermSize=256m"
    ```

4. Update the `common.loader` property located in `$TOMCAT_HOME/conf/catalina.properties` with the following lines of code:

   ```
   common.loader=${catalina.base}/lib,${catalina.base}/lib/*.
   jar,${catalina.home}/lib,${catalina.home}/lib/*.jar,${catalina.
   home}/lib/ext,${catalina.home}/lib/ext/*.jar
   ```

5. Specify the URI encoding as UTF-8 in `$TOMCAT_HOME/conf/server.xml` as follows:

   ```
   <Connector port="8080" protocol="HTTP/1.1"
     connectionTimeout="20000"
     redirectPort="8443" URIEncoding="UTF-8" />
   ```

6. Deploy Liferay Portal using Tomcat manager or manually put the WAR archive into the `$TOMCAT_HOME/webapps` folder. The WAR file is available at `http://www.liferay.com/downloads/liferay-portal/available-releases#additional-versions`.

 More detailed instructions of how to install Liferay on the Tomcat server are available on the official Liferay documentation at `https://www.liferay.com/documentation/liferay-portal/6.2/user-guide/-/ai/installing-liferay-on-tomcat-3`.

See also

For information about running Liferay on the clustered environment, refer to the *Clustering Liferay Portal* recipe in *Chapter 11, Quick Tricks and Advanced Knowledge*, and the *Scalable infrastructure* recipe in *Chapter 12, Basic Performance Tuning*. For information about setting the developer's environment, refer to the next recipe.

The Liferay setup wizard and first login

After successfully running Liferay on the Apache Tomcat server, the system asks users to fill some necessary information to complete the setup wizard. This is only a single screen with basic fields, such as administrator name or portal name.

How to do it...

After running Liferay for the first time, the Liferay platform displays the basic configuration form, which looks like this:

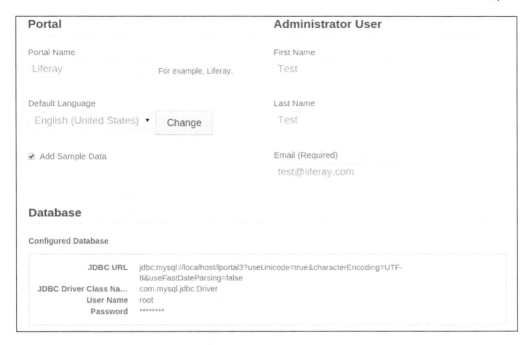

To finish installation, it is necessary to fill in the preceding form as follows:

1. Provide details about **Portal**:

   ❑ **Portal Name**: This is the name of the website, for instance, Enterprise Intranets

   ❑ **Default Language**: This helps in choosing the default language of the portal

   ❑ **Add Sample Date**: This decides to populate the portal with default data

2. Provide details about **Administrator User**:

   ❑ **First Name** and **Last Name**

   ❑ **E-mail** address

3. Choose the database engine (optional). In the previous recipe, we set properties with a MySql connection.

4. Confirm the form.

5. Click on the **Go to My Portal** button.

6. Click on the **I agree** button on the **Terms of Use** screen.

7. Fill in the **Password Reminder** form and confirm the form.

   After confirming the **Password Reminder** form, you will be able to see and use the main Liferay navigation tools.

Follow these steps to navigate to **Control Panel**:

1. Click on the **Admin** button located on the dockbar menu.
2. Click on the **Control Panel** link.

How it works...

After running Liferay for the first time, Liferay needs basic information about the portal, database, and administrator. The database connection was set in `portal-ext.properties`, and it was described in the previous recipe.

All data which was provided on the portal wizard was stored in the `${liferay.home}/portal-setup-wizard.properties` file. The most important settings are described in the following table:

Property name	Description
`admin.email.from.name`	This describes the name of the administrator.
`admin.email.from.address`	This is the e-mail address of the administrator.
`liferay.home`	This is the path to the `${liferay.home}` directory. This property is very important and must be set.
`setup.wizard.enabled`	This flag disables the setup wizard.

After logging in, the user is able to see navigation tools available for authorized users only. Here are the navigation tools:

▶ The dockbar menu is located under the top screen edge. The dockbar consist of three buttons:

□ The **Admin** button that allows us to navigate to the **Site Administration** and **Control Panel** sections

□ The **My Sites** button that lists links to sites that the user is a member of

□ The button with *user name* and *surname* that allows us to navigate to user's profile (**My Profile**), user's dashboard (**My Dashboard**), user's account (**My Account**), and also allows the user to log out

▶ The fast edition menu is located near the left edge of the screen. The menu consists of the following icons:

□ The **Add** icon that allows us to add a new page, a new application to the page, or new content

□ The **Edit** icon that allows us to edit the settings of the currently viewed page

- ❏ The **Preview** icon that allows us to view the currently viewed page in different resolutions and devices
- ❏ The **Edit Controls** icon that allows us to hide or show controls of portlets

There's more...

In internal projects such as intranets, user accounts most often are created and managed in external systems, for instance, LDAP. Therefore, it is unnecessary (and sometimes even unacceptable) to allow users to manage their authentication data (for instance, to set a password-reminder query) or ask them to agree to terms of use directly within Liferay. In Liferay, there are many properties that can help customize the first login action, a few of which are as follows:

Property name	Description
`terms.of.use.required=false`	This turns off the terms of use
`terms.of.use.journal.article.group.id` and `terms.of.use.journal.article.id`	This specifies the group ID and article ID that will be displayed as the terms of use
`users.reminder.queries.enabled=false`	This disables the reminder query functionality

See also

- ▶ For information on adding new users and defining roles and permissions, refer to the *Adding a new user* recipe in *Chapter 3, Working with Liferay User / User Group / Organization*
- ▶ *Creating and configuring roles* and *Assigning user roles* recipes in *Chapter 5, Roles and Permissions*
- ▶ For information on the default login page, refer to the *Overriding the default login page with the administrator defined page* recipe in *Chapter 2, Authentication and Registration Process*

Setting up the developer's environment

Many developers want to customize Liferay Portal to fit it to a client's requirements. Also, in this book, there will be a number of examples of code, so the setting environment is an important step to start with. Liferay mentions that there are two types of development and two ways to get sources:

- ▶ **GitHub**: For contributors
- ▶ **sourceforge.net**: For non-contributors

For the purpose of this book, it is enough to use the non-contributors version only.

Getting ready

The minimal requirements to use Liferay Portal are **Java Development Kit** (**JDK**), Apache Ant with 1.7 version or later, and Eclipse IDE Indigo or later. Make sure that the installation is successful by typing the following lines of code:

```
$ ant -version
Apache Ant(TM) version 1.8.2 compiled on May 18 2012


$ java -version
java version "1.7.0_45"
Java(TM) SE Runtime Environment (build 1.7.0_45-b18)
Java HotSpot(TM) 64-Bit Server VM (build 24.45-b08, mixed mode)
```

How to do it...

This recipe is divided into three sections. The first section contains a description of preparatory activities such as downloading Liferay sources or unpacking them. The second one provides a description about the required configuration. The last section focuses on compiling all Liferay sources and deploying them into Apache Tomcat server.

Import sources to the Eclipse IDE

The first step is importing Liferay sources as a project in our IDE. These steps are based on Eclipse IDE. To achieve this, follow these steps:

1. In `${liferay.home}`, create a `workspace` folder.

2. Go to `http://sourceforge.net/projects/lportal/files/Liferay%20 Portal/` and choose the folder with the newest 6.x version. Next, find the file with the prefix `liferay-portal-src-*` and download it.

3. Unpack this file into the `workspace` folder.

4. Import this project to Eclipse IDE by going to **File | Import | General | Existing Projects into Workspace** and click on the **Next** button. On the next screen, select **Select root directory** and point to the folder with Liferay sources, which is `${liferay.home}/workspace/liferay-portal-src-${VERSION}`. To complete this task, click on the **Finish** button.

5. After this step, it is necessary to create a folder called `/portal-web/test/ functional` in the project. This actions resolves a warning in the Eclipse IDE with the following message: **Build path entry is missing: Liferay-portal-src.6.2-ce-ga2/ portal-web/test/functional**.

Override app.server.properties

To be compatible with the existing Tomcat, which is placed in the `${liferay.home}/tomcat-7.0.42` folder, change the `app.server.parent.dir` properties. To achieve this, follow these steps:

1. Create `app.server.${username}.properties` in the main folder of the project, which is `${liferay.home}/workspace/liferay-portal-src-${VERSION}`.

2. Override `Server directory` properties and set a new value:

   `app.server.parent.dir=${project.dir}/../../`

   It could also be an absolute path to Tomcat's parent folder.

   The `${liferay.home}` folder should have the following hierarchy:

```
.
|-data
|---document_library
|---hsql
|---lucene
|-deploy
|-license
|-logs
|-tomcat-7.0.42
|---bin
|---conf
|---lib
|---logs
|---temp
|---webapps
|-workspace
|---liferay-portal-src-6.2-ce-ga2
```

Compile and deploy

Go to `{$liferay.home}/workspace/liferay-portal-src-${VERSION}` and compile all Liferay sources using the `ant all` target in a command line.

 In this book, we will use a console approach to compile, deploy, and so on. Liferay provides Eclipse with Liferay IDE. For proper understanding, we will use command line as the main tool.

How it works

It could be a source of criticism that Liferay is managed by Apache Ant instead of Maven, Gradle, or other build-automation tools. As a matter of fact, the Apache Ant tool is sufficient to manage and compile the Liferay core. If someone wants to use Maven, they are free to use it in custom portlets. Liferay offers many archetypes to help create Maven projects for multiple plugins.

Let's take a closer look at the project in Eclipse IDE. There are many folders that contain huge bunches of packages. Let's examine the most important folders with regard to Liferay architecture:

Folder name	Description
Definitions	This contains the `dtd` and `xsd` definitions, for instance, the `portlet.xml` definition or the `service.xml` definition.
portal-impl	This is the central core of the portal. It implements all the interfaces that are exposed in global `lib`. Also, it contains model definitions. Never put `portal-impl` anywhere other than where it came from.
portal-service	This provides the interfaces' definitions, which can be used in custom implementation, for instance hooks, portlets, themes, and so on.
util-bridges	This contains bridges and utilities, which can be helpful to implement custom portlets, such as AlloyPortlet, BSFPortlet, MVCPortlet, and so on.
portal-web	This contains the web application root, which has all the configuration files and view tier.

Let's get back to the compile command, `ant all`. What exactly happened here? Portal has its own runtime structure. It provides ready-to-use bundles with Tomcat, JBoss, or other application servers. It gives a tool that can build a runtime bundle. In the main `build.xml` Ant file, there is a definition of Ant target `https://ant.apache.org/manual/targets.html`:

```
<target name="all">
  <antcall target="clean" />
  <antcall target="start" />
  <antcall target="deploy" />
</target>
```

The building process consists of three parts: clean, start, and deploy.

Clean process

The `ant clean` command performs the following steps:

- It cleans Java classes under the following folders: `classes, portal-service, util-bridges, util-java, util-slf4j, util-taglib, portal-impl, portal-pacl, osgi/bootrstap, portal-web` and `sql`
- It deletes files with mask `*.ear, *.jar, *.war,` and `*.zip`
- It cleans the `work, temp,` and `logs` Tomcat folders and removes the `*-hook.xml` and `*-portlet.xml` files from the `/conf/Catalina/localhost` directory

There are some more steps that clean or delete many configuration files depending on the application server. To understand the processes used in this book, it is not important to know every step and deep cleaning process.

Start process

The `ant start` target invokes the following tasks:

- It runs the compile target that compiles sources under the `portal-service, util-bridges, util-java, util-slf4j, util-taglib, portal-impl, portal-pacl,` and `osgi/bootstrap` folders
- It builds a database and rebuilds the hypersonic database
- It builds themes under the `portal-impl` folder
- It calls the `jar` target that generates JAR's and WAR of the Liferay core

Deploy process

This target is strictly dependent on the application server. In general, this build deploys applications into a specific servlet container or application server. Furthermore, this build creates the required folders or files under `${liferay.home}`. The folders that this build creates are as follows:

- The `deploy` folder for the hotdeploy process
- The `data` folder, which contains binary data, such as document library, Jackrabbit, HSQLDB, or Lucene
- The `ROOT.xml` context configuration file in `${app.server.dir}/conf/Catalina/localhost/` and many other tasks depending on the application server

There's more...

As mentioned earlier, it is possible to create a full bundle without manually downloading Tomcat or other application server. There are only two steps in order to achieve this goal:

- ▶ Invoke the `ant -buildfile build-dist.xml unzip-tomcat` task
- ▶ Invoke the `ant all` command

It is possible to deploy Liferay on a different application server. There is a whole range of commands that do this:

```
ant -buildfile build-dist.xml build-dist-geronimo
ant -buildfile build-dist.xml build-dist-glassfish
ant -buildfile build-dist.xml build-dist-jboss
ant -buildfile build-dist.xml build-dist-jboss-eap
ant -buildfile build-dist.xml build-dist-jetty
ant -buildfile build-dist.xml build-dist-jonas
ant -buildfile build-dist.xml build-dist-resin
ant -buildfile build-dist.xml build-dist-tcat
ant -buildfile build-dist.xml build-dist-tomcat
```

Creating a custom portlet

This recipe is very specific, because it shows how to generate a new portlet, install it on Liferay, and import it to the Eclipse IDE. Many recipes from this book assume that the user knows how to generate a new plugin, such as portlet, hook, or web. We will show you how to generate a new portlet using Apache Maven archetypes. The whole book assumes that you use Apache Maven to compile and deploy new portlets.

Getting ready

In order to correctly generate a new portlet, you need to have the following software stack:

- ▶ Java SDK 1.7 or later
- ▶ Apache Maven, we use 3.0.5 version
- ▶ Eclipse IDE (Kepler or later)

We also assume that you properly set the developer's environment, which was described in the previous recipe.

There are three phases to achieve our goal: generating a new portlet, compiling it, and deploying and importing it to the Eclipse IDE.

Generating a new portlet

The first thing we need to do is to create a Maven project. In order to generate it, follow these steps:

1. Go to the `${liferay.home}/workspace` folder.

2. Execute `mvn archetype:generate -Dfilter=liferay-portlet-archetype`.

3. Choose a number for `com.liferay.maven.archetypes:liferay-portlet-archetype`. In our list, it is number `1`:

   ```
   Choose a number or apply filter (format: [groupId:]artifactId,
   case sensitive contains): : 1
   ```

4. Choose the correct Liferay version. In our example, it will be 6.2.2, with the number `24`.

5. Provide all the required Maven project information as follows:

   ```
   Define value for property 'groupId': : com.packtpub.portlet
   Define value for property 'artifactId': : first-portlet
   Define value for property 'version':  1.0-SNAPSHOT: :
   Define value for property 'package':  com.packtpub.portlet: :
   Confirm properties configuration:
   groupId: com.packtpub.portlet
   artifactId: first-portlet
   version: 1.0-SNAPSHOT
   package: com.packtpub.portlet
   Y: : y
   ```

6. In our `workspace` folder, a portlet called `first-portlet` should be generated.

Compiling the portlet and deploying it

With Apache Maven, it is easy to compile and deploy a portlet. Before invoking the Maven command, users have to set specific properties in the `pom.xml` file.

1. Go to the `${liferay.home}/workspace/first-portlet` folder and edit the `pom.xml` file.

2. Under the `<build>` section, add the following properties definition:

```
<properties>
    <liferay.version>6.2.2</liferay.version>
    <liferay.maven.plugin.version>6.2.2</
    liferay.maven.plugin.version>
    <liferay.auto.deploy.dir>${liferay.home}/
    deploy</liferay.auto.deploy.dir>
    <liferay.app.server.deploy.dir>${liferay.home}/tomcat-
    7.0.42/webapps</liferay.app.server.deploy.dir>
    <liferay.app.server.lib.global.dir>${liferay.home}/
    tomcat-7.0.42/lib/ext</liferay.app.server.lib.global.dir>
    <liferay.app.server.portal.dir>${liferay.home}/tomcat-
    7.0.42/webapps/ROOT</liferay.app.server.portal.dir>
</properties>
```

 Replace `${liferay.home}` with the real path to your folders.

3. Save the `pom.xml` file.

4. Build a new project by executing the following command:

   `mvn clean install`

5. Make sure that your Apache Tomcat is running with Liferay.

6. Invoke the `mvn liferay:deploy` command and follow the `catalina.out` logfile. You should see a similar message:

   `[PortletHotDeployListener:343] Registering portlets for first-portlet`

   `[PortletHotDeployListener:490] 1 portlet for first-portlet is available for use`

Importing the portlet to the Eclipse IDE

After successfully generating sources by the Maven archetype plugin, the sources of our portlet can be imported to our Eclipse IDE. To import them, follow these steps:

1. Make sure that you are in the `${liferay.home}/workspace/first-portlet` folder.

2. Run the `mvn eclipse:clean eclipse:eclipse` command.

3. Open your IDE and import `first-portlet` as a project by going to **File | Import | General | Existing Projects into Workspace**.

How it works...

A portlet project created from `com.liferay.maven.archetypes:liferay-portlet-archetype` has ready-to-use portlet implementation. In fact, it is very basic, but the entire folder's structure and configuration files are correctly created. Each portlet has four configuration files: `portlet.xml`, `liferay-portlet.xml`, `liferay-display.xml`, and `liferay-plugin-package.properties`. All of these files are placed in the `first-portlet/src/main/webapp/WEB-INF` folder.

The `portlet.xml` file is a portlet descriptor. It contains a portlet definition, such as name, portlet class, and so on.

The `liferay-portlet.xml` file is a kind of extension of `portlet.xml`. It is only understood by Liferay Portal. It gives additional information such as portlet's icon, path to the `css` and `js` files, and so on.

The `liferay-display.xml` file tells us in which section our portlet will be available. We will describe it later in the book.

The `liferay-plugin-package.properties` file is a metric of our portlet. This is a good place to specify version, tags, page URL, author, and license.

Detailed information on portlets is available in the JSR-168 and JSR-286 specification. There are many examples on how to use portlets, how to establish communication between portlets, or what is a portlet request lifecycle.

See also

For more information on portlets, refer to the following recipes:

▶ The *Creating a role-dependent portlet* recipe in *Chapter 5, Roles and Permissions*

▶ The *Checking permissions in a custom portlet* recipe in *Chapter 5, Roles and Permissions*

▶ The *language properties hook* recipe in *Chapter 11, Quick Tricks and Advanced Knowledge*

▶ The *Using Liferay Service Bus for communication between portlets* recipe in *Chapter 11, Quick Tricks and Advanced Knowledge*

2
Authentication and Registration Process

In this chapter, we will cover the following topics:

- ▸ Changing the default authentication settings
- ▸ Setting up e-mail notifications
- ▸ Customizing the registration form
- ▸ Overriding the default login page with the administrator-defined page
- ▸ Setting up a password policy
- ▸ Integration with CAS SSO
- ▸ CAS and Liferay users' database
- ▸ Liferay and the LDAP integration
- ▸ The magic trio: Liferay, CAS, and LDAP

Introduction

The authentication and registration processes are very important to build intranet systems. In this type of software, it is necessary to protect data against non-authorized users. We decided to describe typical solutions that are commonly used in many projects. It will help you configure the out-of-the box authentication system in Liferay and define the password policy. You will also learn about integration with the most popular single sign-on mechanism (SSO). The purpose of an SSO is to permit a user to access multiple applications while providing their credentials only once. The **Central Authentication Service** (**CAS**) is a single sign-on protocol for the Web. It is also a software package that implements this protocol.

Changing the default authentication settings

Liferay provides a built-in authentication mechanism that, by default, allows users to log in using their e-mail address. Additionally, there are a number of functionalities, such as automatic log in or forgotten password functionality, that assist users and help them go through the authentication process. However, in some cases, the standard authentication behavior must be modified.

Getting ready

Log in to Liferay as a user with administrator credentials. By default, the credentials are as follows:

- ▶ **E-mail**: test@liferay.com
- ▶ **Password**: test

How to do it...

In order to change the default authentication settings, perform the following steps:

1. Log in as an administrator and go to **Admin | Control Panel | Configuration | Portal Settings | Authentication section**:

2. Make sure that you are in the **General** tab.
3. Choose the option that you prefer from the **Authentication type** drop-down list.
4. Enable/disable the **Allow users to automatically login?** option.

5. Enable/disable the **Allow users to request forgotten passwords?** option.
6. Enable/disable the **Allow users to request password reset links?** option.
7. Enable/disable the **Allow strangers to create accounts?** option.
8. Enable/disable the **Allow strangers to create accounts with a company email address?** option.
9. Enable/disable the **Require strangers to verify their email address?** option.
10. Click on the **Save** button.

In order to set only the authentication type for a particular instance of the **Sign In** portlet, you do not need to perform the additional steps in the **Control Panel** scope. In this case, it is enough to change the configuration in the Sign in portlet. Perform these steps:

1. Go to the public page on which the **Sign In** portlet should be placed.
2. Click on the **Add** button.
3. Click on the **Applications** button.
4. Find the **Sign In** portlet using the search option or by browsing the list of available portlets.
5. Click on the **Add** link next to the portlet name. The **Sign In** portlet with basic configuration will be added to the page.
6. Go to the **Sign In** portlet configuration.
7. Choose the option that you prefer from the **Authentication type** list.
8. Click on the **Save** button.

How it works...

In Liferay Portal, a user can be authenticated by their e-mail address, a screen name or a numerical sequence, or an auto-generated user ID. There are two places that allow you to set the preferred authentication method: the portal settings section and the configuration screen of the Sign in portlet. The Control Panel settings enable you to define the default authentication type. This setting can also be modified by the properties in `portal-ext.properties`:

```
company.security.auth.type=emailAddress
company.security.auth.type=screenName
company.security.auth.type=userId
```

Remember that more important configuration comes from GUI (Control Panel) than from `portal-ext.properties`.

However, the Sign in portlet configuration option allows you to decide which way of authentication will be used for a particular Sign in portlet. Within the portlet, it is possible to choose the *default* option or one of the three available options, described previously. The default option is the same as the `company.security.auth.type` property.

In addition to selecting the **Authentication** type, Liferay also allows you to set additional parameters that influence the authorization and authentication processes. By default, all options, except the **Require strangers to verify their email address?** option, are enabled.

The **Allow users to automatically login?** option allows you to decide whether the site should remember the user's login and show the **Remember me** checkbox within the **Sign in** form. This option can be enabled (true) or disabled (false) by setting the following properties:

```
company.security.auto.login=true
```

The **Allow users to request forgotten passwords?** option is responsible for enabling or disabling the forgotten password functionality. This functionality makes it possible for users to request for a new password to be sent to their e-mail addresses. By default, this option is enabled in the following properties:

```
company.security.send.password=true
```

The **Allow users to request password reset links?** option is responsible for enabling or disabling the reset password functionality. This functionality allows users to request for a password reset link to be sent to their e-mail addresses. This option is represented by the following properties:

```
company.security.send.password.reset.link=true
```

The **Allow strangers to create accounts?** option is responsible for the availability of the link to create an account. This option lets you decide whether users who are guests to the site are allowed to create accounts by themselves. By default, it is enabled as follows:

```
company.security.strangers=true
```

The **Allow strangers to create accounts with a company email address?** option allows you to decide whether a new account can be created using the e-mail address in the domain provided in the General section of the Portal settings:

```
company.security.strangers.with.mx=true
```

The **Require strangers to verify their email address?** option enables an e-mail verification functionality. This functionality also can be enabled in `portal-ext.properties` by setting the following properties:

```
company.security.strangers.verify=false
```

Although the **Authentication** section consists of a number of tabs providing a range of additional authentication methods, all the settings gathered on the **General** tab of the **Authentication** tab affect only the Liferay functionality. They have no influence on the integration options grouped on the remaining tabs.

In some cases, the preceding configuration is not enough. For instance, many companies have their own privacy policy that requires an HTTPS connection. Liferay provides several settings in `portal.properties`, which can be overridden in `portal-ext.properties`, they are as follows:

Properties	Description
`company.security.auth.requires.https=false`	Set this to `true` to ensure that users login with HTTPS
`company.security.auto.login.max.age=31536000`	Specify max age (in seconds) of the browser cookie that enables the *Remember me* feature
`company.security.login.form.autocomple=true`	Allows users to autocomplete the login form based on their previously entered values

 Modification in the `portal-ext.properties` file is needed for a server restart.

There's more...

There are two more options strictly connected to the login and logout mechanisms. The first one, the **Default Landing Page** field, is located in the **Portal Settings** web page. This field allows you to indicate the page a user will be redirected to after completing the authorization and authentication. The second, the **Default Logout Page** field, located in **Portal Settings**, allows you to define the page a user will be redirected to after logging out.

In order to set custom values to these fields, follow these steps:

1. Go to **Admin** | **Control Panel** | **Configuration** | **Portal Settings** | **General**.
2. Set **Default Landing Page** to the address of the page you want users to go to after logging in, for example, `/web/guest/login`.
3. Set **Default Logout Page** to the address of the page you want users to go to after logging out, for example, `/web/guest/logout`.
4. Click on the **Save** button.

These settings could also be overridden by `portal-ext.properties` by the following names:

```
default.landing.page.path={PATH}
default.logout.page.path={PATH}
```

See also

For information on overriding the default login page, refer to the *Overriding the default login page with the administrator defined page* recipe.

Setting up e-mail notifications

In Liferay, there are four automatically sent e-mail notifications. They are as follows:

▶ **Account Created Notification**, which is sent when a user successfully creates a new account

▶ **Email Verification Notification**, which provides the e-mail verification link and code

▶ **Password Changed Notification**, which informs a user that their password has been changed

▶ **Password Reset Notification**, which enables a user to reset their current password by providing the password reset URL

This recipe provides information on how these default notifications can be customized.

Getting ready

Make sure that the Java mail session is properly configured. To check whether it works, look at `portal-ext.properties` and find and/or configure the following settings:

```
mail.session.mail.pop3.host=localhost
mail.session.mail.pop3.password=
mail.session.mail.pop3.port=110
mail.session.mail.pop3.user=
mail.session.mail.smtp.auth=false
mail.session.mail.smtp.host=localhost
mail.session.mail.smtp.password=
mail.session.mail.smtp.port=25
mail.session.mail.smtp.user=
mail.session.mail.store.protocol=pop3
mail.session.mail.transport.protocol=smtp
```

How to do it...

In order to change the sender's name and e-mail address, follow these steps:

1. Log in as an administrator and go to **Admin | Control Panel | Configuration | Portal Settings | Email Notifications**.
2. Make sure you are in the **Sender** tab.
3. Provide the sender's name and e-mail address.
4. Click on the **Save** button.

In order to set **Account Created Notification**, perform these steps:

1. Go to **Admin | Control Panel | Configuration | Portal Settings | Email Notifications**.
2. Go to the **Account Created Notification** tab.
3. Set the **Enabled** option.
4. Provide **Subject**.
5. Provide the **Body with Password** message text.
6. Provide the **Body without Password** message text.
7. Click on the **Save** button.

The following screenshot captures the preceding steps

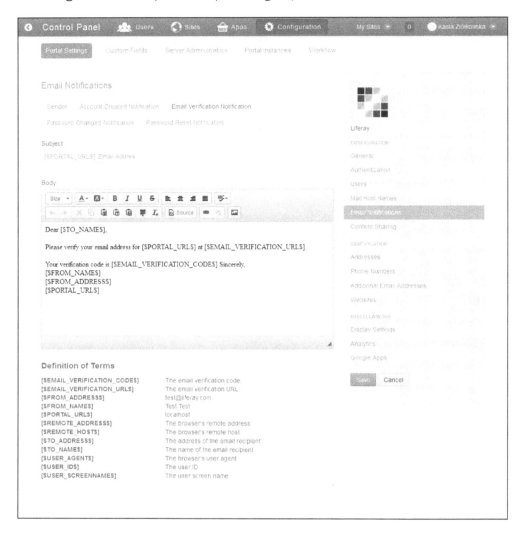

In addition to **Account Created Notification**, Liferay provides three tabs to customize. They are as follows:

- ▶ **Email Verification Notification**
- ▶ **Password Changed Notification**
- ▶ **Password Reset Notification**

In order to set **Email Verification Notification, Password Changed Notification,** or **Password Reset Notification**, perform these steps:

1. Go to **Admin | Control Panel | Configuration | Portal Settings | Email Notifications**.

2. Go to the **Email Verification Notification, Password Changed Notification,** or **Password Reset Notification** tab.

3. Provide the subject and body of the message.

4. Click on the **Save** button.

How it works...

Every e-mail notification consists of the subject and the body of the message. Both the subject and the body of the message can be composed using a set of available variables called terms (different for each notification) and custom text. The text of the body of the message can also be provided with simple text styles.

It is worth noticing that the **Account Created Notification** tab provides an additional **Enabled** option that allows you to decide whether this particular notification should be sent or not.

By default, `portal.properties` contains basic e-mail notification settings (default sender name, default sender e-mail, subject, body, and so on). Of course, all these settings can be customized to specific requirements:

```
admin.email.from.name=Joe Bloggs
admin.email.from.address=test@liferay.com
admin.email.user.added.enabled=true
admin.email.user.added.subject=com/liferay/portlet/admin/dependencies/
email_user_added_subject.tmpl

admin.email.user.added.body=com/liferay/portlet/admin/dependencies/
email_user_added_body.tmpl

admin.email.user.added.no.password.body=com/liferay/portlet/admin/
dependencies/email_user_added_no_password_body.tmpl

admin.email.password.reset.subject=com/liferay/portlet/admin/
dependencies/email_password_reset_subject.tmpl

admin.email.password.reset.body=com/liferay/portlet/admin/
dependencies/email_password_reset_body.tmpl

admin.email.password.sent.subject=com/liferay/portlet/admin/
dependencies/email_password_sent_subject.tmpl
```

```
admin.email.password.sent.body=com/liferay/portlet/admin/dependencies/
email_password_sent_body.tmpl

admin.email.verification.subject=com/liferay/portlet/admin/
dependencies/email_verification_subject.tmpl

admin.email.verification.body=com/liferay/portlet/admin/dependencies/
email_verification_body.tmpl
```

The preceding configuration defines the default settings for every type of notification. For instance, the `admin.email.password.reset.body` property defines the HTML template for the password reset action, which is located in the `com/liferay/portlet/admin/dependencies/email_password_reset_body.tmpl` file.

See also

For information on how to configure SMTP servers, refer to the *Configuring Liferay with the SMTP server* recipe in *Chapter 11, Quick Tricks and Advanced Knowledge.*

Customizing the registration form

The content of the registration form and the behavior of the system after completing the registration process can vary, depending on the system's functional and non-functional requirements. The default configuration of the registration form enables you to gather the data strictly required to create an account. The configuration also provides some additional fields, such as birth date or gender, which may not be always desirable. This recipe describes how to change the default set of registration form fields and modify their basic preferences and system behavior within the registration and authorization processes.

How to do it...

In order to customize the registration form, perform these steps:

1. Login as an administrator and go to **Admin | Control Panel | Configuration | Portal settings | Users**:

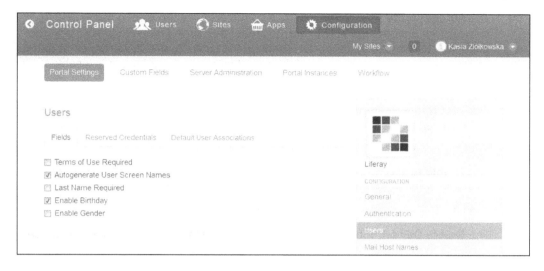

2. Make sure that you are in the **Fields** tab.

3. Enable/disable the **Terms of Use Required** option.

4. Enable/disable the **Autogenerate User Screen Names** option.

5. Enable/disable the **Last Name Required** option.

6. Enable/disable the **Enable Birthday** option.

7. Enable/disable the **Enable Gender** option.

8. Click on the **Save** button.

How it works...

There are three tabs that group the registration form settings: the **Fields** tab, the **Reserved Credentials** tab, and the **Default User Associations** tab.

The **Fields** tab consists of the list of options that are responsible for the content of the registration form and behavior of the system when a user logs in for the first time. Each of these options has its own representation in `portal.properties`, which can be overridden by `portal-ext.properties`. Remember that the highest priorities have settings that come from **Control Panel**. There are following options:

▶   The **Terms of Use Required** option enables and disables the terms of use screen, which is shown after the user's first authorization. By default, it is enabled:

```
terms.of.use.required=true
```

▶ The **Autogenerate User Screen Names** option disables the screen name field in the registration form and sets Liferay to create the screen name automatically from the e-mail address. If this option is enabled, the screen name is generated from the user's e-mail address (local part of the e-mail address). By default, it is disabled:

```
users.screen.name.always.autogenerate=false
```

▶ The **Last Name Required** option sets the last name as a required field. By default, it is disabled:

```
users.last.name.required=false
```

▶ The **Enable Birthday** option allows you to decide whether the birthday field should be available in the registration form. By default, it is enabled:

```
field.enable.com.liferay.portal.model.Contact.birthday=true
```

▶ The **Enable Gender** option allows you to decide whether the gender field should be available in the registration form. By default, it is enabled:

```
field.enable.com.liferay.portal.model.Contact.male=true
```

The **Reserved Credentials** tab allows you to define screen names and e-mail addresses that are reserved and cannot be used to create user accounts both by users and administrators. It also can be overwritten in the following properties:

```
admin.reserved.screen.names
admin.reserved.email.addresses
```

The **Default User Associations** tab provides a set of fields that enable you to assign sites, organization sites, roles, and user groups to each newly created user.

In addition, it is also possible to extend the functionality on existing users using the **Apply to Existing Users** option. However, changes will take effect when the user signs in.

There's more...

It is possible to change the default behavior of the create account link in the Sign in form and use a custom page with the custom create account portlet instead of the default (Sign in portlet) one. In order to do so, define the URL where the custom registration portlet is placed and set a property in the `portal-ext.properties` file as follows:

```
company.security.strangers.url=/create-account
```

See also

For information about adding users, refer to the *Adding a new user* recipe in *Chapter 3, Working with a Liferay User / User Group / Organization*.

Overriding the default login page with the administrator defined page

Liferay provides the possibility to use or replace the default dialog login feature with a custom login page. The custom page can be used to present some additional information such as instructions, description of benefits, and so on. This recipe provides guidelines on how to set such a page within the intranet.

How to do it...

In order to set a custom page in the login process, follow these steps:

1. Log in as an administrator and go to **Admin | Site Administration | Pages**.
2. Make sure that you are in the **Public Pages** tab.
3. Click on the **Add page** button.
4. Provide a name for the page (for instance, login).
5. Enable the **Hide from Navigation Menu** option.
6. Click on the **Add page** button. The new page will be created.
7. Go to the page's details by clicking on the page in the tree that was created and copy the **Friendly URL** value.
8. Go to the created page by typing (or pasting) its address in the browser's address bar.
9. Click on the add button (this is a **+** sign on the left-hand side).
10. Click on the **Applications** tab.
11. Find the Sign in portlet using the search function or by browsing the list of available portlets,
12. Click on the **Add** link next to the portlet name. The Sign in portlet with basic configuration will be added to the page.
13. Set URL to this site in the `portal-ext.properties` file by defining the `auth. login.site.url=/login` property.

 If there is a custom login portlet and custom page to login, it is required that you disable the dialog login functionality by setting the `login. dialog.disabled=true` property.

How it works...

As described previously, the first step is to create a new standard page containing a Sign in portlet. This page will be used as a new login page. The second step is to override the default Liferay configuration and set it to use this newly created login page whenever the user is navigating a site and authentication is needed. In order to do so, you need to set the new link in the `auth.login.site.url` property. It is also important to remember that when redirecting the *Sign in* link to the custom page, it is necessary to disable the standard login popup dialog. It can be achieved by setting the `login.dialog.disabled` property to `true`.

See also

If you want to learn about creating pages or defining page templates, refer to the following recipes from *Chapter 4, Liferay Site Configuration*:

▶ *Creating and customizing private and public pages for the site*

▶ *Using page templates and site templates for quick site and page creation*

Setting up a password policy

The Liferay password policy creator allows you to set the password life cycle and rules of employing it. You can decide whether the password should be changed. You can also specify the password syntax, the expiration rules, the lockout options, and the password history.

The default password policy provided by Liferay is very simple. It enables you to change the password of users and specifies that the reset password link should be valid for one day. This recipe provides a detailed description on how to create a new, more restricted password policy.

The password policy in this example will require the users to provide eight-character passwords, which cannot be found in a dictionary. Users must include numbers and uppercase letters in the password, and it must be changed every sixty days (it should not be possible to set the password that has been used last ten times). Additionally, the system will count the failure login attempts and block the account for 10 minutes after three unsuccessful tries.

How to do it...

In order to set the described password policy, follow these steps:

1. Log in as an administrator and go to **Admin | Control Panel | Users | Password policies**.
2. Click on the **Add** button.

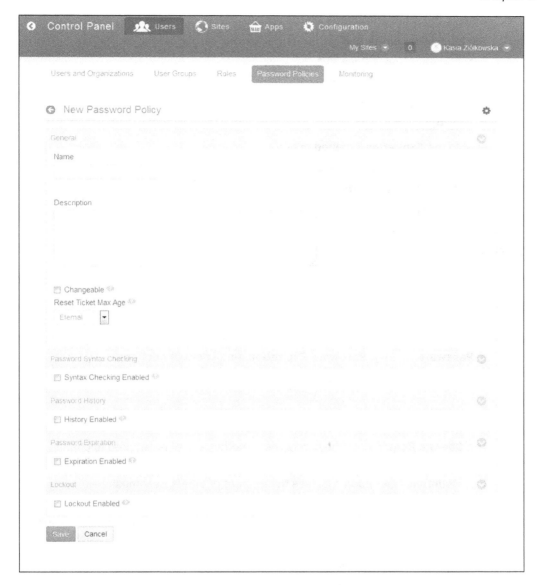

3. Provide a name for the new password policy.

4. Provide a description of the new password policy.

5. Enable the **Changeable** option.

6. Set the **Reset Ticket Max Age** option to **1 Day**.

7. Enable the **Syntax Checking Enabled** option.

8. Disable the **Allow Dictionary Words** option.

9. Set **Minimum Length** to **8**.

10. Set **Minimum Upper Case** to **1**.

11. Set **Minimum Numbers** to **1**.

12. Enable the **History Enabled** option.

13. Set the **History Count** option to **10**.

14. Enable the **Expiration Enabled** option.

15. Set **Maximum Age** to **8 Weeks**.

16. Set **Warning Time** to **6 Days**.

17. Set the **Lockout Enabled** option.

18. Set **Maximum Failure** to **3**.

19. Set **Lockout Duration** to **10 Minutes**.

20. Click on the **Save** button.

How it works...

There are five groups of options in the new password policy form: **General**, **Password Syntax Checking**, **Password History**, **Password Expiration**, and **Lockout sections**.

The General section consists of the following options:

- ▶ The **Changeable** option allows you to decide whether users can change their passwords

- ▶ The **Change Required** option determines whether a user is required to change the password on first login

- ▶ The **Minimum Age** option specifies the amount of time a user must wait before they will be allowed to change the password

- ▶ The **Reset Ticket Max Age** option determines for how long a password reset link is valid

The **Password Syntax Checking** section consists of the following options:

- ▶ The **Syntax Checking Enabled** option determines whether the password syntax should be checked

- ▶ The **Allow Dictionary** option determines whether common words are allowed to be used in passwords

- ▶ The **Minimum Alpha Numeric** option allows you to set the required minimum number of alphanumeric letters in the password

- The **Minimum Length** option determines the required minimum length of the password

- The **Minimum Lower Case** option determines the required minimum number of lowercase letters in the password

- The **Minimum Numbers** option determines the required minimum number of numbers in the password

- The **Minimum Symbols** option determines the required minimum number of symbols in the password

- The **Minimum Upper Case** option determines the minimum number of uppercase letters in the password

- The **Regular Expression** option determines the validation pattern for the user's password

The **Password History** section consists of the following options:

- The **History Enabled** option allows you to decide whether the portal should keep a history of the user's previous passwords in order to prevent them from reusing an old password

- The **History Count** option determines the number of previous passwords, which are kept in the history and cannot be used while setting a new password

The **Password Expiration** section consists of the following options:

- The **Expiration Enabled** option allows you to decide whether users are forced to periodically change their passwords

- The **Maximum Age** option determines for how long a password is valid

- The **Warning Time** specifies the amount of time before the password expiration date; a notification will be sent after this date

- The **Grace Limit** specifies the number of times a user can log in after their password has expired

The **Lockout** section consists of the following options:

- The **Lockout Enabled** option lets you to count the unsuccessful login attempts and enable account-locking mechanisms

- The **Maximum Failure** option specifies the maximum number of unsuccessful login attempts

- The **Reset Failure Count** option specifies the amount of time that an information of unsuccessful logins is kept

- The **Lockout Duration** option indicates the amount of time that a user's account remains blocked and cannot be used

Integration with CAS SSO

CAS is a single sign-on protocol. The official specification introduces it as follows:

> *"The Central Authentication Service (CAS) is a single-sign-on / single-sign-off protocol for the web. It permits a user to access multiple applications while providing their credentials (such as userid and password) only once to a central CAS Server application."*

Liferay provides ready-to-use functionality based on JASIG CAS (CAS became a **Java in Administration Special Interest Group (JASIG)** project in December 2004 and is now also known as JASIG CAS). In many projects, especially internal ones (for instance, intranet) it is necessary to provide single sign-on. CAS integrates with the following authentication mechanisms:

- Active Directory
- Generic
- JAAS
- JDBC
- LDAP
- Legacy
- RADIUS
- SPNEGO
- Trusted
- X.509 certificates

This recipe covers the basic steps to install a CAS server and to integrate it with Liferay.

How to do it...

In order to install and run a CAS server that works with Liferay, there are four main steps:

1. Install the CAS system on the Tomcat server.
2. Configure an HTTPS connection.
3. Set the CAS server.
4. Configure Liferay Portal.

Installing the CAS system

The first step is installing the CAS system on the Apache Tomcat server. The CAS can be deployed in the same instance as Liferay, but in the real-world example, it is a dedicated application server. We assume the first approach. The second important assumption is that we rely on Tomcat hot-deploy of archives. So, make sure that the `autoDeploy` option is set to `true`. This is a default setting. To install CAS, follow these steps:

1. Download the newest version of CAS from `http://downloads.jasig.org/cas/` and unzip archive. At this moment, 4.0 is the newest version.

2. Deploy `cas-server-4.0.0/modules/cas-server-webapp-4.0.0.war` into the Tomcat server by copying the `cas-server-webapp-4.0.0.war` application into the `${TOMCAT_HOME}/webapps` folder or using Tomcat Manager (if it is available). In the `catalina.out` logfile, you should see similar information:

   ```
   INFO: Deploying web application archive /home/user/apps/liferay/
   liferay-portal-6.2-ce-ga2/tomcat-7.0.42/webapps/cas-server-webapp-
   4.0.0.war
   ```

Configuring the HTTPS connection

The next important step is to establish an HTTPS connection between Liferay and CAS. By default, CAS sends the single sign-on cookie (CASTGC) only over secure connections. In our case, we will use a Java *keytool* to generate the SSL certificate. Java keytool is a key and certificate-management utility. It allows users to manage their own public/private key pairs and certificates. Basically, this tool stores keys and certificates in the *keystore*. This is a repository implemented as a file and placed on the local hard drive. Our goal is to generate a certificate, export it as a file, and place it in the truststore (`$JAVA_HOME/jre/lib/security/cacerts`). These instructions set up Tomcat's keystore file with a self-signed certificate (self-signed certificates should *never* be used for anything beyond development environment):

1. In any directory, type the command that generates a new key and puts it in the local keystore called `keystore.jks`:

   ```
   keytool -genkey -alias tomcat -keypass changeit -keyalg RSA
   -keystore keystore.jks
   ```

 Make sure that you provide the `$JAVA_HOME/jre/lib/security/cacerts` keystore password. Both passwords must be the same.

The following list shows how the key-generation process looks:

```
Enter keystore password:
Re-enter new password:
What is your first and last name?
  [Unknown]:  $REPLACE_WITH_FULL_MACHINE_NAME
What is the name of your organizational unit?
  [Unknown]:  IT
What is the name of your organization?
  [Unknown]:  Liferay
What is the name of your City or Locality?
  [Unknown]:  Warsaw
What is the name of your State or Province?
  [Unknown]:
What is the two-letter country code for this unit?
  [Unknown]:  PL
Is CN=$FULL_MACHINE_NAME, OU=IT, O=Liferay, L=Warsaw, ST=, C=PL
correct?
  [no]:  yes
```

 The value of the `first and last name` field mentioned previously must be set to a fully qualified domain name. On Windows, the fully qualified machine name appears as a full computer name. On Linux, this is a host name.

2. Export the key to a file called `tomcat.cert`:

```
keytool -export -alias tomcat -keypass changeit -file tomcat.cert
-keystore keystore.jks
```

3. Import the key to the `$JAVA_HOME/jre/lib/security/cacerts` truststore:

```
keytool -import -alias tomcat -file tomcat.cert -keypass changeit
-keystore $JAVA_HOME/jre/lib/security/cacerts
```

4. Check whether your certificate was successfully imported in the Java truststore:

```
keytool -list -v -alias tomcat -keystore $JAVA_HOME/jre/lib/
security/cacerts
```

5. Edit the `server.xml` file in the `${TOMCAT_HOME}/conf` folder and uncomment the SSL section to open up port **8443**:

```
<Connector port="8443" protocol="HTTP/1.1" SSLEnabled="true"
maxThreads="150" scheme="https" secure="true" clientAuth="false"
sslProtocol="TLS" />
```

Setting the CAS server

In this step, we will define a map of users that can be authenticated in our Liferay system. To achieve it, go to the `${TOMCAT_HOME}/webapps/cas-server-webapp-4.0.0/WEB-INF` folder, edit `deployerConfigContext.xml`, and modify the bean definition.

Set users list by adding them into `users` property. Here is an example:

```
<bean id="primaryAuthenticationHandler"
class="org.jasig.cas.authentication.
AcceptUsersAuthenticationHandler">
  <property name="users">
    <map>
      <entry key="casuser" value="Mellon"/>
      <entry key="joebloggs" value="test" />
    </map>
  </property>
</bean>
```

 Remember that a user must be created in the Liferay Portal.

Configuring Liferay Portal

The last set of steps is a Liferay configuration. Our goal is to change the authentication type, which should be based on `screenName` (login), and enable the CAS authentication method. To achieve this, follow these steps:

1. In Liferay, set the authentication type based on `screenName` (login). The portal can authenticate users based on their e-mail addresses, `screenName`, or `userId`. Change the default option and set a new value of the authentication type in `${liferay.home}/portal-ext.properties`:

    `company.security.auth.type=screenName`

2. Enable the CAS authentication by setting specific properties in `${liferay.home}/portal-ext.properties`:

    ```
    cas.auth.enabled=true
    cas.import.from.ldap=false
    cas.login.url=https://localhost:8443/cas-server-webapp-4.0.0/login
    cas.logout.url=https://localhost:8443/cas-server-webapp-4.0.0/
    logout
    cas.server.name=localhost:8443
    cas.server.url=https://localhost:8443/cas-server-webapp-4.0.0
    cas.no.such.user.redirect.url=https://localhost:8443
    cas.logout.on.session.expiration=false
    ```

3. Start the CAS server and Liferay. When the homepage loads, click on the login link. The system should redirect the user to the CAS login page with the HTTPS protocol.

4. Try authenticating yourself with the following credentials:

```
Login: joebloggs
Password: test
```

How it works...

The **Central Authentication Service** (**CAS**) provides a single sign-on for the applications. The main purpose of SSO is to provide user's credentials only once and permit them to access all the client's applications that support the SSO protocol. Therefore, CAS is divided into two parts: CAS client and CAS server. For clarity sake, this means that the CAS Client component (jar) is placed in the Liferay libraries, and the CAS server is a standalone application. The CAS server is responsible for authenticating users. The CAS client acquires and protects the identity of the granted users. Communication between clients and server can be implemented by four protocols:

▸ CAS 3.0 (enabled by default)

▸ SAML 1.1

▸ OpenID

▸ OAuth (1.0, 2.0)

Let's try analyzing the login process step by step:

1. User clicks on the **login** button in the Liferay site. The system redirects the user to the CAS application at `https://localhost:8443/cas-server-webapp-4.0.0/login?service=https://localhost:8443/c/portal/login`.

2. User types the correct login and password and invokes the submit action. The CAS server authenticates the user and sets the CASTGC cookie (for example, `CASTGC=TGT-4-HASH-cas01.example.org`). Then, the authenticated user goes back to Liferay with the Service Ticket (ST) ticket parameter: `https://localhost:8443/c/portal/login?ticket=ST-6-HASH-cas01.example.org`.

3. The next step is calling the validation. It is a background process that sends the GET request via back-channel communication and gets an XML response with username details: `https://localhost:8443/cas-server-webapp-4.0.0/proxyValidate?{PARAMETERS}`.

4. User is successfully logged in into the Liferay system.

In Liferay, there are two classes that implement CAS authentication:

▸ `com.liferay.portal.servlet.filters.sso.cas.CASFilter`

▸ `com.liferay.portal.security.auth.CASAutoLogin`

`CASFilter` is responsible for the CAS authentication process, especially for login action. The most important piece of code calls validation:

```
TicketValidator ticketValidator = getTicketValidator(companyId);
Assertion assertion = ticketValidator.validate(ticket,
serviceUrl);
if (assertion != null) {
  AttributePrincipal attributePrincipal =
  assertion.getPrincipal();
  login = attributePrincipal.getName();
  session.setAttribute(WebKeys.CAS_LOGIN, login);
}
```

Filter validates ticket and sets login as a session attribute.

`CASAutoLogin` reads the session `CAS_LOGIN` attribute and tries to find the user in the database. If the user exists in the database, the `AutoLogin` process returns the user's credentials and successfully logs them in into Liferay Portal.

The CAS server, without any external authentication handler, is useless. So, the following recipes will show how to integrate the CAS server and Liferay users' database or LDAP server.

See also

For more information on CAS and LDAP configuration, refer to the following recipes:

► *CAS and the Liferay user's database*
► *Liferay and the LDAP integration*
► *The magic trio: Liferay, CAS, and LDAP*

CAS and the Liferay user's database

The following recipe presents an idea on how to use the Liferay user functionality so it is authenticated by the CAS server. This idea may be used instead of LDAP or Active Directory systems. In small companies, where Liferay will be the main system that contains all user details, it would be a great concept to implement SSO in the following way:

► Liferay provides user details such as login and password to the CAS server
► When a user tries to login to the Liferay Portal, the CAS server *asks* the Liferay database and checks the user's data correctness

Getting ready

This recipe is in continuation with the previous one. To be ready, check whether the CAS server is correctly installed and is communicating with Liferay (the CAS client). To check it, try authenticating yourself as a default Liferay user via CAS by invoking `https://localhost:8443/cas-server-webapp-4.0.0/login`.

How to do it...

Since 6.2 version, Liferay uses the PBKDF2WithHmacSHA1/160/128000 algorithm for password encryption. To configure the CAS server without any customization, it is necessary to change the password encryption (for instance, the SHA algorithm).

 Warning! Changing the encryption is dangerous for existing accounts. All passwords stored in the database will be lost. If this happens, it is necessary to set a new password for every user.

In order to configure the CAS server to work with the Liferay database follow these steps:

1. Add the following libraries to `${TOMCAT_HOME}/webapps/cas-server-webapp-4.0.0/WEB-INF/lib`:

   - c3p0 (for instance, `c3p0-0.9.1.2.jar`): Download it from `https://github.com/swaldman/c3p0`

   - `cas-server-support-jdbc-4.0.0.jar`: Copy it from `cas-server-4.0.0/modules/`

2. Change the password encryption by setting the new one in `${liferay.home}/portal-ext.properties`:

   ```
   passwords.encryption.algorithm=SHA
   passwords.digest.encoding=hex
   ```

3. Set the `passwordEncoder` bean in the CAS server. Open `${TOMCAT_HOME}/webapps/cas-server-webapp-4.0.0/WEB-INF/deployerConfigContext.xml` and define the bean:

   ```
   <bean id="passwordEncoder" class="org.jasig.cas.authentication.
   handler.DefaultPasswordEncoder"
   c:encodingAlgorithm="SHA1"
   p:characterEncoding="UTF-8" />
   ```

4. The last thing is to set `dataSource` and change `primaryAuthenticationHandler` in `deployerConfigContext.xml`.

   ❏ Set a new bean with `id="dataSource"`:

   ```
   <bean id="dataSource"
   class="com.mchange.v2.c3p0.ComboPooledDataSource"
   p:driverClass="org.mysql.jdbc.driver"
   p:jdbcUrl="jdbc:mysql://HOST:3306/lportal?useUnicode=true&am
   p;characterEncoding=UTF-8"
   p:user="USERNAME"
   p:password="PASSWORD"
   p:initialPoolSize="6"
   p:minPoolSize="6"
   p:maxPoolSize="18"
   p:maxIdleTimeExcessConnections="120"
   p:checkoutTimeout="10000"
   p:acquireIncrement="6"
   p:acquireRetryAttempts="5"
   p:acquireRetryDelay="2000"
   p:idleConnectionTestPeriod="30"
   p:preferredTestQuery="1" />
   ```

   ❏ Find and change the bean with `id="primaryAuthenticationHandler"`:

   ```
   <bean id="primaryAuthenticationHandler" class="org.jasig.cas.
   adaptors.jdbc.QueryDatabaseAuthenticationHandler"
   p:dataSource-ref="dataSource"
   p:passwordEncoder-ref="passwordEncoder"
   p:sql="select password_ from User_ where screenName=? and
   status=0" />
   ```

How it works...

The CAS server supports many common kinds of authentication systems, such as database, LDAP, OpenID, OAuth, Radius, Windows (NTLM), and so on. In this recipe, we have shown an example configuration, where Liferay database provides user detail to the CAS server. This type of handler is called `QueryDatabaseAuthenticationHandler`. CAS provides two other database handlers called `SearchModeSearchDatabaseAuthenticationHandler` and `BindModeSearchDatabaseAuthenticationHandler`. Information about these handlers is available at `https://github.com/Jasig/cas/wiki/Configuring-Authentication-Components`.

As mentioned at the beginning, both Liferay and CAS have to use the same password encryption algorithm (SHA1). It has to be the same because the CAS server authenticates users by comparing the (hashed) user's password against the password stored in the database. To define database connection, it was necessary to create a new bean called `dataSource`.

The last and most important step was defining the handler with the following query:

```
select password_ from User_ where screenName=? and status=0
```

This query returns an encrypted password by the SHA1 algorithm from the Liferay users database. It is enough to correctly compare encoded passwords and authenticate the user.

There's more...

Many systems provide authentication by e-mail address instead of `screenName` (login). By default, Liferay implements this kind of authentication. So, let's change the earlier recipe and deploy e-mail authentication. To achieve it, there are two steps:

1. Change the authentication type in `${liferay.home}/portal-ext.properties`: `company.security.auth.type=emailAddress`.

2. Modify `primaryAuthenticationHandler` in the CAS `deployerConfigContext.xml` file:

```
<bean id="primaryAuthenticationHandler" class="org.jasig.cas.
adaptors.jdbc.SearchModeSearchDatabaseAuthenticationHandler">
  <property name="tableUsers">
    <value>User_</value>
  </property>
  <property name="fieldUser">
    <value>emailAddress</value>
  </property>
  <property name="fieldPassword">
    <value>password_</value>
  </property>
  <property name="passwordEncoder" ref="passwordEncoder" />
  <property name="dataSource" ref="dataSource"></property>
</bean>
```

At this time, we decided to use a different `authenticationHandler` called `SearchModeSearchDatabaseAuthenticationHandler` to show a variety of possible ways to achieve database communication.

The second and very important fact is that it is not a good idea (for security purposes) to use the SHA1 or MD5 algorithm without SALT. Moreover, Liferay developers decided to use very strong encryption:

"PBKDF2 (Password-Based Key Derivation Function 2) is a key derivation function that's part of RSA's PKCS (Public-Key Cryptography Standards) series: PKCS #5, version 2.0. It's also described in the IETF's RFC 2898. The PBKDF2WithHmacSHA1/160/128000 algorithm uses a keyed-hash message authentication code using SHA-1 and generates 160-bit hashes using 128,000 rounds."

If someone wants to use the same algorithm in the CAS Server, it is necessary to implement new `passwordEncoder` and define it in the CAS `deployerConfigContext.xml`:

```
<bean id="passwordEncoder" class="com.example.LiferayPasswordEncoder"
   c:encodingAlgorithm="PBKDF2WithHmacSHA1/160/128000"
   p:characterEncoding="UTF-8" />
```

`LiferayPasswordEncoder` must implement the `org.jasig.cas.authentication.handler.PasswordEncoder` interface.

See also

For information on CAS and LDAP, refer to the *Liferay and the LDAP integration* and *The magic trio: Liferay, CAS, and LDAP* recipes.

Liferay and the LDAP integration

In many companies, LDAP (OpenLDAP, Active Directory, or other LDAP implementations) is the system that keeps users' details, especially login, password, e-mail address, name, and surname. It is a good idea to integrate Liferay with LDAP. Fortunately, Liferay developers thought about it. Liferay provides out-of-the-box functionality that can read and import users from LDAP.

Getting ready

To start the configuration, you need to correctly install an LDAP server such as OpenLDAP or Active Directory, or ApacheDS. As an example of integration, it will be used online as a LDAP test server:

- Server: `ldap.forumsys.com`
- Port: `389`
- Bind DN: `cn=read-only-admin,dc=example,dc=com`
- Bind Password: `password`
- All user passwords are: `password`.

How to do it...

There are two ways of configuration: by GUI or by portal properties. In this case, we will show configuration via **Control Panel**.

1. Log in to your Liferay instance as a super administrator (by default, it is `joebloggs/test`).

2. Go to **Admin | Control Panel | Configuration | Portal Settings | Authentication**.

3. Select the **LDAP** tab.

4. Select the **Enabled** option.

5. Click on the **Add** button in the LDAP servers section.

6. Fill in the form with the following data:

   ❏ **Server name**: `<YOUR_SERVER_NAME>` (for example, `ldap.forumsys.com`).

   ❏ **Default values**: `<CHOOSE ONE OF THEM>` (for example, other directory server).

   ❏ **Connection section**: These settings contain the basic connection to LDAP.

   ❏ **Base Provider URL**: `<ldap://host:port>` (for example, `ldap://ldap.forumsys.com:389`).

   ❏ **Base DN**: `<Distinguished Name>` (for example, `dc=example,dc=com`).

   ❏ **Principal**: `<LDAP administrator ID>` (for example, `cn=read-only-admin,dc=example,dc=com`).

   ❏ **Credentials**: `<LDAP administrator's password>` (in our case is `password`).

   ❏ Check the configuration and click on the **Test LDAP Connection** button. It should be displaying the following message:

   Liferay has successfully connected to the LDAP server.

   ❏ **Users section**: These settings cover search filter and user mapping functionality.

 Values in this form strictly depend on the LDAP directory schema. Administrator should know which fields from LDAP can map as Liferay values.

   ❏ **Authentication Search Filter**: `<Search criteria for users login>` (for example, `(uid=@screen_name@)`).

   ❏ **Import Search Filter**: `<Way to identify users>` (for example, `(objectClass=inetOrgPerson)`).

❑ **User Mapping section** (maps the LDAP attribute as a Liferay value):

Screen Name = uid

Email Address = mail

Password = userPassword

First Name = cn

Last Name = sn

After configuration, try to check the correctness by clicking on **Test LDAP Users**. The system should list users from the LDAP directory.

▶ **Groups section**: These settings map LDAP user groups to Liferay user groups. It is not required to fill this form. If an administrator wants to configure it, the steps are very similar to the example shown previously. There may be a problem with the **Import search filter** field. There is usually the (objectClass=groupOfNames) or (objectClass=groupOfUniqueNames) value.

7. Save the **LDAP Servers** and **Portal Settings** forms.

8. Log out and try to log in as an LDAP user, such as newton/password.

> There are several parameters that are unavailable in the GUI. If there are any problems with configuration, check out portal.properties under the key prefix, ldap.*. LDAP configuration is a vast subject and could be difficult to understand and properly configure.

How it works...

Liferay provides an Authentication Pipeline mechanism that allows you to define many authentication types. By default, there is an enabled LdapAuth authenticator, as follows:

```
auth.pipeline.pre=com.liferay.portal.security.auth.LDAPAuth
```

In general, every login process, instead of default authentication, tries to invoke a list of authenticators defined in auth.pipeline.pre. If any authenticator returns a success, it means the user is correctly logged in to the Liferay Portal.

The LDAPAuth class implements the com.liferay.portal.security.auth. Authenticator interface, which provides the following methods:

▶ authenticateByEmailAddress

▶ authenticateByScreenName

▶ authenticateByUserId

To communicate with the LDAP server, Liferay uses classes from the javax.naming.ldap package. It provides support for LDAPv3 extended operations and controls.

The magic trio: Liferay, CAS, and LDAP

The next challenge is to connect Liferay, CAS, and LDAP authentication. In this combination, the CAS system provides single sign-on mechanism, the LDAP system stores the user's credentials, and Liferay uses both systems to authenticate users coming from LDAP. This configuration is used in many deployments. Furthermore, we dare to say that it should be considered as a standard solution when people think about intranet in their companies.

Getting ready

Study the *Integration with CAS SSO* and *Liferay and the LDAP integration* recipes explained previously. Set up the system in accordance with these recipes. Check out the connection to the LDAP Server from Liferay and verify that the CAS authentication is enabled.

How to do it...

To integrate Liferay with CAS Server where LDAP is the authentication provider, follow these steps:

1. Find the archive with the CAS server downloaded from `http://downloads. jasig.org/cas/`. Copy `cas-server-4.0.0/modules/cas-server-support-ldap-4.0.0.jar` to the `${TOMCAT_HOME}/webapps/cas-server-webapp-4.0.0/WEB-INF/lib` directory.

2. By default, CAS uses the `ldaptive` library for communication with LDAP. Download `ldaptive.jar` (`http://central.maven.org/maven2/org/ldaptive/ldaptive/1.0.3/ldaptive-1.0.3.jar`) and place this archive in the `${TOMCAT_HOME} /webapps/cas-server-webapp-4.0.0/WEB-INF/lib` directory.

3. Open the `${TOMCAT_HOME}/webapps/cas-server-webapp-4.0.0/WEB-INF/deployerConfigContext.xml` file and specify the following beans:

   First, define the bean that will be a primary authentication handler and set it as LDAP authentication.

   [Make sure that you are not using a previously configured database authentication handler.]

   The primary authentication handler contains mapping fields between LDAP and CAS. Keys are LDAP attribute names, and values are CAS attribute names. This definition has a reference to the authenticator bean, which will be described in the next section:

```
<bean id="primaryAuthenticationHandler"
      class="org.jasig.cas.authentication.
      LdapAuthenticationHandler"
      p:principalIdAttribute="uid"
      c:authenticator-ref="authenticator">
    <property name="principalAttributeMap">
      <map>
        <entry key="uid" value="username" />
        <entry key="givenname" value="first_name" />
        <entry key="sn" value="last_name" />
        <entry key="mail" value="email" />
      </map>
    </property>
</bean>
```

The authenticator bean defines the method of authentication. It contains references to the DN (distinguished name) resolver and authentication handler, which is responsible for establishing connection. It should be included in our `deployerConfigContext.xml` file:

```
<bean id="authenticator" class="org.ldaptive.auth.Authenticator"
      c:resolver-ref="dnResolver"
      c:handler-ref="authHandler" />
```

Distinguished name resolver defines resolution implementation. In this case, `FormatDnResolver` is used:

```
<bean id="dnResolver"
      class="org.ldaptive.auth.FormatDnResolver"
      c:format="uid=%s,${ldap.authn.baseDn}" />
```

Next, bean definitions are responsible for establishing connection with LDAP. There are many settings, which are described in the `ldaptive` library documentation:

```
<bean id="authHandler" class="org.ldaptive.auth.
PooledBindAuthenticationHandler"
  p:connectionFactory-ref="pooledLdapConnectionFactory" />

<bean id="pooledLdapConnectionFactory"
  class="org.ldaptive.pool.PooledConnectionFactory"
  p:connectionPool-ref="connectionPool" />

<bean id="connectionPool"
  class="org.ldaptive.pool.BlockingConnectionPool"
  init-method="initialize"
  p:poolConfig-ref="ldapPoolConfig"
```

```
        p:blockWaitTime="${ldap.pool.blockWaitTime}"
        p:validator-ref="searchValidator"
        p:pruneStrategy-ref="pruneStrategy"
        p:connectionFactory-ref="connectionFactory" />

    <bean id="ldapPoolConfig"   class="org.ldaptive.pool.PoolConfig"
    p:minPoolSize="${ldap.pool.minSize}"
    p:maxPoolSize="${ldap.pool.maxSize}"
    p:validateOnCheckOut="${ldap.pool.validateOnCheckout}"
    p:validatePeriodically="${ldap.pool.validatePeriodically}"
    p:validatePeriod="${ldap.pool.validatePeriod}" />

    <bean id="connectionFactory" class="org.ldaptive.
    DefaultConnectionFactory"
        p:connectionConfig-ref="connectionConfig" />

    <bean id="connectionConfig" class="org.ldaptive.ConnectionConfig"
        p:ldapUrl="${ldap.url}"
        p:connectTimeout="${ldap.connectTimeout}"
        />


    <bean id="pruneStrategy" class="org.ldaptive.pool.
    IdlePruneStrategy"
        p:prunePeriod="${ldap.pool.prunePeriod}"
        p:idleTime="${ldap.pool.idleTime}" />

    <bean id="searchValidator" class="org.ldaptive.pool.
    SearchValidator" />
```

4. Add the following properties to the ${TOMCAT_HOME}/webapps/cas-server-webapp-4.0.0/WEB-INF/cas.properties file:

```
#=========================================
# General properties
#=========================================
ldap.url=ldap://ldap.forumsys.com

# LDAP connection timeout in milliseconds
ldap.connectTimeout=3000

# Whether to use StartTLS (probably needed if not SSL connection)
ldap.useStartTLS=false
```

```
#========================================
# LDAP connection pool configuration
#========================================
ldap.pool.minSize=3
ldap.pool.maxSize=10
ldap.pool.validateOnCheckout=false
ldap.pool.validatePeriodically=true

# Amount of time in milliseconds to block on pool
# exhausted condition before giving up.
ldap.pool.blockWaitTime=3000

# Frequency of connection validation in seconds
# Only applies if validatePeriodically=true
ldap.pool.validatePeriod=300

# Attempt to prune connections every N seconds
ldap.pool.prunePeriod=300

# Maximum amount of time an idle connection is allowed to #be in
pool before it is liable to be removed/destroyed
ldap.pool.idleTime=600


#========================================
# Authentication
#========================================

# Base DN of users to be authenticated
ldap.authn.baseDn=dc=example,dc=com

# Manager DN for authenticated searches
ldap.authn.managerDN=cn=read-only-admin,dc=example,dc=com

# Manager password for authenticated searches
ldap.authn.managerPassword=password

# Search filter used for configurations that require searching for
DNs
ldap.authn.searchFilter=(uid={user})

# Search filter used for configurations that require searching for
DNs
ldap.authn.format=uid=%s,dc=example,dc=com
```

5. Check in the `portal-ext.properties` file whether CAS authentication is enabled:

   `cas.auth.enabled=true`

6. Restart the Tomcat server.

After finishing the configuration described previously, it should be possible to authenticate to Liferay by the CAS server and LDAP user credentials (login and password) such as `newton/password`.

How it works...

Configuration for the LDAP schema in many cases is different. It is not possible to provide the correct configuration that will be flexible. In the configuration mentioned previously, highlighted phrases are sensitive and should be fitted to a specific LDAP schema.

The biggest advantage of this solution is that there is only one place that stores users' credentials (LDAP server) and exactly one place that provides authentication mechanism (CAS SSO). Liferay is just a client of these services.

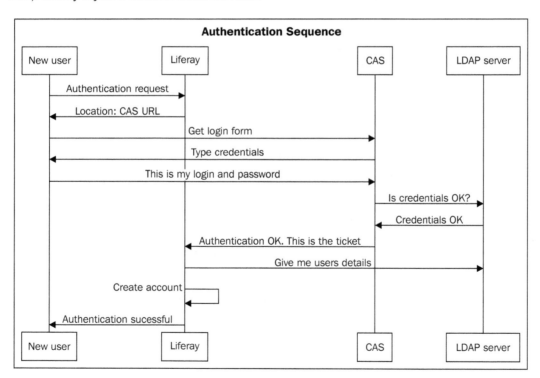

Let's follow this process:

1. A new user wants to log in to the Liferay system. Liferay doesn't have any information about this user.

2. Liferay checks whether CAS SSO is enabled and redirects the user to the CAS authentication provider.

3. The CAS authentication provider renders the login form.

4. The user types the LDAP login and LDAP password and sends the request to the CAS server.

5. The CAS server asks the LDAP server for credentials and checks the answer from LDAP.

6. If the answer is OK, the CAS server sends a success message to the Liferay authentication ticket.

7. Liferay checks whether it has that user in its database. If it doesn't, it asks the LDAP server about user details such as login, name, surname, e-mail address, and so on.

8. Liferay creates account in its database and successfully logs in a new user.

See also

- For information on how to export Liferay users, refer to the *Exporting users* recipe in *Chapter 3, Working with a Liferay User / User Group / Organization*.

- For information on how to build a scalable infrastructure, refer to the *Scalable infrastructure* recipe in *Chapter 12, Basic Performance Tuning*.

3
Working with a Liferay User / User Group / Organization

In this chapter, we will cover the basic functionalities that will allow us to manage the structure and users of the intranet. In this chapter, we will cover the following topics:

- ▶ Managing an organization structure
- ▶ Creating a new user group
- ▶ Adding a new user
- ▶ Assigning users to organizations
- ▶ Assigning users to user groups
- ▶ Exporting users

Introduction

The first step in creating an intranet, beyond answering the question of who the users will be, is to determine its structure. The structure of the intranet is often a derivative of the organizational structure of the company or institution. Liferay Portal CMS provides several tools that allow mapping of a company's structure in the system. The hierarchy is built by organizations that match functional or localization departments of the company. Each organization represents one department or localization and assembles users who represent employees of these departments. However, sometimes, there are other groups of employees in the company. These groups exist beyond the company's organizational structure, and can be reflected in the system by the User Groups functionality.

Managing an organization structure

Building an organizational structure in Liferay resembles the process of managing folders on a computer drive. An organization may have its suborganizations and—except the first level organization—at the same time, it can be a suborganization of another one. This folder-similar mechanism allows you to create a tree structure of organizations.

Let's imagine that we are obliged to create an intranet for a software development company. The company's headquarter is located in London. There are also two other offices in Liverpool and Glasgow. The company is divided into finance, marketing, sales, IT, human resources, and legal departments. Employees from Glasgow and Liverpool belong to the IT department.

How to do it...

In order to create a structure described previously, these are the steps:

1. Log in as an administrator and go to **Admin | Control Panel | Users | Users and Organizations**.

2. Click on the **Add** button.

3. Choose the type of organization you want to create (in our example, it will be a regular organization called software development company, but it is also possible to choose a location):

4. Provide a name for the top-level organization.

5. Choose the parent organization (if a top-level organization is created, this must be skipped).

6. Click on the **Save** button:

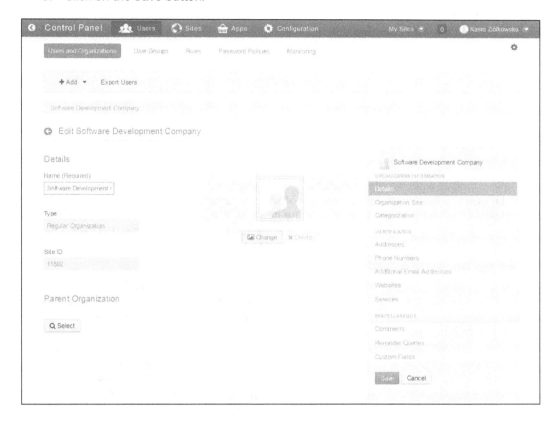

7. Click on the **Change** button and upload a file, with a graphic representation of your company (for example, logo).

8. Use the right column menu to navigate to data sections you want to fill in with the information.

9. Click on the **Save** button.

10. Go back to the **Users and Organizations** list by clicking on the back icon (the left-arrow icon next to the **Edit Software Development Company** header).

11. Click on the **Actions** button, located near the name of the newly created organization.

12. Choose the **Add Regular Organization** option.

13. Provide a name for the organization (in our example, it is IT).

14. Click on the **Save** button.

15. Go back to the **Users and Organizations** list by clicking on the back icon (left-arrow icon next to **Edit IT** header).

16. Click on the **Actions** button, located near the name of the newly created organization (in our case, it is IT).

17. Choose the **Add Location** option.

18. Provide a name for the organization (for instance, IT Liverpool).

19. Provide a country.

20. Provide a region (if available).

21. Click on the **Save** button.

How it works...

Let's take a look at what we did throughout the previous recipe. In steps 1 through 6, we created a new top-level organization called software development company. With steps 7 through 9, we defined a set of attributes of the newly created organization. Starting from step 11, we created suborganizations: standard organization (IT) and its location (IT Liverpool).

Creating an organization

There are two types of organizations: regular organizations and locations. The regular organization provides the possibility to create a multilevel structure, each unit of which can have parent organizations and suborganizations (there is one exception: the top-level organization cannot have any parent organizations). The localization is a special kind of organization that allows us to provide some additional data, such as country and region. However, it does not enable us to create suborganizations. When creating the tree of organizations, it is possible to combine regular organizations and locations, where, for instance, the top-level organization will be the regular organization and, both locations and regular organizations will be used as child organizations.

 When creating a new organization, it is very important to choose the organization type wisely, because it is the only organization parameter, which cannot be modified further.

As was described previously, organizations can be arranged in a tree structure. The position of the organization in a tree is determined by the parent organization parameter, which is set by creating a new organization or by editing an existing one. If the parent organization is not set, a top-level organization is always created.

There are two ways of creating a suborganization. It is possible to add a new organization by using the **Add** button and choosing a parent organization manually. The other way is to go to a specific organization's action menu and choose the **Add Regular Organization** action. While creating a new organization using this option, the parent organization parameter will be set automatically.

Setting attributes

Similarly, just like its counterpart in reality, every organization in Liferay has a set of attributes that are grouped and can be modified through the organization profile form. This form is available after clicking on the **Edit** button from the organization's action list (see the *There's more...* section). All the available attributes are divided into the following groups:

- The **ORGANIZATION INFORMATION** group, which contains the following sections:

  - The **Details** section, which allows us to change the organization name, parent organization, country, or region (available for locations only). The name of the organization is the only required organization parameter. It is used by the search mechanism to search for organizations. It is also a part of an URL address of the organization's sites.

  - The **Organization Sites** section, which allows us to enable the private and public pages of the organization's website.

  - The **Categorization** section, which provides tags and categories. They can be assigned to an organization (for more information about tags and categories, refer to the *Tagging and categorizing content* recipe from *Chapter 8, Search and Content Presentation Tools*).

- **IDENTIFICATION**, which groups the **Addresses, Phone Numbers, Additional Email Addresses, Websites**, and **Services** sections.

- **MISCELLANEOUS**, which consists of:

  - The **Comments** section, which allows us to manage an organization's comments

  - The **Reminder Queries** section, in which reminder queries for different languages can be set

  - The **Custom Fields** section, which provides a tool to manage values of custom attributes defined for the organization

Customizing an organization functionalities

Liferay provides the possibility to customize an organization's functionality. In the `portal.properties` file located in the `portal-impl/src` folder, there is a section called **Organizations**. All these settings can be overridden in the `portal-ext.properties` file. We mentioned that top-level organization cannot have any parent organizations. If we look deeper into portal settings, we can dig out the following properties:

```
organizations.rootable[regular-Organization]=true
organizations.rootable[location]=false
```

These properties determine which type of organization can be created as a root organization.

In many cases, users want to add a new organization's type. To achieve this goal, it is necessary to set a few properties that describe a new type:

```
organizations.types=regular-Organization,location,my-Organization
organizations.rootable[my-organization]=false
organizations.children.types[my-organization]=location
organizations.country.enabled[my-organization]=false
organizations.country.required[my-organization]=false
```

The first property defines a list of available types. The second one denies the possibility to create an organization as a root. The next one specifies a list of types that we can create as children. In our case, this is only the location type. The last two properties turn off the country list in the creation process. This option is useful when the location is not important.

Another interesting feature is the ability to customize an organization's profile form. It is possible to indicate which sections are available on the creation form and which are available on the modification form. The following properties aggregate this feature:

```
organizations.form.add.main=details,organization-site
organizations.form.add.identification=
organizations.form.add.miscellaneous=

organizations.form.update.main=details,organization-site,categorization
organizations.form.update.identification=addresses,phone-numbers,additional-email-addresses,websites,services
organizations.form.update.miscellaneous=comments,reminder-queries,custom-fields
```

There's more...

It is also possible to modify an existing organization and its attributes and to manage its members using actions available in the organization **Actions** menu.

There are several possible actions that can be performed on an organization:

- ▸ The **Edit** action allows us to modify the attributes of an organization.
- ▸ The **Manage Site** action redirects the user to the **Site Settings** section in **Control Panel** and allows us to manage the organization's public and private sites (if the organization site has been already created).
- ▸ The **Assign Organization Roles** action allows us to set organization roles to members of an organization.
- ▸ The **Assign Users** action allows us to assign users already existing in the Liferay database to the specific organization.

- The **Add User** action allows us to create a new user, who will be automatically assigned to this specific organization.

- The **Add Regular Organization** action enables us to create a new child regular organization (the current organization will be automatically set as a parent organization of a new one).

- The **Add Location** action enables us to create a new location (the current organization will be automatically set as a parent organization of a new one).

- The **Delete** action allows us to remove an organization. While removing an organization, all pages with portlets and content are also removed.

 An organization cannot be removed if there are suborganizations or users assigned to it.

In order to edit an organization, assign or add users, create a new suborganization (regular organization or location) or delete an organization. Perform the following steps:

1. Log in as an administrator and go to **Admin | Control panel | Users | Users and Organizations**.

2. Click on the **Actions** button, located near the name of the organization you want to modify:

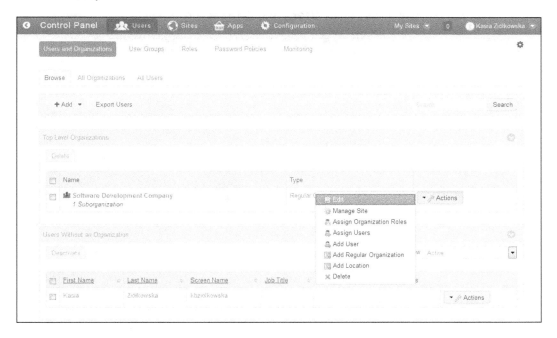

3. Click on the name of the chosen action.

See also

For information on Organization Sites, refer to the *Creating an organization and a stand alone site* and the *Site configuration* recipes from *Chapter 4, Liferay Site Configuration*.

Creating a new user group

Sometimes, in addition to the hierarchy, within the company, there are other groups of people linked by common interests or occupations, such as people working on a specific project, people occupying the same post, and so on. Such groups in Liferay are represented by user groups. This functionality is similar to the LDAP users group where it is possible to set group permissions. One user can be assigned into many user groups.

How to do it...

In order to create a new user group, follow these steps:

1. Log in as an administrator and go to **Admin | Control panel | Users | User Groups**.
2. Click on the **Add** button.
3. Provide **Name** (required) and **Description** of the user group.
4. Leave the default values in the **User Group Site** section.

5. Click on the **Save** button.

How it works...

The user groups functionality allows us to create a collection of users and provide them with a public and/or private site, which contain a bunch of tools for collaboration. Unlike the organization, the user group cannot be used to produce a multilevel structure. It enables us to create non-hierarchical groups of users, which can be used by other functionalities. For example, a user group can be used as an additional information targeting tool for the announcements portlet, which presents short messages sent by authorized users (the announcements portlet allows us to direct a message to all users from a specific organization or user group).

It is also possible to set permissions to a user group and decide which actions can be performed by which roles within this particular user group.

It is worth noting that user groups can assemble users who are already members of organizations. This mechanism is often used when, aside from the company organizational structure, there exist other groups of people who need a common place to store data or for information exchange.

There's more...

It is also possible to modify an existing user group and its attributes and to manage its members using actions available in the user group **Actions** menu.

There are several possible actions that can be performed on a user group. They are as follows:

- The **Edit** action allows us to modify attributes of a user group
- The **Permissions** action allows us to decide which roles can assign members of this user group, delete the user group, manage announcements, set permissions, and update or view the user group
- The **Manage Site Pages** action redirects the user to the site settings section in **Control Panel** and allows us to manage the user group's public and private sites
- The **Go to the Site's Public Pages** action opens the user group's public pages in a new window (if any public pages of User Group Site has been created)
- The **Go to the Site's Private Pages** action opens the user group's private pages in a new window (if any public pages of User Group Site has been created)
- The **Assign Members** action allows us to assign users already existing in the Liferay database to this specific user group
- The **Delete** action allows us to delete a user group

 A user group cannot be removed if there are users assigned to it.

In order to edit a user group, set permissions, assign members, manage site pages, or delete a user group, perform these steps:

1. Go to **Admin | Control panel | Users | User Groups**.

2. Click on the **Actions** button, located near the name of the user group you want to modify:

3. Click on the name of the chosen action.

See also

For information on user group sites, refer to the *Creating an organization and a stand alone site* and the *Site configuration* recipes from *Chapter 4, Liferay Site Configuration*.

Adding a new user

Each system is created for users. Liferay Portal CMS provides a few different ways of adding users to the system that can be enabled or disabled depending on the requirements, as seen in *Chapter 2, Authentication and Registration Process*. The first way is to enable users by creating their own accounts via the **Create Account** form. This functionality allows all users who can enter the site containing the form to register and gain access to the designated content of the website. In this case, the system automatically assigns the default user account parameters, which indicate the range of activities that may be carried by them in the system. The second solution (which we presented in this recipe) is to reserve the users' account creation to the administrators, who will decide what parameters should be assigned to each account.

How to do it...

To add a new user, you need to follow these steps:

1. Log in as an administrator and go to **Admin | Control panel | Users | Users and Organizations**.

2. Click on the **Add** button.

3. Choose the **User** option.

4. Fill in the form by providing the user's details in the **Email Address (Required)**, **Title**, **First Name (Required)**, **Middle Name**, **Last Name**, **Suffix**, **Birthday**, and **Job Title** fields (if the **Autogenerated User Screen Names** option in the **Portal Settings | Users** section is disabled, the screen name field will be available):

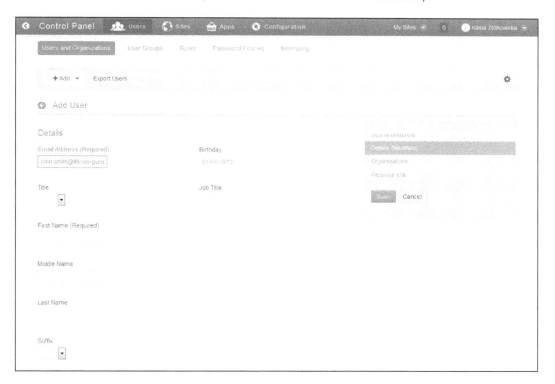

5. Click on the **Save** button:

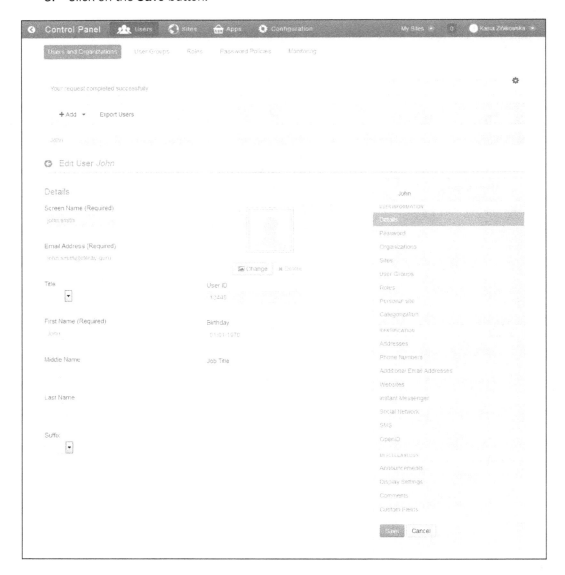

6. Using the right column menu, navigate to the data sections you want to fill in with the information.

7. Click on the **Save** button.

How it works...

In steps 1 through 5, we created a new user. With steps 6 and 7, we defined a set of attributes of the newly created user. This user is active and can already perform activities according to their memberships and roles. To understand all the mechanisms that influence the user's possible behavior in the system, we have to take a deeper look at these attributes.

User as a member of organizations, user groups, and sites

The first and most important thing to know about users is that they can be members of organizations, user groups, and sites. The range of activities performed by users within each organization, user group, or site they belong to is determined by the roles assigned to them. All the roles must be assigned for each user of an organization and site individually. This means it is possible, for instance, to make a user the administrator of one organization and only a power user of another.

User attributes

Each user in Liferay has a set of attributes that are grouped and can be modified through the user profile form. This form is available after clicking on the **Edit** button from the user's actions list (see, the *There's more...* section).

All the available attributes are divided into the following groups:

- ▶ **USER INFORMATION**, which contains the following sections:
    - ❑ The **Details** section enables us to provide basic user information, such as **Screen Name, Email Address, Title, First Name, Middle Name, Last Name, Suffix, Birthday, Job Title**, and **Avatar**
    - ❑ The **Password** section allows us to set a new password or force a user to change their current password
    - ❑ The **Organizations** section enables us to choose the organizations of which the user is a member
    - ❑ The **Sites** section enables us to choose the sites of which the user is a member
    - ❑ The **User Groups** section enables us to choose user groups of which the user is a member
    - ❑ The **Roles** tab allows us to assign user roles
    - ❑ The **Personal Site** section helps direct the public and private sites to the user
    - ❑ The **Categorization** section provides tags and categories, which can be assigned to a user

> ▶ **IDENTIFICATION** allows us to to set additional user information, such as **Addresses, Phone Numbers, Additional Email Addresses, Websites, Instant Messenger, Social Network, SMS,** and **OpenID**

> ▶ **MISCELLANEOUS,** which contains the following sections:

>> ❑ The **Announcements** section allows us to set the delivery options for alerts and announcements

>> ❑ The **Display Settings** section covers the **Language, Time Zone,** and **Greeting text** options

>> ❑ The **Comments** section allows us to manage the user's comments

>> ❑ The **Custom Fields** section provides a tool to manage values of custom attributes defined for the user

User site

As it was mentioned earlier, each user in Liferay may have access to different kinds of sites: organization sites, user group sites, and standalone sites. In addition to these, however, users may also have their own public and private sites, which can be managed by them. The user's public and private sites can be reached from the user's menu located on the dockbar (the **My Profile** and **My Dashboard** links). It is also possible to enter these sites using their addresses, which are `/web/username/home` and `/user/username/home`, respectively.

Customizing users

Liferay gives us a whole bunch of settings in `portal.properties` under the **Users** section. If you want to override some of the properties, put them into the `portal-ext.properties` file.

It is possible to deny deleting a user by setting the following property:

```
users.delete=false
```

As in the case of organizations, there is a functionality that lets us customize sections on the creation or modification form:

```
users.form.add.main=details,Organizations,personal-site
users.form.add.identification=
users.form.add.miscellaneous=

users.form.update.main=details,password,Organizations,sites,user-
groups,roles,personal-site,categorization
users.form.update.identification=addresses,phone-numbers,additional-
email-addresses,websites,instant-messenger,social-network,sms,open-id
users.form.update.miscellaneous=announcements,display-
settings,comments,custom-fields
```

There are many other properties, but we will not discuss all of them. In `portal.` `properties`, located in the `portal-impl/src` folder, under the **Users** section, it is possible to find all the settings, and every line is documented by comment.

There's more...

Each user in the system can be active or inactive. An active user can log into their user account and use all resources available for them within their roles and memberships. Inactive user cannot enter his account, access places and perform activities, which are reserved for authorized and authenticated users only.

It is worth noticing that active users cannot be deleted. In order to remove a user from Liferay, you need to to deactivate them first.

To deactivate a user, follow these steps:

1. Log in as an administrator and go to **Admin | Control panel | Users | Users and Organizations**.
2. Click on the **Actions** button located near the name of the user.
3. Go to the **All Users** tab.
4. Find the active user you want to deactivate.
5. Click on the **Deactivate** button.
6. Confirm this action by clicking on the **Ok** button.

To activate a user, follow these steps:

1. Log in as an administrator and go to **Admin | Control panel | Users | Users and Organizations**.
2. Go to the **All Users** tab.
3. Find the inactive user you want to activate.
4. Click on the **Actions** button located near the name of the user.
5. Click on the **Activate** button.

Sometimes, when using the system, users report some irregularities or get a little confused and require assistance. You need to look at the page through the user's eyes. Liferay provides a very useful functionality that allows authorized users to impersonate another user. In order to use this functionality, perform these steps:

1. Log in as an administrator and go to **Control Panel | Users | Users and Organizations**.
2. Click on the **Actions** button located near the name of the user.
3. Click on the **Impersonate user** button.

See also

▶ For more information on actions that users can perform, refer to the *Assigning user roles* recipe from *Chapter 5, Roles and Permissions* and *The Single Approver workflow for the user creation process* recipe from *Chapter 9, Liferay Workflow Capability*

▶ For information on how to customize and use user registration form, refer to the *Customizing the registration form* recipe from *Chapter 2, Authentication and Registration Process*

▶ For more information on managing users, refer to the following recipes

❑ The *Exporting users* recipe from this chapter

❑ The *Assigning user roles* recipe from *Chapter 5, Roles and Permissions*

❑ The *Customizing the registration form* recipe from *Chapter 2, Authentication and Registration Process*

Assigning users to organizations

There are several ways a user can be assigned to an organization. It can be done by editing the user account that has already been created (see the *User attributes* section in *Adding a new user* recipe) or using the **Assign Users** action from the organization actions menu. In this recipe, we will show you how to assign a user to an organization using the option available in the organization actions menu.

Getting ready

To go through this recipe, you will need an organization and a user (refer to *Managing an organization structure* and *Adding a new user* recipes from this chapter).

How to do it...

In order to assign a user to an organization from the organization menu, follow these steps:

1. Log in as an administrator and go to **Admin | Control panel | Users | Users and Organizations**.

2. Click on the **Actions** button located near the name of the organization to which you want to assign the user.

3. Choose the **Assign Users** option.

4. Click on the **Available** tab.

5. Mark a user or group of users you want to assign.

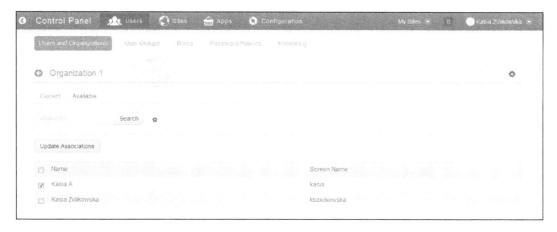

6. Click on the **Update Associations** button.

How it works...

Each user in Liferay can be assigned to as many regular organizations as required and to exactly one location. When a user is assigned to the organization, they appear on the list of users of the organization. They become members of the organization and gain access to the organization's public and private pages according to the assigned roles and permissions. As was shown in the previous recipe, while editing the list of assigned users in the organization menu, it is possible to assign multiple users.

It is worth noting that an administrator can assign the users of the organizations and suborganizations tasks that she or he can manage. To allow any administrator of an organization to be able to assign any user to that organization, set the following property in the `portal-ext.properties` file:

```
Organizations.assignment.strict=true
```

In many cases, when our organizations have a tree structure, it is not necessary that a member of a child organization has access to the ancestral ones. To disable this structure set the following property:

```
Organizations.membership.strict=true
```

See also

▸ For information on how to create user accounts, refer to

 ❑ *Adding a new user* recipe from this chapter

 ❑ *Customizing the registration form* recipe from *Chapter 2, Authentication and Registration Process*

> ▶ For information on assigning users to user groups, refer to the *Assigning users to a user group* recipe from this chapter

Assigning users to a user group

In addition to being a member of the organization, each user can be a member of one or more user groups. As a member of a user group, a user can profit by getting access to the user group's sites or other information directed exclusively to its members, for instance, messages sent by the Announcements portlet. A user becomes a member of the group when they are assigned to it. This assignment can be done by editing the user account that has already been created (see the *User attributes* description in *Adding a new user* recipe) or using the **Assign Members** action from the **User Groups** actions menu. In this recipe, we will show you how to assign a user to a user group using the option available in the **User Groups** actions menu.

Getting ready

To step through this recipe, first, you have to create a user group and a user (see the *Creating a new user group* and *Adding a new user* recipes).

How to do it...

In order to assign a user to a user group from the **User Groups** menu, perform these steps:

1. Log in as an administrator and go to **Admin | Control panel | Users | User Groups**.
2. Click on the **Actions** button located near the name of the user group to which you want to assign the user.
3. Click on the **Assign Members** button.
4. Click on the **Available** tab.

5. Mark a user or group of users you want to assign.

6. Click on the **Update Associations** button.

How it works...

As was shown in this recipe, one or more users can be assigned to a user group by editing the list of assigned users in the user group menu. Each user assigned to a user group becomes a member of this group and gains access to the user group's public and private pages according to assigned roles and permissions.

See also

▸ For information on how to create user accounts, refer to

❑ The *Adding a new user* recipe from this chapter

❑ The *Customizing the registration form* recipe from *Chapter 2, Authentication and Registration Process*

▸ For information about assigning users to organization, refer to the *Assigning users to organizations* recipe from this chapter

Exporting users

Liferay Portal CMS provides a simple export mechanism, which allows us to export a list of all the users stored in the database or a list of all the users from a specific organization to a file.

How to do it...

In order to export the list of all users from the database to a file, follow these steps:

1. Log in as an administrator and go to **Admin | Control Panel | Users | Users and Organizations**.

2. Click on the **Export Users** button.

In order to export the list of all users from the specific organization to a file, follow these steps:

1. Log in as an administrator and go to **Admin | Control Panel | Users | Users and Organizations**.
2. Click on the **All Organizations** tab.
3. Click on the name of an organization to which the users are supposed to be exported.
4. Click on the **Export Users** button.

How it works...

As mentioned previously, Liferay allows us to export users from a particular organization to a .csv file. The .csv file contains a list of user names and corresponding e-mail addresses. It is also possible to export all the users by clicking on the **Export Users** button located on the **All Users** tab. You will find this tab by going to **Admin | Control panel | Users | Users and Organizations**.

See also

▶   For information on how to create user accounts, refer to

   ❑   The *Adding a new user* recipe from this chapter

   ❑   The *Customizing the registration form* recipe from *Chapter 2, Authentication and Registration Process*

▶   For information on how to assign users to organizations, refer to the *Assigning users to organizations* recipe from this chapter

4
Liferay Site Configuration

In this chapter, we will cover the following topics:

- ▶ Creating an organization and a standalone site
- ▶ Site configuration
- ▶ Creating and customizing private and public pages for the site
- ▶ Using page templates and site templates for quick site and page creation
- ▶ Enabling local live staging
- ▶ Enabling remote live staging
- ▶ Enabling page versioning

Introduction

In the previous chapter, we described how to model an organizational structure in the intranet using organizations and user groups. We also discussed their attributes, such as address, phone numbers, websites, services, and so on. There is one attribute that makes organizations and user groups a very important component of Liferay Portal CMS. This attribute is site. A site is set of pages that may contain applications and content. Users gathered within an organization or user group can have their site, which stores and presents information that is produced and published by its users (files, articles, calendar events, bookmarks, and so on). There are also sites that are not connected to any structured collection of users. In this chapter, we will discuss how to create, customize and manage sites.

Creating an organization and a standalone site

Each organization and user group can have a site, which consists of a group of public and private pages organized into a tree-like structure. Public pages are pages accessible by anyone who has a link to the site. Private pages are pages that can only be accessed by logged-in users, who are members of the organization, user group, or standalone site. It is also possible to create a standalone site that is not assigned to any organization or user group. Standalone sites can additionally form a structure of sites, similar to the organization structure described in the previous chapter (for example, there can be a top-level site that has subsites). Organization sites are often created to store and present content and provide tools for users from a specific department or localization of the company. User group sites group information and tools used by people sharing common interests or people who are a part of the same project team. Standalone sites or site structures are used to provide a site or group of sites outside the organizational structure and are common for members of different user groups.

How to do it...

In this recipe, we will show you how to create an organization site and a standalone site. User group sites are created while setting up a user group. Unlike the organization, it is not possible to create a user group without the site.

In order to create a site for an existing organization, perform these steps:

1. Login as an administrator and go to **Admin** | **Control Panel** | **Users**| **Users and Organizations**.
2. Click on the **Actions** button located near the name of the organization you want to modify.
3. Choose the **Edit** option.

4. Click on the **Organization Site** link in the right menu.

5. Check the **Create Site** checkbox:

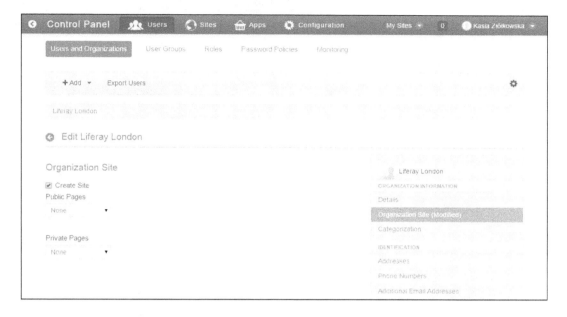

6. Click on the **Save** button.

In order to create a standalone site, perform the following steps:

1. Login as an administrator and go to **Admin | Control Panel | Sites**.

2. Click on the **Add** button.

3. Choose the **Blank Site** option.

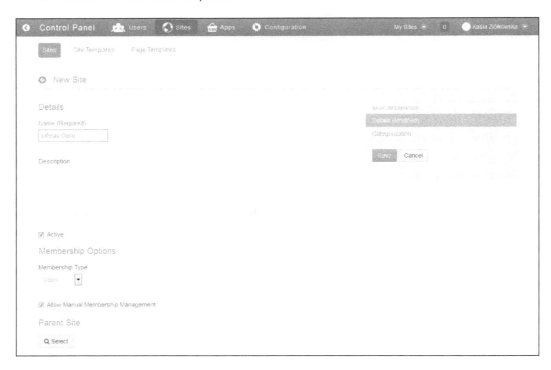

4. Provide the **Name (Required)** and **Description** for the site.

5. Enable the **Active** option.

6. Choose the **Membership Type**.

7. Enable the **Allow Manual Membership Management** option.

8. Choose the parent site.

9. Click on the **Save** button.

Once the site has been created, it is possible to add pages, place and configure portlets on them, and present content. However, it is not possible to enter the site before the first page is added. For more information on adding pages to the site, refer to the *Creating and customizing private and public pages for the site* recipe. To enter the site after adding the first page, execute these steps:

1. Go to **Admin | Control Panel | Sites**.

2. Click on the **Actions** button next to the particular site name.

3. Click on the **Site Administration** action.

4. Go to the **Pages | Site Pages** section.

5. Choose the set of pages you want to enter by clicking on the **Public Pages** or **Private Pages** tab.

6. Click on the **Public Pages** or **Private Pages** link (depending on the tab chosen in step 5).

7. Click on the **View pages** link.

You can also enter the site by typing the URL. The default URL addresses are as follows:

- `http://localhost:8080/web/site-name` for public pages
- `http://localhost:8080/group/site-name` for private pages

How it works...

In the first part of the recipe, we created an organization site. The second part of the recipe describes how to add a standalone site. Both the organization and standalone sites we created are empty and require us to add and configure pages and portlets. All the organization and standalone sites can be accessed by going to **Admin | Control Panel | Sites**.

Active and inactive sites

Each site can be set as active or inactive. The active site is accessible for users. An inactive site cannot be entered by users, but it is still available and can be activated any time. The activation option can be used when we want to switch the site off temporarily or when we need to turn it off permanently while keeping all the content as an archive.

Public and private pages and their membership type

Each organization, user group, or standalone site consists of public and private pages, which are organized in two separate trees. Public pages are pages accessible by anyone who has a link to the site. In Liferay, these users are called guests. Private pages are pages that can only be accessed by logged-in users, who are members of the organization, user group, or standalone site. Users can become members of organizations, user groups, or standalone sites when they are assigned to them by an administrator or they join by themselves using the My Sites portlet. The My Sites portlet is one of the many applications available for administrators to place on a site's pages. Its main purpose is to show the sites of which the user is a member and list other sites that the user can join or request membership to.

The way a user becomes a member of the site is defined by the type of membership; the parameter can be specified while adding a new site.

There are three types of membership:

- **Open**: This allows any user to join and leave the site. The open sites are shown in the My Sites portlet.

- **Restricted**: In this type of membership, the administrator or the owner manages the user's membership of the site. Although users do not have the ability to join the site, they can request membership and leave it by themselves. What is important is whether their membership can be granted by the administrator. The restricted sites are also listed in the My Sites portlet.

  If users want to join to the site, they can request membership. When a user sends a request or when an administrator approves the request, the system sends an e-mail message. It is possible to define the templates of notification in `portal-ext. properties`:

  ```
  sites.email.from.name=
  sites.email.from.address=

  sites.email.membership.reply.subject=com/liferay/portlet/sites/
  dependencies/email_membership_reply_subject.tmpl
  sites.email.membership.reply.body=com/liferay/portlet/sites/
  dependencies/email_membership_reply_body.tmpl

  sites.email.membership.request.subject=com/liferay/portlet/sites/
  dependencies/email_membership_request_subject.tmpl
  sites.email.membership.request.body=com/liferay/portlet/sites/
  dependencies/email_membership_request_body.tmpl
  ```

- **Private**: Denies users the chance to join, request membership from, or leave the site. Users must be assigned to the site manually by its administrator. The private site does not appear in the My Sites portlet.

The membership type is strictly connected to the **Allow Manual Membership Management** option, which determines whether users can be manually added to and removed from the site by its administrators. If the option is enabled (except manual membership management), it also allows users to join open sites or request membership to restricted sites using the My Sites portlet. By default, the option is enabled for standalone sites and disabled for organization sites, where the users section of site administration is not available.

Creating an empty site versus creating a site using site templates

When a new site is created, the tree of pages is empty. It is worth noting that when an empty site is created (as described in this recipe), it is not possible to enter the site before adding its first page. What's more, newly created sites are by default set as active, which means that users can immediately access them. However, it is possible to create a preconfigured set of public and/or private pages using site templates, which consist of preconfigured sites that can consist of pages, portlets, and content. You can find more about templates in the *Using page templates and site templates for quick site and page creation* recipe.

Technical view

From the technical point of view, a site is a group of layouts. In the database, each site is stored in the `Group_` table. Understanding this concept may be difficult. However, it is one of the most important functionalities in Liferay.

Liferay allows the administrator to run many portal instances on the same server. In the basic installation, it is called Liferay.com. Remember that portal instances keep their data separately from every portal instance (in the same database or in a different database).

Each portal instance can aggregate many groups: organizations, user groups, teams, users, and sites. All of these settings have a different `groupId`, but all of them are stored in the same table called `Group_`. Moreover, layouts (pages) can be created from templates (page templates or/and sites templates). Furthermore, users can have their private and public pages. This information is stored in the `Group_` table too. To sum up, `Group_` contains the following settings:

- Group (site)
- Organization
- User group
- User
- Team
- Layout prototype
- Layout set prototype

To distinguish these records in the `Group_` table, there are two columns:

- `classNameId` contains the ID of the `className` (names of classes are stored in the `ClassName_`) table
- `classPK` is the primary key of the specific class, for instance, user, team, or just group

Every site can have only private pages or only public pages, or both. Public pages are accessible to anyone, especially users who aren't logged in. Private pages are only accessible to the users who belong to the organization where this site is. Each of them is a set of the pages (layouts) that define the default theme, language, logo, and so on. Liferay contains this information in the `LayoutSet` table. These settings are the default settings of each layout. For example, if a layout does not define a theme, this setting comes from `LayoutSet`.

There's more...

It is also possible to manage the site using actions available in the site actions menu.

There are several possible actions that can be performed on a site:

- ► The **Site Administration** action redirects the user to the site settings section in **Control Panel** and allows them to manage an organization's public and private sites
- ► The **Add Child Site** action allows us to create a subsite
- ► The **View Child Sites** action allows us to browse the list of child sites
- ► The **Go to Public Pages** action opens the site's public pages in a new window
- ► The **Go to Private Pages** action opens the site's private pages in a new window
- ► The **Activate** action allows us to activate the site
- ► The **Deactivate** action allows us to deactivate the site
- ► The **Delete** action allows us to delete a site
- ► The **Leave** action allows users to leave the site. This option is available only if the user is a member of the site

In order to perform one of the actions listed earlier, perform these steps:

1. Go to **Control Panel | Sites**.
2. Click on the **Actions** button, located near the name of the site you want to modify.

3. Click on the name of the chosen action.

See also

You may also refer to the following recipes:

- For information on creating organizations and user groups, refer to the *Managing an organization structure* and *Creating a new user group* recipes from *Chapter 3, Working with a Liferay User / User Group / Organization*

- For information on customizing the site and adding pages to it, refer to the the *Site configuration* and *Creating and customizing private and public pages for the* site recipes

- For more information on creating sites, refer to the *Using page templates and site templates for quick site and page creation* recipe

Site configuration

When a site is created, it is possible to configure each site parameter, but the range of possible options is determined by the origin of the site (whether it is an organization, users group, or a standalone site). After creating an organization site, the link to the **Site Settings** section will appear on the organization menu and its actions menu. All the new organizations and standalone sites are also visible on the list that you can see by going to **Admin | Control Panel | Sites**. The user group pages are not included in this list, but can be accessed from the actions menu of the particular user group by going to **Admin | Control Panel | User Group**.

Getting ready

To step through this recipe, you have to create a site first (for more information on how to create a site, refer to the *Creating an organization and a standalone site* recipe).

How to do it...

In this recipe, we will show you how to set parameters of an organization site and a standalone site.

In order to configure a site of an organization, follow these steps:

1. Login as an administrator and go to **Admin | Control Panel | Users and Organizations**.
2. Click on the **Actions** button, located near the name of the organization, for which you want to configure the site.
3. Choose the **Manage Site** option.
4. Fill in the **Details**, **Search Engine Optimization**, **Advanced**, and **Miscellaneous** fields.

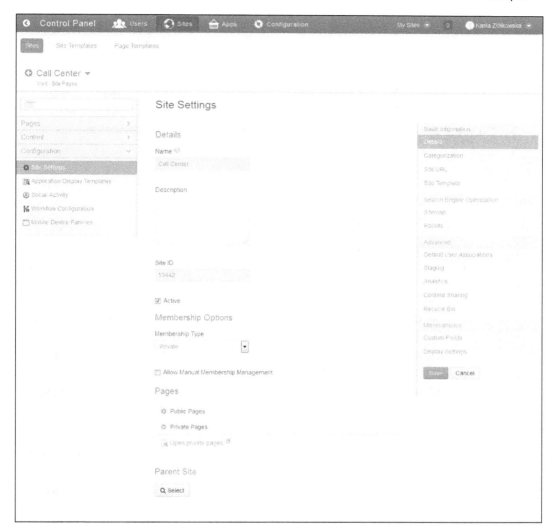

5. Click on the **Save** button.

In order to configure a standalone site, perform these steps:

1. Login as an administrator and go to **Admin | Control Panel | Sites**.
2. Click on the **Actions** button, located near the name of the site.
3. Choose the **Site Administration** option.
4. Go to the **Configuration** section.
5. Fill in the **Details**, **Search Engine Optimization**, **Advanced** and **Miscellaneous** fields.
6. Click on the **Save** button.

How it works...

All the available parameters are divided into the following groups:

- The **Basic information** group, which contains the following sections:
  - The **Details** section contains a set of options that allow changing the Name, Description, Membership Options, create Public and Private pages, choose Parent Site or activate and deactivate the site
  - The **Categorization** section, which provides tags and categories that can be assigned to a site
  - The **Site URL** section, which allows the user to enter the friendly URL that will be used by both public and private pages
  - The **Site Template** section, which shows the names of templates used to create public and private pages and their basic settings

- **Search Engine Optimization**, which consists of the following sections:
  - The **Sitemap** section, which allows the user to send sitemap information to preview
  - The **Robots** section, which allows us to set robot parameters for public and private pages

- **Advanced**, which consists of the following sections:
  - The **Default User Associations** section, which allows us to define the default site roles and teams that should be assigned to the site's users
  - The **Staging** section, which allows us to enable the staging functionality
  - The **Analytics** section, which allows the user to define the Google Analytics ID or Piwik script that will be used for this set of pages
  - The **Content Sharing** section, which allows us to decide whether subsites can display content from this site

- ❑ The **Recycle Bin** section, which allows the user to enable the recycle bin functionality and also move entries in trash; the trash automatically deletes the stored content after the indicated number of days

▶ **Miscellaneous**, which contains the following sections:

- ❑ The **Custom Fields** section, which provides a tool to manage values of custom attributes defined for the site.
- ❑ The **Display Settings** section, which allows the user to set the language of the site. It is possible to use the default language option or define a custom default language and additional available languages for this site.

Each section can be customized in `portal-ext.properties` by setting the following properties:

```
sites.form.add.main=details,categorization
sites.form.add.seo=
sites.form.add.advanced=
sites.form.add.miscellaneous=

sites.form.update.main=details,categorization,site-url,site-template
sites.form.update.seo=sitemap,robots
sites.form.update.advanced=default-user-associations,staging,analytics
,content-sharing,recycle-bin
sites.form.update.miscellaneous=custom-fields,display-settings
```

Another interesting feature is sharing content between sites (from parent to children). It can be set by the `sites.content.sharing.with.children.enabled` property. Here are the possible values:

▶ **0** disables the sharing of content with subsites for all sites

▶ **1** disables the sharing of content by default while allowing site administrators to enable it per site

▶ **2** enables the sharing of content by default while allowing site administrators to disable it per site

The next setting corresponds to the earlier one. The administrator can be a member of many sites. It is possible to allow or deny content sharing across the sites that an administrator manages. To enable or disable this feature, set the following property:

```
sites.content.sharing.through.administrators.enabled=true
```

The last property settings correspond to the site map. Every site map can be refreshed by particular units of time (always, hourly, daily, weekly, monthly, yearly or newer). In the site map, pages can have a default priority (ranging between 0.0 to 1.0). Set the following properties to order these settings:

```
sites.sitemap.default.change.frequency=daily

sites.sitemap.default.priority=
```

See also

For more information on creating sites, refer to the *Creating an organization and a standalone site* and *Using page templates and site templates for quick site and page creation* recipes.

Creating and customizing private and public pages for the site

As was mentioned earlier, there are two groups of pages within a site: public pages and private pages. Each page in a group is a part of a separate tree-like structure, reflecting levels in the website's information architecture. Pages in a tree can differ, depending on their purpose and origin. The page could be just a place where the information arranged in portlets is shown. It can provide a range of tools for users who manage the content of the website. It is also possible to add a page that is the link to another page of the same or a separate site. In addition, pages can be created as empty pages, copies of already existing ones, or can be based on defined templates.

Getting ready

To step through this recipe, you have to create a site first (for more information how to create a site, refer to the *Creating an organization and a standalone site* recipe).

How to do it...

The following recipe will illustrate how to create pages and arrange their structure.

In order to create public pages, follow these steps:

1. Login as an administrator and go to **Admin | Control Panel | Sites**.
2. Click on the **Actions** button, located near the name of the site.
3. Choose the **Site Administration** option.
4. Click on the **Site Pages** link in the **Pages** section of the left menu.
5. Make sure you are in the **Public Pages** tab.

6. Click on the **Add Page** button (indicated by **+** icon).

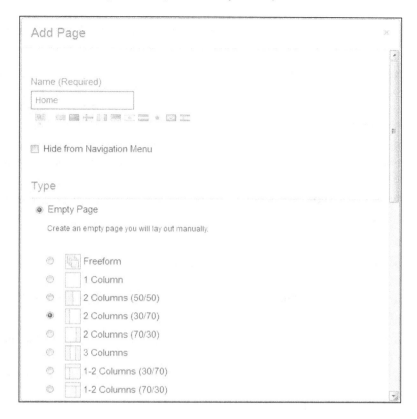

7. Provide the name of the page (in our example, it is **Home**).

8. Enable the **Hide from Navigation Menu** option.

9. Choose the **Empty Page** type.

10. Choose the page layout.

11. Click on the **Add Page** button.

12. Click on the newly added page's name on the **Public Pages** tree.

13. Click on the **Add Child Page** button.

14. Provide the name of the page (for instance, News).

15. Disable the **Hide from Navigation Menu** option.

16. Choose the **Empty page** type.

17. Choose the page layout.

18. Click on the **Add Page** button.

How it works...

As shown in the previous recipe, the creation of a page is a very simple action that requires us to provide some basic information, such as:

- The **Name**, which identifies the page. The name will be shown in all the portlets listing pages and (if the page title is not set) will be used as a page HTML title.

- The layout of the page determines whether it should consist of one, two, or other combinations of columns.

- The **Hide from Navigation Menu** option allows us to manage the visibility of the page. If the option is enabled, the page is not visible in the navigation menu, navigation portlet, site map portlet, and so on.

- The **Type** option allows the user to choose the type of newly created page. There are the following types of pages:

  - **Empty Page**: An empty page will be added
  - **Panel**: This allows us to create a page with predefined applications and navigation
  - **Embedded page**: This presents content from another website
  - **Link to URL**: This is a link to another website
  - **Link to a Page of This Site**: This is a link to another page within the current site
  - **Copy of a Page of This Site**: This is a copy an existing page from this site

  There is also a list of page templates that can be used.

It is worth noting that as was shown in a previous example, the level of the page is determined by the page that is chosen and marked before we click on the **Add Child Page** button. If we want to create a top-level page, the public pages or (private pages) branch must be selected. What's more, it is also possible to manage the localization of the page within a tree by simply dragging and dropping pages on different tree levels.

There are many others parameters that influence the page's appearance and behavior. These parameters can be managed by going to **Admin | Control Panel | Sites | Pages | Site Pages**.

Page parameters

Page customization options (available after clicking on the page name link on the appropriate tab by going to **Admin | Control Panel | Sites | Pages | Site Pages**) are divided into the following sections:

- ▶ The **Details** sections, which allows us to change the parameters set while adding the page, such as **Name, Type, Friendly URL, Layout of the page**, for example **1 Column, 2 Columns (50/50)**, **2 Columns (30/70)** and so on, and decide whether to hide the page from the navigation menu.

- ▶ The **SEO** section, which allows us to provide information that helps to optimize the page for search engines, such as HTML title, meta tags, and description, keywords, robot information, and sitemap options.

- ▶ The **Look and Feel** section, which allows us to decide what look and feel should be used for the site. It is possible to use the same look and feel configuration as that of the whole tree (**Use the same look and feel of the public pages** option) or customize it by choosing the **Define a specific look and feel for this page** option.

- ▶ The **JavaScript** section, which allows us to define JavaScript code that will be executed at the bottom of the page.

- ▶ The **Custom Fields** section, which provides a tool to manage the values of custom attributes defined for the page.

- ▶ The **Advanced** section, which allows us to set the target and icon for the page that appears in the navigation menu.

- ▶ The **Mobile Device Rules** section, which allows us to decide whether to use the mobile device rules of the public pages or define specific mobile device rules for this page.

- ▶ The **Customization Settings** section, which allows us to decide which sections of the page will be customizable for users having required permissions.

Whole-tree parameters

There are also some parameters that can be set for the whole tree of pages (available after clicking on the public pages or private pages link on the corresponding tab by going to **Admin | Control Panel | Sites | Pages | Site Pages**). These parameters are as follows:

- ▶ The **Look and Feel** section, which allows us to choose the graphical theme, bullet styles, and color schemes for this group of pages; decide whether portlet borders should be visible by default; or insert custom CSS to be loaded after the theme

- ▶ The **Logo** section, which allows us to set the logo of this particular tree of pages and decide whether the name of the site should be shown

- The **JavaScript** section, which allows us to define JavaScript code that will be executed at the bottom of the page
- The **Advanced** section, which allows us to merge the public pages of our portal's default site with the public pages of the current site
- The **Mobile Device Rules** section, which allows the user to define groups of devices and corresponding rules

Technical view

Layouts are stored in the `Layout` table. This table has the following columns:

- `plid`: Unique identified
- Audit fields (`groupId`, `companyId`, `userId`, `userName`, `createDate`, `modifiedDate`)
- `name`: Layout name
- `type_`: One of the values—`portlet`, `panel`, `embedded`, `url`, `link_to_layout`
- `friendlyURL`: Friendly URL to the specific layout
- `typeSettings`: Aggregate layout settings
- Any other columns that are not important to understand this recipe

There's more...

It is also possible to manage the page using available actions.

There are several possible actions that can be performed on a site page:

- The **Permissions** action allows us to set permissions for the site page
- The **Copy Applications** action is used to copy all the portlets (and their configurations) from another page
- The **Go to Private Pages** action opens the site's private pages in a new window
- The **Delete** action allows us to delete a page

In order to perform one of the actions listed earlier, perform these steps:

1. Login as an administrator and go to **Admin** | **Control panel** | **Sites**.
2. Click on the **Actions** button, located near the name of the site whose page you want to modify.

3. Click on the **Site Administration** option.

4. Select the page to modify.

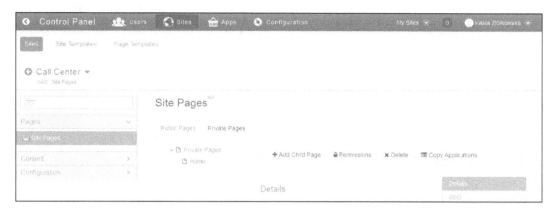

5. Click on the name of the chosen action.

Using page templates and site templates for quick site and page creation

In some cases, selected groups or even all sites within the intranet should contain the same set of pages, including the same set of portlets. This model can be employed, for example, when sites are used as department websites or project spaces. Liferay provides a very effective tool that allows us to create whole preconfigured sites or pages from templates prepared earlier. It is also possible to enable the connection between the template and the site, which will ensure live propagation of changes.

How to do it...

In this recipe, we will show you how to create a standalone site using site templates and how to create a single page from the page template.

In order to create a standalone site using a site template, perform these steps:

1. Login as an administrator and go to **Admin | Control Panel | Sites**.

2. Click on the **Add** button.

3. Choose the template you want to use from the drop-down list (for example, **Community Site**).

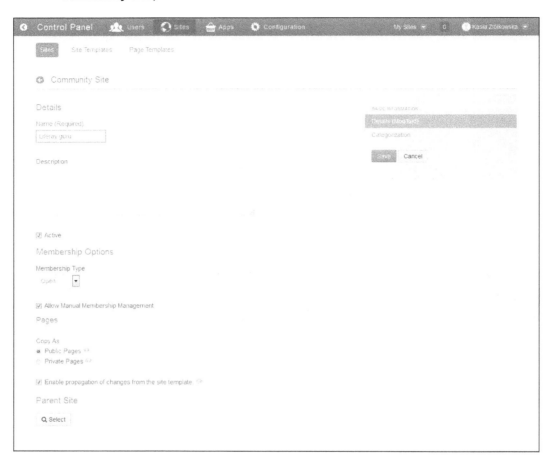

4. Provide the **Name (Required)** and **Description** for the site.

5. Make sure the **Active** option is enabled.

6. Choose **Membership Type**.

7. Enable or disable the **Allow Manual Membership Management** option.

8. Choose the **Copy As | Public Pages** option.

9. Set the **Enable propagation of changes from the site template** option.

10. Choose **Parent Site**.

11. Click on the **Save** button.

In order to create a page using a page template, perform these steps:

1. Click on the **Actions** button, located near the name of the site.
2. Choose the **Site administration** option.
3. Click on the **Site pages** section.
4. Click on the **Public Pages** tab.
5. Click on the **Add Page** button:

6. Provide the **Name** of the page (for example, **Blog**).
7. Enable the **Hide from Navigation Menu** option.
8. Choose the **Blog** page type of the page.
9. Click on the **Add Page** button.

How it works...

There are two types of templates: **Page Templates** and **Site Templates**.

The page template is a base for creating single pages and can be chosen when creating a new page. It can be configured by going to **Admin | Control Panel | Page Templates**. A page template stores not only page configurations, but also portlets with their configuration and, in some cases, content.

The site template is used for creating whole sites and can be managed by going to **Admin | Control Panel | Site Templates**. The list of templates is available when creating a standalone site, user group, or organization site. The site template may contain a group of pages with their configurations, portlets, and content.

Propagation of changes

When creating a site form template, it is important to decide whether the propagation of changes from the site template should be enabled or not. When the propagation is enabled, the changes made in the template are automatically applied to sites connected to it.

It is also worth noting that templates may allow site administrators to modify sites based on a template. When the template allows modifications (the **Enable propagation of changes from the site template** option is enabled) each modification of the pages of a site (site configuration and configuration of portlets) causes disconnection from the template. When template modifications are not allowed, administrators of sites cannot change the configuration of pages and their portlets.

Technical view

Site templates and page templates are stored in the `LayoutSetPrototype` and `LayoutPrototype` tables. `LayoutSetPrototype` contains default information about layouts that belong to a specific Layout Set. As mentioned earlier, site templates define a set of pages that can be copied after creating the new site.

A page template is a page created to be copied in other pages. The `LayoutPrototype` table stores all the required information about the page prototype.

See also

For information on creating new empty sites, refer to the *Creating an organization and a standalone site* recipe.

Enabling local live staging

Staging is a powerful tool that allows users to change, deploy, and test a new site's configuration before it goes into production. In other words, it provides a testing environment that is visible only to administrators. Users can stage their work; this means they have the ability to work on the working copy of the website.

Liferay provides the site administrator with the possibility to use local live staging and remote live staging. When we are talking about local live staging, the staging site and live site are in the same Liferay instance and on the same server. Remote live staging provides the possibility to configure and test changes in a different host (which is invisible in the production environment) and deploy changes to the production environment.

How to do it...

To enable local live staging, follow these steps:

1. Login as an administrator and go to **Admin | Site Administration | Configuration | Site Settings**.
2. Choose the **Staging** tab in the **Advanced** section.

 Staging cannot be used for sites where propagation of changes from the site template is enabled.

3. Select the **Local Live** option.
4. Decide if page versioning is necessary.
5. Select portlets that should be staged. Liferay defines the following rule:

 When a portlet is checked, its data will be copied to staging and it may not be possible to edit it directly in live. When unchecking a portlet, make sure that any changes done in staging are published first; otherwise, they might be lost.

6. After saving this configuration, there should be two additional buttons on the site dockbar: **Staging** and **Live**.

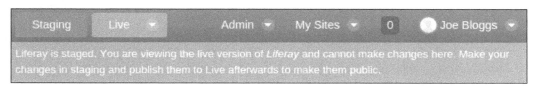

How it works...

Staging is a powerful functionality that gives users a tested area. After enabling staging, the portal gives users two areas:

- **Live**: Which gives a real-world view
- **Staging**: Which gives an area to test and configure a specific layout or portlet

Live view is a real view that is presented to all users who have access to the page. The staging view is a technical area where a user can change settings without life view influence. If an administrator is ready to submit and publish changes, they do it by clicking on the **Publish to Live** button.

Technically, it is a simple mechanism. Liferay creates a new group, which *friendlyURL* value has suffix *-staging* (for instance, */guest-staging*) This group contains its layouts, portlet preferences, content, and so on.

After enabling staging, Liferay invokes a background process, which copies layouts, portlet preferences, and specific content to the staging group (with a new `groupId`).

 This process can be quite long, so Liferay gives the following information:
An initial staging publication is in progress. The status of the publication can be checked on the publish screen.

Additionally, Liferay stores information about staging in the `Group_.typeSettings` column:

```
staged-portlet_{NUMBER}=true
stagedRemotely=false
staged=true
```

After enabling staging, Liferay duplicates a lot of data in the database. If you have a large amount of data, be careful and track database performance.

See also

If you want to configure remote live staging, refer to the next recipe. For information on how to enable page versioning, refer to the *Enabling page versioning* recipe

Enabling remote live staging

Liferay provides remote live staging for separate testing areas and production environments. In the local server, we can configure and test a new layout or a whole site after publish event changes are propagated into the production environment. To achieve this, both servers have to know about themselves.

How to do it...

Let's assume that the local server for the test environment is called `STAGING_SERVER` and the server machine for the production environment is `PRODUCTION_SERVER`.

To properly configure remote live staging, go through following steps:

1. On the local server (`STAGING_SERVER`) in `portal-ext.properties`, set the following properties:

   ```
   tunnel.servlet.hosts.allowed=127.0.0.1,PRODUCTION_SERVER_IP
   axis.servlet.hosts.allowed=127.0.0.1, PRODUCTION_SERVER_IP
   tunneling.servlet.shared.secret=SHARED_SECRET
   auth.verifier.TunnelingServletAuthVerifier.hosts.allowed=
   ```

2. On the remote server (`PRODUCTION_SERVER`) in `portal-ext.properties`, set the following properties:

   ```
   tunnel.servlet.hosts.allowed=127.0.0.1,LOCAL_SERVER_IP
   axis.servlet.hosts.allowed=127.0.0.1, LOCAL_SERVER_IP
   tunneling.servlet.shared.secret=SHARED_SECRET
   auth.verifier.TunnelingServletAuthVerifier.hosts.allowed=
   ```

 Make sure that the `SHARED_SECRET` phrase has 16, 32, or 64 characters.

3. Restart both servers.

4. On the local (`STAGING_SERVER`) server, go to **Admin | Site Administration | Configuration** and open the **Staging** tab from the right menu.

5. Choose the **Remote Live** radio button.

6. Fill in the following inputs on the form:

   ❏ **Remote Host/IP**: IP address of `PRODUCTION_SERVER`

   ❏ **Remote Port**: Port number of `PRODUCTION_SERVER`

       ❏ **Remote Path Context**: Context name of Liferay instance (if it is the root (/) context, leave blank)

       ❏ **Remote Site ID**: A site identifier (`groupId`) of the site that our configuration will install. If the site doesn't exist, create it.

 The `groupId` number can be found by going to **Site | Administration | Configuration | Site Settings | Site ID**.

7.   Click on the **Save** button.

8.   After successful configuration in the dockbar area, we should have the following view:

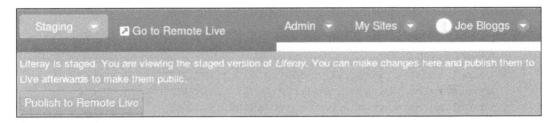

How it works...

Remote staging is a more difficult process than the local one. Liferay Portal uses two out-of-the-box mechanisms:

▶ Export layouts to the LAR file on a local server and import it on a remote server

▶ Transfer file by soap API using the `StagingServiceHttp` class

Properties that we set in `portal-ext.properties` allow us to invoke the portal API by an external client. In order to allow it, we set `PRODUCTION_SERVER_IP` and `LOCAL_SERVER_IP`. There is another property called: `tunneling.servlet.shared.secret`, which is used to create an authorization context (permission checker) to help secure the remote publication process.

After establishing a connection between servers, the system exports all the setting into the LAR file (a special file called Liferay Archive File) and transfers it by invoking `updateStagingRequest`. The entire process is implemented in the `com.liferay.portal.lar.backgroundtask.LayoutRemoteStagingBackgroundTaskExecutor` class.

Information about remote staging is kept in the `Group_.typeSettings` database column with the following properties:

```
staged-portlet_{NUMBER}=true
staged=true
stagedRemotely=true
remoteGroupId=GROUP_ID
remoteAddress=ADDRESS
remotePort=PORT_NUMBER
secureConnection=false
```

 Users in the local instance and remote instance must be the same, with the same credentials as well as roles and permissions.

Enabling page versioning

Page versioning works only if staging is enabled. This functionality has two main advantages:

► Allows users to work in a parallel way on a different version of the page

► Keeps a history of the page and gives users a backup point

How to do it...

Enabling page versioning is a simple process. Perform the following steps:

1. Login as an administrator, go to **Admin | Site Administration | Configuration** and open the **Staging** tab.

2. Select **Enabled On Public Pages** in the **Versioning** section.

3. Confirm by clicking on the **Save** button.

4. After enabling versioning, the dockbar should present the following information:

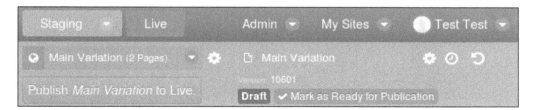

How it works...

Working with page versioning is similar to working with code repositories such as Git or Subversion. This mechanism is connected with all sites (`LayoutSet`) and with specific pages (`Layout`). This means that it is possible to version the entire site or a single page. Moreover, Liferay provides a feature to branch changes. This functionality will be useful if a user wants to reorganize the whole site. The next important button is the undo/redo arrow in the top-right corner of the dockbar.

From a technical point of view, Liferay defines another table that keeps branches and versions:

- `LayoutSetBranch`: Stores site branches
- `LayoutBranch`: Stores layouts (pages) branches
- `LayoutRevision`: Stores layout (page) revision—undo/redo and versioning functionality

See also

If you want to configure staging, refer to the *Enabling local live staging* and *Enabling remote live staging* recipes.

5

Roles and Permissions

In this chapter, we will cover the following topics:

- ▶ Creating and configuring roles
- ▶ Assigning user roles
- ▶ Creating role-dependent portlet
- ▶ Checking permissions in a custom portlet

Introduction

Just like employees of companies in the real world, users in the system can carry out different tasks. Some of them may deal with the management of the entire intranet—creating new organizations, locations, user groups, and sites; assigning users; and setting permissions. The others may be responsible for the configuration of specific sites and their pages, and managing portlets. There can also be a group of users who are responsible for creating and posting content. What is more, it is also possible that the same user can be an administrator of one of the sites, but at the same time, not be able to do anything except view the content of another. To enable the management of such a complex net of allowances, Liferay introduced the role functionality, which allows us to define what actions can be performed by which users in defined places.

A role is a collection of actions that can be performed by users assigned to that particular role. There are three types of roles defined at the portal level available in Liferay: regular roles, site roles, and organization roles. Regular roles define a list of actions that can be performed in areas (scopes) of the system specified in its definition. Using the regular role allows us to perform actions within one particular scope only. Site roles include actions performed within the site. Organization roles group actions that can be performed within an organization (for more information about organizations and sites, refer to *Chapter 3, Working with a Liferay User / User Group / Organization*, and *Chapter 4, Liferay Site Configuration*).

Creating and configuring roles

Regardless of the type of the role with which we are dealing, the process of creating a new role consists of two steps—creating a new, empty role and defining a set of permissions for the role.

How to do it...

In this recipe, we will show you how to create a new regular site and organization roles and how to define a set of permissions for them.

In order to create a new regular role, perform the following steps:

1. Go to **Admin | Control Panel | Roles**.
2. Click on the **Add** button.
3. Choose the **Regular Role**, **Site Role** or **Organization Role** option.

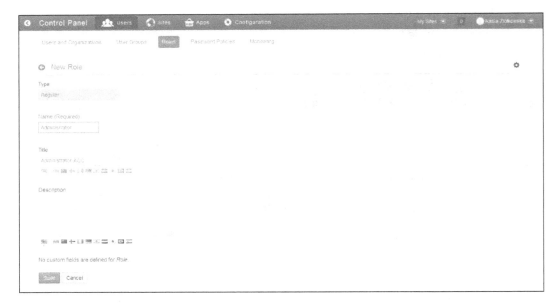

4. Provide **Name (Required)**, **Title**, and **Description** for the role.
5. Click on the **Save** button, and you will come back to a list containing all the roles defined.
6. Click on the **Actions** button next to the newly created role.
7. Choose the **Edit** action.
8. Click on the **Define Permissions** tab.

9. Using the left column navigation menu, choose the categories (such as **Site Administration | Pages | Site Pages**) for which you want to define permissions.

10. For each chosen category, mark the checkboxes next to the permissions for which you'd like to add the role.

 If you already know what categories you are searching for, then you could use the **Search** text field to filter functionalities accordingly.

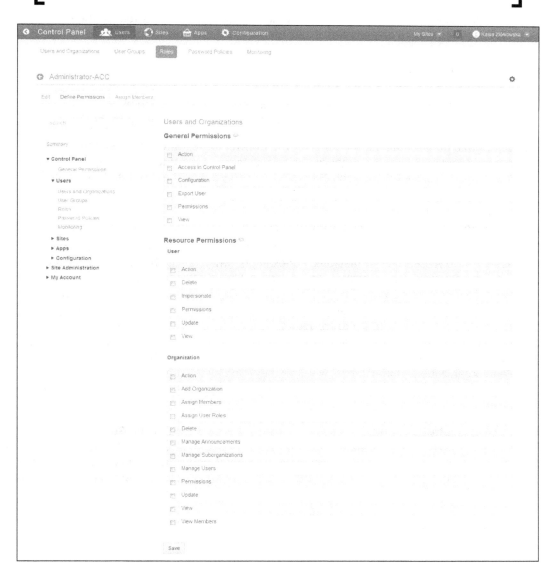

When setting regular role permissions for categories within the **Site Administration** group, you additionally need to choose the list of sites for which this role will be able to perform the action.

11. Click on the **Save** button.

How it works...

In the first part of the recipe, we showed you how to create a new empty role. In the second part, we described how to define permissions for this newly created role.

Role parameters

Each role has a name, title, and description. The description identifies the role in the system and consists of permissions. These permissions define what actions can be performed by users assigned to this role. Regular roles also have a list of users assigned to them.

The regular role may contain permissions for the **Control Panel**, **Site Administration**, and **My Account** functionalities. The organization role consists of the **Users and Organizations** and **Site Administration** permissions. Site roles may only define the **Site Administration** permissions.

Control Panel, Site Administration, and My Account permissions

The majority of **Control Panel** category permissions are divided into two groups: **General Permissions** and **Resource Permissions**. For example, when configuring permissions for the **Users and Organizations** functionality, we can define what actions can be performed for all applications in this group—whether they can be viewed, accessed in the **Control Panel**, configured, whether users assigned to the role can perform user export action or set permissions for the **Users and Organizations** functionality, and so on. All these are general permissions. Additionally, for the **Users and Organizations** functionality, it is also possible to set **Resource Permissions**. This defines which actions users having this role can perform on users and organizations, for instance, whether they can delete, impersonate, update, or view users; add organizations; assign members; manage suborganizations using the **Users and Organization** section; and so on.

The **Site Administration** permissions, in most cases, are also divided into **General Permissions** and **Resource Permissions**. However, in addition, when defining the **Site Administration** permissions, we can decide for which sites users having this role may perform actions. For example, it is possible to set the regular role, which allows users to manage pages or add content only for chosen sites.

The **My Account** permissions are concerned with application actions only.

There's more...

It is also possible to manage a role using actions available in the **Roles** actions menu.

There are several possible actions that can be performed on a role:

- ▶ The **Edit** action allows us to change the **Name**, **Title**, and **Description** of the role, define permissions, and assign members for the role.
- ▶ The **Permissions** action allows us to set permissions for actions that can be performed on this role.
- ▶ The **Define** permissions action allows us to define permissions for the role.
- ▶ The **Assign Members** action allows us to assign the role for users. It is available for regular roles only.
- ▶ The **View Users** action opens the list of all users having this particular role. It is available for regular roles only.
- ▶ The **Delete** action allows us to delete a role. Out-of-the-box Liferay roles cannot be deleted.

In order to perform one of the preceding actions, follow these steps:

1. Go to **Control Panel | Roles**.
2. Click on the **Actions** button located near the name of the role you want to modify:

3. Click on the name of the chosen action.

See also

For more information on organizations and sites, refer to the following recipes:

▶ *Managing an organization structure* recipe in *Chapter 3, Working with a Liferay User / User Group / Organization*

▶ *Creating an organization and a standalone site* in *Chapter 4, Liferay Site Configuration*

Assigning user roles

In order to define what users can do, you need to assign roles for them. Each user can have multiple roles, including regular, site, and organization roles. Each role assigned to a user is available in the roles section of the user account.

How to do it...

In this recipe, we will show you how to assign members to regular roles.

In order to assign members for a regular role, follow these steps:

1. Go to **Admin | Control Panel | Roles**.
2. Click on the **Actions** button located near the name of the role to which you want to assign users.
3. Click on the **Assign Members** action, and you will see a list of the current members of this role.
4. Click on the **Available** tab:

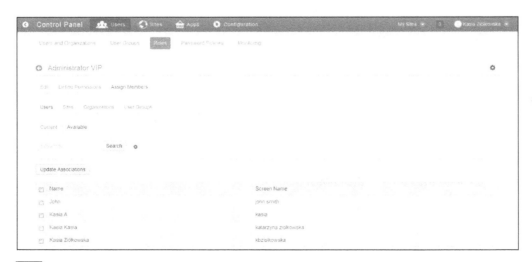

5. Choose the **Users**, **Sites**, **Organizations**, or **User Groups** tab.

6. Mark users, sites, organizations, or user groups to which you want to assign the role.

7. Click on the **Update Associations** button.

How it works...

Regular roles can be assigned to users or collections of users, such as **Organizations**, **Sites**, and **User Groups**. If the role is assigned to a user, this user gains all the permissions defined for this role. You can see the role by going to **Roles | Regular Roles** in the edit user form (to enter the edit user form go to **Users and Organizations | All Users** and click on the name of the user whose account you want to see). If a role is assigned to a collection of users, each member of that site, organization, or user group inherits this role. You can see this information by navigating to **Roles | Inherited Roles** in the edit user form.

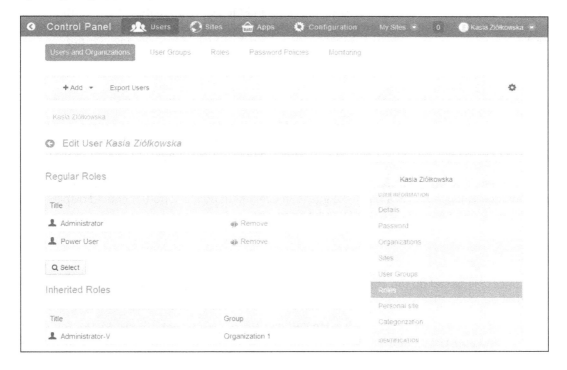

The **Roles** section in **Control Panel** allows us to assign users or a collection of users to **Regular Roles** only. **Organization Roles** can be assigned using the **Assign Organization Roles** action available in the **Organization** action menu. **Site Roles** can be assigned in the **Site Membership** section of **Site Administration**. It is important to remember that it is not possible to assign organization and site roles to collections of users.

See also

For more information on assigning organization roles and site roles, refer to the following recipes:

- ▶ *Managing an organization structure* in *Chapter 3, Working with a Liferay User / User Group / Organization*
- ▶ *Creating an organization and a standalone site* in *Chapter 4, Liferay Site Configuration*

Creating a role-dependent portlet

Liferay provides two ways to check permissions. The first mechanism implements the **Java Portlet Specification 2.0 (JSR 286)** and provides an XML definition to map a Liferay role and portlet role. The second mechanism uses the Liferay permission checker to verify users and the actions that they perform. In this recipe, we will show you how the Java Portlet Specification and Liferay work together.

Getting ready...

Generate or create an empty portlet using the Maven archetype generator. We described it in *Chapter 1, Installation and Basic Configuration*. It is not important which `PortletBridge` will be used. We will decide to use a simple one called `MVCPortlet`.

Let's assume that our goal is to write a greeting portlet that can recognize whether the current user is logged in as a user or a guest. In every situation, our portlet should display the greeting, **Welcome Guest!** or **Welcome User**.

How to do it...

Our concept is based on the approach that every kind of greeting will be in a different `JSP` file and that our controller will decide which `JSP` file should be used. Follow these steps:

1. Open `portlet.xml`, which is located in the `src/main/webapp/WEB-INF` folder, and add `init` parameters to it:

```
<init-param>
  <name>view-user-template</name>
  <value>/html/user.jsp</value>
</init-param>
<init-param>
  <name>view-guest-template</name>
  <value>/html/guest.jsp</value>
</init-param>
```

Chapter 5

2. Create the `src/main/webapp/html` folder and add two files, `user.jsp` and `guest.jsp`. In each file, define the greeting. In the `guest.jsp` file, add the following content:

```
<h1>Welcome Guest!</h1>
```

In the `user.jsp` file, add this line:

```
<h1>Welcome User!</h1>
```

3. Define roles in the `<security-role-ref>` tag in `portlet.xml`:

```
<security-role-ref>
  <role-name>logged-user</role-name>
</security-role-ref>
<security-role-ref>
  <role-name>guest-user</role-name>
</security-role-ref>
```

 We have changed the default role names on purpose to show you that the previous roles are different from the Liferay ones.

4. Open `liferay-portlet.xml` and map portlet roles into Liferay roles as follows:

```
<role-mapper>
  <role-name>guest-user</role-name>
  <role-link>Guest</role-link>
</role-mapper>
<role-mapper>
  <role-name>logged-user</role-name>
  <role-link>User</role-link>
</role-mapper>
```

5. Define the portlet render method as follows:

```
public void render(RenderRequest request, RenderResponse response)
throws PortletException, IOException {
  String renderPagePath = getInitParameter("view-guest-
  template");
  if (request.isUserInRole("logged-user")) {
    renderPagePath = getInitParameter("view-user-
    template");
  }

  include(renderPagePath, request, response);
  super.render(request, response);
}
```

6. Compile and deploy the portlet.

7. Put our portlet on the welcome site and test it. Our greeting should be on the site depending on whether the user is authenticated or not.

How it works...

Portlet specification JSR-286 defines a set of the methods of the `PortletRequest` interface. These methods allow us to check the user's principal name or role:

- `getUserPrincipal`
- `getRemoteUser`
- `isUserInRole`

The `getUserPrincipal` method returns the principal name of the current authenticated user and returns the `java.security.Principal` object. Similarly, `getRemoteUser` returns the name of the logged-in user. As a matter of fact, both methods return the same value, which is the `userId`, in the Liferay implementation. If a user is not authenticated, both methods return null. The third method expects a string parameter with the role name that is defined in `portlet.xml`. It checks the current user role and returns a `boolean` value.

The JSR-286 specification determines that every `security-role-ref` definition should be mapping into the internal system roles depending on the portlet container implementation. This mapping can be specified in `web.xml` as a pair of tags: `role-name` and `role-link`. Here is an example:

```
<role-mapper>
  <role-name>logged-user</role-name>
  <role-link>User</role-link>
</role-mapper>
```

Liferay specifies these mappings in `liferay-portlet.xml`.

However, this approach has a limitation. JSR-286 documents contain the following sentence:

"The developer must be aware that the use of this default mechanism may limit the flexibility in changing role-names in the application without having to recompile the portlet making the call."

See also

If you want to learn how to create new portlets or hooks, refer to these recipes:

- *Creating a custom portlet* in *Chapter 1, Installation and Basic Configuration*
- *The language properties hook* in *Chapter 11, Quick Tricks and Advanced Knowledge*
- *Using Liferay Service Bus for communication between portlets* in *Chapter 11, Quick Tricks and Advanced Knowledge*

Checking permissions in a custom portlet

Permissions in Liferay are very flexible but very complex to understand. In this recipe, we will show you only the basic use of permissions, but we hope this tutorial will be a start-up to implement more complex permissions. Let's assume that our goal is extending the previous portlet to display a secret message only for the users who have a specific permission. This permission should be configurable in the portlet permissions.

Getting ready...

We assume that you have a ready-to-use Maven portlet generated from Maven archetypes. In *Chapter 1, Installation and Basic Configuration*, we described how to achieve this.

How to do it...

To achieve our goal, we have to define and add a specific permission to our portlet from the previous recipe. Next, we should register our list of permissions. At the end, we will use those permissions to display the secret area in our portlet. Perform these steps:

1. Create the `src/main/resources/resource-actions` folder.

2. Create a file called `roles.xml` in the `resource-actions` folder with the following content:

```xml
<?xml version="1.0"?>
<!DOCTYPE resource-action-mapping PUBLIC "-//Liferay//DTD Resource
Action Mapping 6.2.0//EN" "http://www.liferay.com/dtd/liferay-
resource-action-mapping_6_2_0.dtd">

<resource-action-mapping>
  <portlet-resource>
    <portlet-name>roles-portlet</portlet-name>
    <permissions>
      <supports>
        <action-key>ADD_SECTION</action-key>
        <action-key>CONFIGURATION</action-key>
        <action-key>VIEW</action-key>
        <action-key>ACCESS_IN_CONTROL_PANEL</action-key>
      </supports>
      <site-member-defaults>
        <action-key>VIEW</action-key>
      </site-member-defaults>
      <guest-defaults>
        <action-key>VIEW</action-key>
      </guest-defaults>
```

```
        <guest-unsupported>
          <action-key>ACCESS_IN_CONTROL_PANEL</action-key>
          <action-key>CONFIGURATION</action-key>
        </guest-unsupported>
      </permissions>
    </portlet-resource>
  </resource-action-mapping>
```

3. Create the `default.xml` file in the `resource-actions` folder with the following content:

```
<?xml version="1.0"?>
<!DOCTYPE resource-action-mapping PUBLIC "-//Liferay//DTD Resource
Action Mapping 6.2.0//EN" "http://www.liferay.com/dtd/liferay-
resource-action-mapping_6_2_0.dtd">

<resource-action-mapping>
  <resource file="resource-actions/roles.xml" />
</resource-action-mapping>
```

4. Create the `portlet.properties` file in the `src/main/resources` folder (if it doesn't exist yet) and set the following property:

```
resource.actions.configs=resource-actions/default.xml
```

5. Edit `liferay-portlet.xml` and add the following tag in the `<portlet>` section:

```
<add-default-resource>true</add-default-resource>
```

6. Compile and deploy the portlet.

7. Put the portlet on the layout and go to **Options | Configuration menu.**

8. Set the `action.ADD_SECTION` permission for **Power User**.

9. Go back to the Eclipse IDE. In the portlet render method, add the following code:

```
ThemeDisplay themeDisplay = (ThemeDisplay) request.
getAttribute(WebKeys.THEME_DISPLAY);
boolean secretSection = true;
try {
  PermissionChecker permissionChecker =
  themeDisplay.getPermissionChecker();
  String portletId =
  themeDisplay.getPortletDisplay().getId();
  PortletPermissionUtil.check(permissionChecker, portletId,
  "ADD_SECTION");
} catch (PrincipalException pe) {
  secretSection = false;
} catch (SystemException | PortalException e) {}
request.setAttribute("secretSection", secretSection);
```

In our example, the render method is placed in the `com.packtpub.portlet.RolesPortlet` class.

10. Create the `secret.jspf` file in the `src/main/webapp/html` folder with the following content:

```
<c:if test="${requestScope.secretSection}">
  <h2>Secret section</h2>
</c:if>
```

11. Include this file in `guest.jsp` and `user.jsp`:

```
<%@ include file="/html/secret.jspf" %>
```

12. Compile, deploy, and run your portlet.

 You have to also define `c.tld` in both JSP files and in `liferay-plugin-package.properties`. A ready-to-use portlet is included in this book.

How it works...

In general, Liferay divides permissions as `portlet-resources` and `model-resources`. Portlet resources are connected with the portlet and possible operations on the portlet itself (for instance, view, configuration). Model resources describe the possible permissions on the specific model (for instance, create, update, and delete). In this example, we showed only the `portlet-resources` definition, but `model-resources` is similar.

Portlet resources and model resources should be defined in the XML file and put in the classpath. In this recipe, we created two files: `default.xml` and `roles.xml`. This is the typical notation that Liferay applies in the core implementation. The first file lists all the resources where permissions are defined. The second one defines real permissions. It is possible to have just one file including the content of `roles.xml`. Typical resource action mapping consists of:

▸ The portlet name, whose definition should be the same as in the `portlet.xml` file

▸ The `portlet-resource` section, which specifies supported permissions in our portlet, default permissions for a specific role, and unsupported permissions for a specific role

▸ The `model-resource` section, which was not used in this recipe

A very useful option is `<add-default-resource>true</add-default-resource>`, which we added in `liferay-portlet.xml`. The Liferay DTD definition explains this tag as follows:

> *"If the add-default-resource value is set to false and the portlet does not belong to the page but has been dynamically added, then the user will not have permissions to view the portlet. If the add-default-resource value is set to true, the default portlet resources and permissions are added to the page, and the user can then view the portlet. This is useful (and necessary) for portlets that need to be dynamically added to a page. However, to prevent security loopholes, the default value is false."*

The last thing is checking permissions. Liferay gives us a class called `PermissionChecker`, which is enabled in every portlet. `ThemeDisplay` aggregates this implementation. To check for permissions, Liferay provides a method that implements the `PermissionChecker` interface:

```
permissionChecker.hasPermission(groupId, name, primKey, actionId);
```

Arguments of this method are as follows:

- `groupId`: This is the primary key of the group containing the resource
- `name`: This is the resource's name, which can be either a class name or a portlet ID
- `primKey`: This is the primary key of the resource
- `actionId`: This is the action ID

It is possible to use this type of checking in a direct way or to invoke the permission checker from `PortletPermissionUtil`. The second way is recommended by Liferay. The utility class has at least nine static methods called `check` with many variations of arguments depending on the situation. The `check` method doesn't return any value. If there is no permission, the method throws `PrincipalException`.

The second static method is `contain`, which returns `true` if a specific permission is enabled or `false` if the permission is disabled.

As a matter of fact, this recipe only touched upon the basics of permissions in Liferay. On the Internet, there are a lot of tutorials on how to use Liferay permissions and how to implement new functionalities. If we use a *service builder* mechanism with a Liferay-based model, it is quite simple to implement the correct permissions. Liferay adds many things by default.

See also

If you want to learn how to create new portlets or hooks, refer to these recipes:

- The *Creating a custom portlet* in *Chapter 1, Installation and Basic Configuration*
- The *language properties hook* and *Using Liferay Service Bus for communication between portlets* in *Chapter 11, Quick Tricks and Advanced Knowledge*

6

Documents and Media in Liferay

In this chapter, we will cover the following topics:

- ▸ Managing files in Liferay using the Documents and Media portlet
- ▸ Managing document types and metadata sets
- ▸ Integration with the Amazon S3 cloud
- ▸ Data migration between storage hooks

Introduction

The primary task of any intranet is to allow efficient exchange of information between the employees of a company. In most cases, business knowledge is stored in the form of files and—if the company does not have a dedicated system—distributed between mailboxes, network drives, FTP servers, employees' computer drives, and external data carriers. In such cases, there is often a problem in determining who has the current version of the file, whether such documents exist at all, or where to find them. Liferay helps in coping with the dispersal of information by providing an internal repository of files.

Managing files in Liferay using the Documents and Media portlet

Each site in Liferay has its own separate repository, accessible by going to **Admin | Site Administration | Content | Documents and Media**. In addition, it is also possible to place the Documents and Media portlet on one of the pages where it can be shared between users who do not have access to the admin functionalities. The Documents and Media portlet allow us to manage all the folders and documents that can be published within a site.

How to do it...

The Documents and Media portlet provides tools to create, edit, and delete folders, documents, and shortcuts. It also enables us to create multiple documents by uploading whole groups of files. This recipe will cover all the basic actions that can be performed in order to create an efficient and easy-to-search structure of documents and folders.

Creating a new folder

To add a new folder, perform the following steps:

1. Log in as an administrator and go to **Admin | Site Administration | Content | Documents and Media**.

2. Click on the **Add** button.

3. Select the **Folder** or **Subfolder** option.

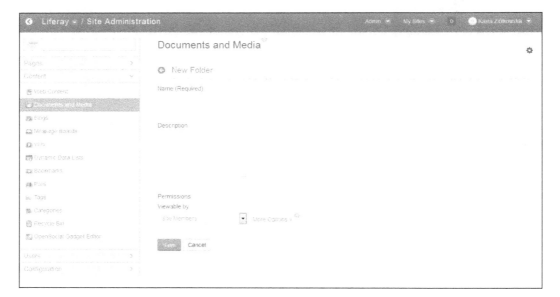

4. Enter the **Name (Required)** of the folder.

5. Enter the **Description** of the folder.

6. Determine the **Permissions** for the folder by setting all actions that may be performed by specific roles (you can find more permissions after clicking on the **More options** link).

7. Click on the **Save** button.

Editing a folder

To edit a folder, perform these steps:

1. Log in as an administrator and go to **Admin | Site Administration | Content | Documents and Media**.

2. Go to the folder you want to edit.

3. Click on its actions icon (the down arrow icon visible when hovering on the folder miniature).

4. Click on the **Edit** button.

5. Provide a new **Name** for the folder.

6. Enter a new **Description** of the folder.

7. Determine the way in which document type restrictions and wokflow definition settings work for this particular folder. You can do this by setting **Use document type restrictions and workflow of the parent folder** by going to the **Document Type Restrictions and Workflow** option.

8. Click on the **Save** button.

Adding a new document

To add a new document, perform these steps:

1. Log in as an administrator and go to **Admin** | **Site Administration** | **Content** | **Documents and Media**.

2. Click on the **Add** button.

3. Select the appropriate document type, for example, Basic Document.

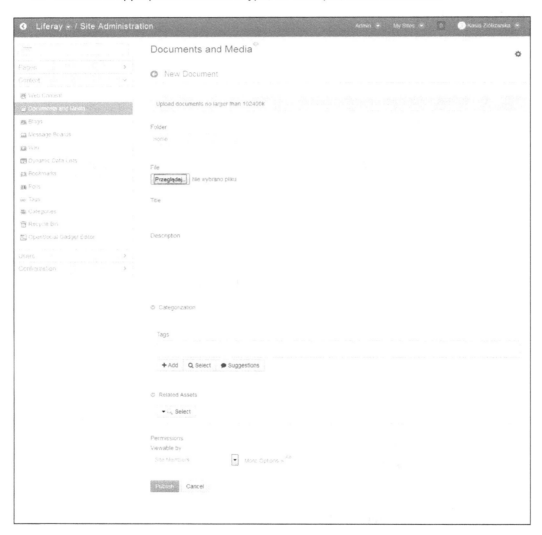

4. Click on the **Select File** button and choose a file from your drive to be added to the repository.

5. Enter the **Title** of the document (if you do not provide a title, the filename will be used as the title).

6. Enter the **Description** of the document.

7. Expand the **Categorization** section.

8. Select **Categories** and type or select **Tags** that describe the document.

    If there are no visible categories that can be assigned to the document, it means that either the categories for the specific site have not been created or the account of the user who is working on it does not have access to the existing dictionaries category.

9. Determine the permissions for the document by setting all actions that may be performed by specific roles.

10. Click on the **Related Assets** button, and find and choose documents (or other content types) that will be set as related content.

11. Click on the **Publish** button.

Uploading multiple documents

It is also possible to add more than one document and set metadata for multiple documents at a time.

To add multiple documents, go to the **Documents and Media** section. Then, follow these steps:

1. Log in as an administrator and go to **Admin | Site Administration | Content | Documents and Media**.

2. Click on the **Add** button.

3. Select the **Multiple Documents** option.

4. Click on the **Select Files** button and choose all the files you want to upload.

 It is also possible to choose the group of files that should be uploaded using drag-and-drop.

5. After uploading all the files, mark the checkboxes next to the names of files that will have the same type, set of tags and categories, and permissions:

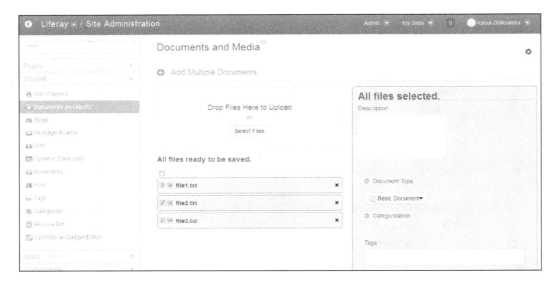

6. Enter the description, choose a document type, and define categories, tags, and permissions for these documents.

7. Click on the **Save** button.

8. Repeat steps 6 and 7 until all the uploaded files are saved.

Editing documents

To edit a document, perform these steps:

1. Log in as an administrator and go to **Admin | Site Administration | Content | Documents and Media**.

2. Go to the document you want to edit.

3. Click on its actions icon:

4. Click on the **Edit** button.

5. Provide a new **Title** and **Description**, choose **Document Type**, define **Categories** and **Tags**, and choose **Related Content** for the edited document.

6. Click on the **Publish** button.

Removing folders and documents

Each folder and document can be temporarily or permanently removed from the repository. Both temporary and permanent removal are done through the *Recycle Bin* mechanism.

To temporarily remove a folder or document, perform these steps:

1. Go to the folder or document you want to delete.

2. Click on its actions icon.

3. Click on the **Move to the Recycle Bin** action.

 You can undo this action by clicking on the undo button that will appear just after moving a document to the trash. By default, trash is enabled and keeps removed items for 30 days. The trash availability for the particular site and the maximum age of trash entries can be changed by going to **Admin | Site Administration | Configurations | Site Settings | Recycle Bin**.

To permanently remove a folder or document, follow these steps:

1. Go to **Admin | Site Administration | Content | Recycle Bin**.

2. Click on the **Actions** button located near the name of the document you want to delete:

3. Click on the **Delete** action and confirm your wish by clicking on **Ok**.

 Note that when removing a folder, its whole content is also removed. It is also possible to restore a document using the **Restore** action available in the **Actions** menu.

How it works...

Liferay's documents and media library allows us to create a tree-like structure of folders and documents. This means that each folder can contain subfolders and documents. Each document in Liferay Portal consists of a file and a set of metadata describing it.

Liferay provides many properties to configure the Documents and Media portlet. They are localized in the `portal-impl/src/portal.properties` file, which can be overridden by `portal-ext.properties` located in the `${liferay.home}` folder. One of the properties is to deny names of files or folders, regardless of the extension:

```
dl.name.blacklist=con,prn,aux,nul,com1,com2,com3,com4,com5,com6,com7,c
om8,com9,lpt1,lpt2,lpt3,lpt4,lpt5,lpt6,lpt7,lpt8,lpt9
```

It is also possible to define the extension's restriction and permit the addition only of defined extensions (by default, this property permits all file extensions). To reduce or add available extensions, set the following property:

```
dl.file.extensions=.bmp,.css,.doc,.docx,.dot,.gif,.gz,.htm,.html,.
jpg,.js,.lar,.odb,.odf,.odg,.odp,.ods,.odt,.pdf,.png,.ppt,.pptx,.rtf,.
swf,.sxc,.sxi,.sxw,.tar,.tiff,.tgz,.txt,.vsd,.xls,.xlsx,.xml,.zip,.
jrxml
```

The next important and useful property is the definition of the maximum size of files. By default, it is unlimited. To change it, define how many bytes are allowed:

```
dl.file.max.size=3072000
```

The Liferay search indexer tries to index the content of the file. It is possible to define which types of extensions should be ignored. You can also define the size for indexing files:

```
dl.file.indexing.ignore.extensions=.exe,.sh,.pdf
dl.file.indexing.max.size=10485760
```

More settings are available in `portal-impl/src/portal.properties` in the Document Library portlet section.

Types of documents

There are five default types of documents: Basic Document, Contract, Marketing Banner, Online Training, and Sales Presentation. Each type of document may contain a different set of metadata. For instance, when adding a new contract, the user can provide data such as effective date, expiration date, contract type, legal reviewer, status, and so on. The Basic Document contains only the basic information, such as name, description, tags, categories and permissions.

Very often, these default document types or metadata sets provided by Liferay are not sufficient. It is required to compose personalized types of documents containing very specific metadata information. This can be achieved using the Document Types and Metadata Sets that create tools, as described in the following recipe.

It is possible to restrict folders to contain documents of one or more particular types. The document type restrictions can be set separately for each folder or inherited from parent folders.

Permissions

Each folder and document has its own permissions set, which defines the list of actions that can be performed on it by users assigned to different roles. For example, it is possible to set such permissions so that users with a specific role will have access to a specific folder, but will not see some of the files stored there.

[For more information on permissions, refer to *Chapter 5, Roles and Permissions*.]

Categories and tags

If an intranet groups a very large number of documents, a well-designed structure cannot sufficiently help users get to the correct documents. Categories and tags provide an additional mechanism to mark, list, and search files and allow their subsequent selection with the help of dedicated portlets, such as Category Navigation, Asset Publisher, or Tag Cloud. Categories as well as documents can create a tree-like structure. Each category is placed in the dictionary and can have subcategories. Tags, on the contrary, are not stored in dictionaries and create a flat structure. It is possible to assign one or more categories and tags to a document.

Related assets

In Liferay, an asset is a piece of content that can be shown on a page, such as a document, web content, blog entry, and so on. Each document can be connected to another document (or other types of assets). These documents will be listed by portlets, such as the Asset Publisher.

Additional information

Let's understand in detail how Liferay stores files with the default configuration. First of all, the system reads a file's metadata, such as extension, title, size. Next, it recognizes the mime type of a file (`image/png`, `audio/mpeg`, `application/pdf`, and so on). This setting depends on the file's extension. The next thing that the portlet does is create a version. By default, the first uploaded file has the version 1.0. Liferay also recognizes in which folder and in which repository a file is added. All of this information is stored in the `DLFileEntry` table. This type of data is called metadata.

By default, physically each file is stored on a local hard drive in the `${liferay.home}/data/document_library` folder. A hierarchy of the folders is very specific. It is difficult to recognize where each file is stored. Let's examine one of the paths to the file: `data/document_library/10157/11501/303/1.0`.

As we said earlier, each file is placed in the `data/document_library` folder. The next folder name is an `instanceId`, which can be set by going to **Admin | Control Panel | Configuration | Portal Instances**. The next identifier is `folderId`. It is good to know that this identifier is exactly a parent folder of this file. If the file is placed in the folder's hierarchy, it is the last folder's identifier. 303 is a number stored in the `DLFileEntry.name` column. Each file has only the version name. In this example, the name of the file is 1.0. In the real world, this is a PNG image. All the necessary data for this file, such as its name, is placed in the database.

 Be careful and remember that a file entry consists of metadata stored in the database and bytes stored on the hard drive in the specific location.

There's more...

It is also possible for the user to create a shortcut to any document that they can access. The permissions set on the shortcut enable the user to access the original document through the shortcut.

In order to create a shortcut, use these steps:

1. Log in as an administrator and go to **Admin | Site Administration | Content | Documents and Media**.
2. Click on the **Add** button.
3. Select the appropriate shortcut.

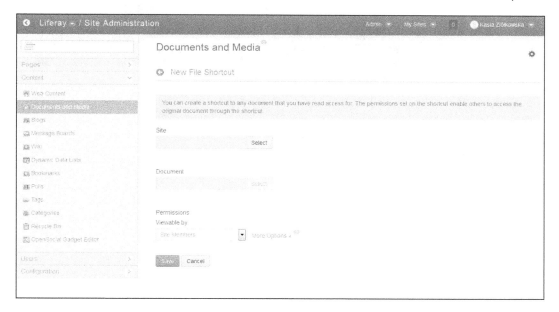

4. Click on the **Site** button and choose the site containing the document for which you want to create a shortcut.

5. Click on the **Document** button and choose the document.

6. Determine the permissions for the shortcut by setting all actions that may be performed by specific roles.

7. Click on the **Save** button.

See also

▶ For information on permissions, refer to the *Creating and configuring roles* recipe from *Chapter 5, Roles and Permissions*

▶ The *Kaleo Web installation* recipe from *Chapter 9, Liferay Workflow Capability*

▶ For more information on categorizing documents, refer to the *Tagging and categorizing content* recipe from *Chapter 8, Search and Content Presentation Tool*

Managing document types and metadata sets

As was mentioned in the previous recipe, each file, while provided with metadata, becomes a document. By default, each document consists of information, such as name, description, category, tags, permissions, or related assets. Very often, the basic set is not sufficient. In such cases, it may be necessary to create a new document type, which allows us to provide a file with specific additional information.

How to do it...

It this recipe, we will describe how to define different types of documents and teach how to compose and use metadata sets.

Creating a new document type using metadata sets

To add a new document type, perform these steps:

1. Log in as an administrator and go to **Admin | Site Administration | Content | Documents and Media**.
2. Click on the **Manage** button.
3. Select the **Document Types** option.
4. Click on the **Add** button.
5. Enter the **Name** of the type of document.
6. Enter a description of the type of document.
7. Determine **Metadata Fields**, which will be available in this type of document, by dragging and dropping fields from the left column menu to the area on the right-hand side.
8. Set all the added fields by clicking on each field and defining its properties (**Field Label**, **Show Label**, **Required**, **Name**, **Predefined Value**, **Tip**, **Indexable**, **Repeatable**, **Options**, and **Multiple**).

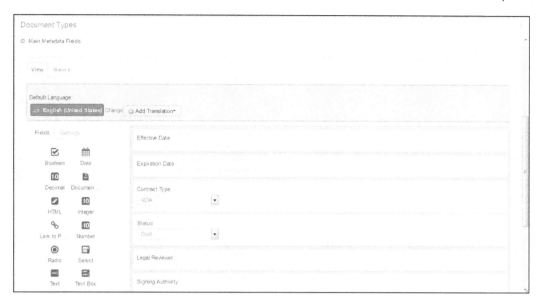

9. Click on **Select Additional Metadata Set** and choose one of the available metadata sets (see the next section of this recipe to understand how to work with metadata sets).

10. Determine the permissions for the document type by setting all actions that may be performed by specific roles.

11. Click on the **Save** button.

Defining metadata sets

To define a new metadata set, perform the following steps:

1. Log in as an administrator and go to **Site Administration | Content | Documents and Media**.

2. Click on the **Manage** button.

3. Select the **Metadata Sets** option.

4. Click on the **Add** button.

5. Enter the **Name (Required)** of the metadata set.
6. Enter the **Description** of the metadata set.
7. Choose **Parent Metadata Set**.
8. Determine **Metadata Fields**, which will be available in this type of document.
9. Click on the **Save** button.

How it works...

When defining a new type of document, we not only define the scope of information that is stored with the file, but also compose a form that allows us to enter the information. Both document type forms and the metadata set form can be composed using a simple form editor. This editor contains a small library of different form fields, such as **Boolean, Date, Decimal, Documents and Media, HTML, Integer, Link to Page, Number, Radio, Select, Text**, and **Text Box**. It is worth noticing that it is also possible to create groups of fields by dragging and dropping one field (or more) onto another.

When defining a new type of document, we have to decide whether the set of fields we want to include will be used in this particular document only or with different document types. In the first case, we can compose the form directly within the new document type. In the second case, it is better to create a metadata set that can be used as a part of many document types, but is managed in one place. Similarly as in case of Liferay assets, metadata sets may be created and used in one particular scope only or, when created in global scope, may be used in all scopes within one Liferay Portal instance.

Additionally, metadata sets can inherit a set of fields from other metadata sets.

Fields can be defined by the following properties:

Type	Defines the type of the field
Field Label	This allows us to provide a label for the field
Show Label	This lets you decide whether the label should be shown or not
Required	This lets you decide whether filling the field is necessary or optional
Name	This allows us to define the name of the field
Predefined Value	This allows us to define they value that will be shown by default before a user enters their own value
Tip	This lets you provide a short text, which will be shown as a tooltip for the field
Indexable	This lets you decide whether the content of the file should be indexed and searched
Repeatable	This allows us to determine whether the field can be repeated
Options	This lets you provide possible options for all the fields that allows users to choose options from a defined list
Multiple	This allows us to determine whether a user can choose more than one option

See also

For information on document management, refer to the *Managing files in Liferay using the Documents and Media portlet* recipe.

Integration with the Amazon S3 cloud

Liferay provides a built-in capability to communicate with the Amazon S3 cloud. This feature gives users a really powerful tool to store their documents in a cloud-based solution. The **Amazon Simple Storage Service** (**Amazon S3**) is a scalable, high-speed, low-cost, and web-based service designed for online backup and archiving of data such as documents, presentations, spreadsheets, pictures, photos, and so on. The greatest feature of the **Amazon Storage** is the fact that it claims 99.99 percent availability of objects over a given year. Moreover, these services provide highly scalable storage that can be easily increased as data increases. The whole infrastructure has secure SSL data transfer and encryption. Amazon Simple Storage Service is a part of the bigger project called **Amazon Web Services** (http://aws.amazon.com). This is a collection of many web services, such as computing cloud, storage cloud, databases, networking, and administration and security.

Liferay gives users a feature to store and manage documents in remote repositories. This type of repository can be Amazon S3. In order to allow communication between a portal and Amazon S3, Liferay uses *JetS3t toolkit*. It is an open source project based on Java. More details about this solution are available at `http://www.jets3t.org/`. Technically, it is a `jets3t.jar` archive placed in the `ROOT/WEB-INF/lib/` folder of the deployed Liferay instance.

How to do it...

Communication between Liferay and Amazon S3 works with Amazon S3 API. In order to properly configure this access, you need to have three things: access key, secret key, and bucket name. To generate this data (access key, secret key, and bucket name), follow these steps:

1. Log in to the Amazon Web Service console: `https://console.aws.amazon.com`.

2. Go to **Your Name** | **Security Credentials** on the dockbar.

3. Expand **Access Keys** (access key ID and secret access key).

4. Click on the **Create New Access Key** button.

5. On the popup window, you will see the following message:

   Your access key (access key ID and secret access key) has been created successfully.

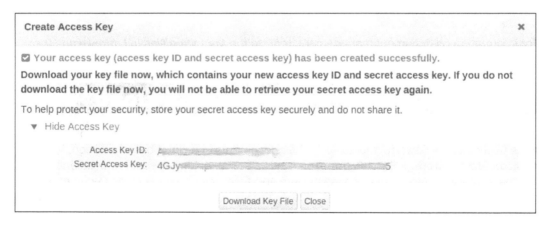

6. Click on **Show Access Key** and copy **Access Key ID** and **Secret Access Key**. This pair of keys will be used a little later.

The next few steps are responsible for creating a new bucket, where Liferay will store its files:

1. In `https://console.aws.amazon.com`, go to **Services | S3**.

2. To create a new bucket, click on the **Create Bucket** button.

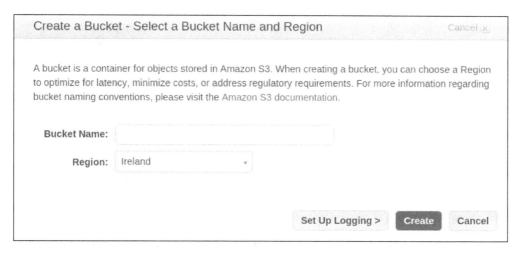

3. Fill in all required fields and save the form.

4. Remember your bucket name.

The last thing is Liferay Portal configuration. As we said in the beginning, Liferay provides a built-in capability to communicate with Amazon, so the configuration is not difficult. It is only a simple setting with `${liferay.home}/portal-ext.properties`:

```
dl.store.impl=com.liferay.portlet.documentlibrary.store.S3Store
dl.store.s3.access.key=<ACCESS KEY ID>
dl.store.s3.secret.key=<SECRET ACCESS KEY>
dl.store.s3.bucket.name=<BUCKET NAME>
```

Finally, restart your portal instance and try to upload a file in the Documents and Media portlet. From the user's point of view, it should not be any different with the upload action. In order to see the difference, you can log in to the S3 storage bucket to check out the uploaded file.

How it works...

The portal provides many configurable hooks to upload and put documents into various persistence systems. All of them are implemented as Liferay core functionalities. The basic and default persistence system is `FileSystemStore`, which keeps data in the local hard drive. Liferay provides other implementations, such as `AdvancedFileSystemStore`, `CMISStore`, `DBStore`, `JCRStore`, and `S3Store`. One of these types can be set in `portal-ext.properties`:

```
dl.store.impl=com.liferay.portlet.documentlibrary.store.
AdvancedFileSystemStore
dl.store.impl=com.liferay.portlet.documentlibrary.store.CMISStore
dl.store.impl=com.liferay.portlet.documentlibrary.store.DBStore
dl.store.impl=com.liferay.portlet.documentlibrary.store.
FileSystemStore
dl.store.impl=com.liferay.portlet.documentlibrary.store.JCRStore
dl.store.impl=com.liferay.portlet.documentlibrary.store.S3Store
```

The following description shows differences in storage implementation:

- `FileSystemStore`: This saves documents directly to the local filesystem.
- `AdvancedFileSystemStore`: Similar to `FileSystemStore`, but divides the data into buckets (folders), thus avoiding the many-files-in-one-directory limitation.
- `DBStore`: Keeps binary data in the database as blobs.
- `CMISStore`: **Content Management Interoperability Services** (**CMIS**) is a specification to improve the interoperability between **Enterprise Content Management** (**ECM**) systems. Documents and Media allow users to connect to multiple third-party repositories that support CMIS 1.0 with **AtomPub** and web service protocols. It is possible to integrate Liferay with many CMIS-compliant ECM vendors, such as SharePoint, Alfresco, Documentum, IBM FileNet, and so on.
- `JCRStore`: Implements content repository API for Java. The well-known implementation is **Apache Jackrabbit**. So, if this hook is set, it is possible to keep binary data in the Apache Jackrabbit content repository.
- `S3Store`: Keeps data in the Amazon Simple Storage Service.

Let's examine a code that is responsible for this integration. The `S3Store` class implements the `Store` interface. Thus, it provides all the necessary operations on files, for instance, `addFile`, `addDirectory`, `deleteFile`, `deleteDirectory`, and so on. In `portal-ext.properties`, we set the `dl.store.impl` property as the `S3Store` class.

Liferay uses the JetS3t toolkit to communicate with Amazon services. This toolkit is responsible for transferring files from/to Amazon Cloud.

In the Amazon S3 repository, the structure of the folders and files looks the same as in the local filesystem. The following screenshot shows an example of the folder hierarchy:

There's more...

Integration with Amazon S3 Cloud works perfectly if the document library repository is small. The problems occur when the number of concurrent users and number of files is huge. The problem is between `HttpClient` and S3 and their parallel communication (concurrent communication threads). It is possible to increase the number of connections by overriding `jets3t.properties`. To properly change it, put this file in the Tomcat classpath, for instance, in the `${CATALINA_BASE}/lib` folder. Afterwards, change the following properties and try to fit the values to your environment:

```
s3service.internal-error-retry-max=10 (Liferay 6.0 and 6.1)
cloudfront-service.internal-error-retry-max=10 (Liferay 6.2)
threaded-service.max-thread-count=100
httpclient.retry-max=10
httpclient.connection-timeout-ms=90000
httpclient.socket-timeout-ms=90000
httpclient.max-connections=100
```

The official documentation at `https://jets3t.s3.amazonaws.com/toolkit/configuration.html` describes the properties as follows:

Property name	Description
`s3service.internal-error-retry-max`	This refers to the maximum number of concurrent communication threads that will be started by the `ThreadedStorageService`/`SimpleThreadedStorageService` services for upload and download operations. This value should not be too high. Otherwise, you risk I/O errors due to bandwidth starvation when transferring many large files. *It works only with Liferay 6.0 and Liferay 6.1.*
`cloudfront-service.internal-error-retry-max`	This refers to the maximum number of retries that will be attempted when a CloudFront connection fails with an InternalServer error. To disable retries of InternalError failures, set this to 0. *It works only with Liferay 6.2.*

Property name	Description
`threaded-service.max-thread-count`	This is the maximum number of concurrent communication threads that will be started by the `ThreadedStorageService`/`SimpleThreadedStorageService` services for upload and download operations. This value should not be too high. Otherwise, you risk I/O errors due to bandwidth starvation when transferring many large files. The default value is `2`. This value must not exceed the maximum number of HTTP connections available to JetS3t, as set by the `httpclient.max-connections` property.
`httpclient.retry-max`	This determines the number of times to retry connections when they fail with I/O errors. Set this to `0` to disable retries. The default value is `5`.
`httpclient.connection-timeout-ms`	This determines the number of milliseconds to wait before a connection times out. `0` means infinity. The default value is `60000`.
`httpclient.socket-timeout-ms`	This determines the number of milliseconds to wait before a socket connection times out. `0` means infinity. The default value is `60000`.
`httpclient.max-connections`	This refers to the maximum number of simultaneous connections to be allowed globally. The default value is `20`. If you have a fast Internet connection, you can improve the performance of your S3 client by increasing this setting and the corresponding S3 Service properties, `s3service.max-thread-count` and `s3service.admin-max-thread-count`. However, be careful because, if you increase this value too much for your connection, you may exceed your available bandwidth and cause communication errors.

See also

For information on building scalable systems, refer to the *Scalable infrastructure* recipe in *Chapter 12, Basic Performance Tuning*.

Data migration between storage hooks

This recipe is dedicated to administrators who have to change from one store implementation to another for any reason. This example shows you how we can migrate binary files stored in the document library to other storage repositories. In our example, we will examine migration from S3Store (Amazon S3) to the local `FileSystemStore` repository hook.

How to do it...

Liferay has a built-in functionality to migrate documents between storage hooks. Let's assume that our Liferay instance is already started, and the library is connected to the Amazon S3 cloud. In order to migrate documents to the filesystem, go through the following steps:

1. Log in as an administrator to the Liferay instance.
2. Go to **Admin | Control Panel**.
3. Then go to **Configuration | Server Administration | Data Migration**.
4. Scroll to the **Migrate documents from one repository to another** section.
5. Select a new repository hook called **com.liferay.portlet.documentlibrary.store. FileSystemStore**.

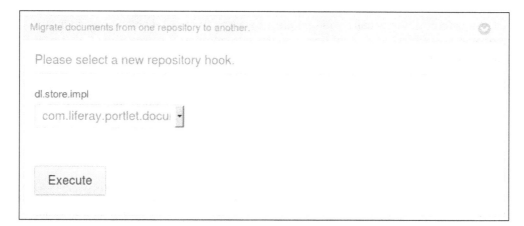

6. Click on the **Execute** button.
7. Liferay temporarily changes the status to maintenance mode.

8. Look into the `catalina.out` log and check the execution. The log file should look like this:

```
DEBUG [liferay/convert_process-1][MaintenanceUtil:64] Please set
dl.store.impl in your portal-ext.properties to use com.liferay.
portlet.documentlibrary.store.FileSystemStore
[liferay/convert_process-1] [ConvertProcess:47] Finished conversion
for com.liferay.portal.convert.ConvertDocumentLibrary in 3010 ms
```

How it works...

Liferay provides powerful features to migrate data between store hooks. It is an important tool when our Liferay instance works and our project manager or product owner wants to change the storage system to another, such as Amazon S3 or even SharePoint. Moreover, it is possible to do it without your developers having to write custom scripts. This functionality is implemented in the `com.liferay.portal.convert.ConvertDocumentLibrary` class. The `doConvert` method invokes migration processes for the following files:

▸ Migrate images

▸ Migrate document libraries

▸ Migrate message board attachments

▸ Migrate wiki attachments

In fact, these four methods call *Dynamic Query* to get all the file definitions placed in the database and physically copy them from one place to another. The structure of all the folders and files is mapped one by one.

 Carefully study your logfile in order to make sure that all of the data is moved correctly.

See also

For information on how to change a database engine, refer to the *Migrating content from one database to another database* recipe in *Chapter 11, Quick Tricks and Advanced Knowledge*.

7

Working with Content

In this chapter, we will cover the following topics:

- ▸ Managing and displaying web contents
- ▸ Creating a new structure
- ▸ Creating a new template

Introduction

As was described in the previous chapter, Liferay provides a whole set of tools that allows us to manage files that store data exchanged between the employees of the company. However, in many cases, it is not quite convenient for end users to operate on the information stored in files. For example, it is much easier to navigate through the content available directly on the web page than in a file while reading the news or browsing the corporate knowledge base. Information such as news, project descriptions, procedures, and so on can be provided using web content. The web content can be displayed on a page using some specific portlets, such as the Web Content Display portlet or the Asset Publisher portlet.

Managing and displaying web contents

Each site in Liferay has its own separate set of web contents, which can be accessed by going to **Admin** | **Site Administration** | **Content** | **Web Content**. All the web contents stored in the **Web Content** section can be organized in a tree-like folder structure. The web content can contain text, graphics, tables, lists, and links to other web contents, documents, or pages. Additionally, every web content can be tagged and categorized or provided with the list of assets related to it. This list will be listed in the related assets section under the main content of the web content. It is also possible to define permissions that specify which actions can be performed on web contents by users assigned to different roles.

How to do it...

This recipe will cover all the basic actions that can be performed in order to manage web contents within a site.

Creating a new folder

To add a new folder, perform these steps:

1. Log in as an administrator and go to **Admin | Site Administration | Content | Web Content**.

2. Click on the **Add** button.

3. Select the **Folder** option (if you add a folder inside one that is already created, the **Subfolder** option will be available instead).

4. Enter the **Name (Required)** of the folder.

5. Enter the **Description** of the folder.

6. Determine **Permissions** for the folder by setting all actions that may be performed by specific roles (you can find more permissions after clicking on the **More Options** link).

7. Click on the **Save** button.

Downloading the example code

You can download the example code files from your account at `http://www.packtpub.com` for all the Packt Publishing books you have purchased. If you purchased this book elsewhere, you can visit `http://www.packtpub.com/support` and register to have the files e-mailed directly to you.

Editing a folder

To edit a folder, follow these steps:

1. Log in as an administrator and go to **Admin | Site Administration | Content | Web Content**.

2. Find the folder that you want to edit.

3. Click on its actions icon (the down-arrow icon visible when hovering on the folder miniature).

4. Click on the **Edit** button.

5. Provide a new **Name (required)** for the folder.

6. Enter a new **Description** of the folder.

7. Determine new **Permissions** for the folder by setting all actions that may be performed by specific roles.

8. Leave the **Merge with Parent Folder** option unchecked.

9. Click on the **Save** button.

Creating a new web content

To create a new basic web content, perform these roles:

1. Log in as an administrator and go to **Admin | Site Administration | Content | Web Content**.

2. Click on the **Add** button.

3. Choose the **Basic web content** option.

4. Provide the **Title (Required)** and **Content**.

5. Navigate to the **Abstract** tab.

6. Provide a **Summary**.

7. Set the small image by providing a URL or by uploading it from your computer drive. Then, select the **Use Small Image** option.

8. Navigate to the **Categorization** tab.

9. Choose **Type** from the type drop-down list, for example, **News**.

10. Choose **Categories** from the available category dictionaries (represented by a name and a related **Select** button) by clicking on the button beside the dictionary and marking the categories.

If there are no visible categories that can be assigned to the document, it means that either the categories for the specific site have not been created or the account user, who is working on it, does not have access to the existing category's dictionaries.

11. Provide **Tags** by adding new tags. You can choose them from the list of existing tags or use the suggestions function.

12. Navigate to the **Schedule** tab.

13. Set the **Display date**, **Review date**, and **Expiration date** functions (or enable the **Never expire** and **Never review** functions).

14. Navigate to the **Display Page** tab.

15. Choose the page on which you want the web content to be displayed in full.

The display page will be available if there is at least one page containing the Asset Publisher portlet with the **Set as the Default Asset Publisher for This Page** option enabled. Page names without an Asset Publisher portlet are shown in gray instead of black. For more information, refer to the *Asset Publisher as a search-based tool for content presentation* recipe from *Chapter 8, Search and Content Presentation Tools*.

16. Navigate to the **Related Assets** tab.

17. Choose **Related Assets**, which should be listed under the full text of your web content.

18. Click on the **Publish** button.

It is possible to preview web content before publishing it using the basic preview option. This option becomes available after saving the first draft of the web content. However, the basic preview function does not allow us to preview web content in a theme context. Instead, it is presented in default view.

Displaying web content in the Web Content Display portlet

In order to display web content in the Web Content Display portlet, perform these steps:

1. Go to the page on which you want to display the web content.

2. Click on the add icon (this is a **+** sign on the left-hand side).

3. Click on the **Applications** tab.

4. Find the **Web Content Display** portlet using the search feature or by browsing the list of available portlets.

5. Click on the **Add** link located next to it or drag and drop it on the page you want.

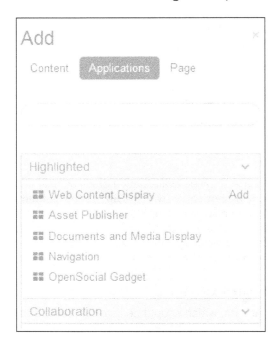

6. Click on the added portlet options icon (this will be a gear icon in the top-right corner of the portlet).

7. Choose the **Configuration** option.

8. From the list, choose the web content (by clicking on its name) that you want to display in a portlet.

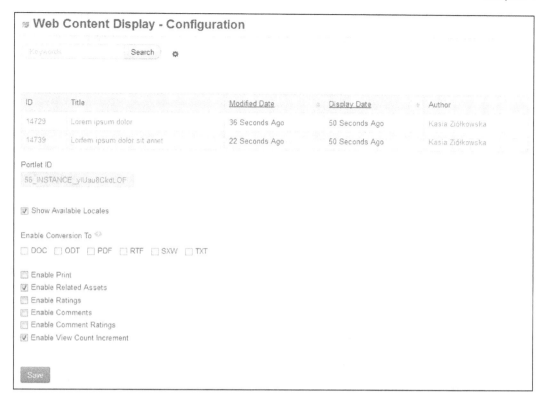

9. Choose the list of additional functionalities that should be available in a portlet (for example, the **Enable Print** or **Enable Comments** option).

10. Click on the **Save** button.

Editing web content

In order to modify existing web content, follow these steps:

1. Log in as an administrator and go to **Admin | Site Administration | Content | Web Content**.

2. From the list of available web contents, choose the one you want to modify.

3. Click on the name of the chosen web content or choose the **Edit** action from its **Actions** menu.

4. When the form opens, edit the field you want to change.

5. Click on the **Publish** button.

Adding translation to an existing web content

To add a translation to an existing web content, perform these steps:

1. Log in as an administrator and go to **Admin | Site Administration | Content | Web Content**.

2. From the list of available web contents, choose the one you want to define a translation for.

3. Click on the name of the chosen web content or choose the **Edit** action from its actions menu.

4. Click on the **Add Translation** button.

5. Choose the language you want to create a translation for (if you want, change the available languages by referring to *The language properties hook* recipe from *Chapter 11, Quick Tricks and Advanced Knowledge*).

6. Provide a **Title**, **Content**, and **Summary** for this language.

7. Click on the **Save** button.

All the available translations are listed in the available translations section placed just after the **Add Translation** button in the edit content page. It is possible to manage (including removing) the translation using a form that can be accessed after clicking on the translation name in this section.

8. Click on the **Publish** button.

Expiring web content

There are two ways of expiring web content. The first way, described previously, is to set the expiration date while adding or editing a web content. The second option is to use the expire action available in the **Web Content** actions menu. Go through the following steps to follow this option of expiring web content:

1. Log in as an administrator and go to **Admin | Site Administration | Content | Web Content**.

2. From the list of available web contents, choose the one you want to modify.

3. Click on the **Actions** menu of the chosen web content.

Choose the **Expire** action. To make the expired web content available for users, it is required that you edit and publish it again.

Removing folders and web content

Each folder and web content can be temporarily or permanently removed. Both temporary and permanent removal are done through the **Recycle Bin** mechanism.

To temporarily remove a folder or web content, follow these steps:

1. Go to the folder or web content that needs to be deleted.
2. Click on its actions icon.
3. Click on the **Move to the Recycle Bin** action.

 You can undo this action by clicking on the **Undo** button that will appear just after moving a web content to the trash.

To permanently remove a folder or web content, follow these steps:

1. Log in as an administrator and go to **Admin | Site Administration | Content | Recycle Bin**.
2. Click on the **Actions** button, which is located near the name of the web content or folder you want to delete:

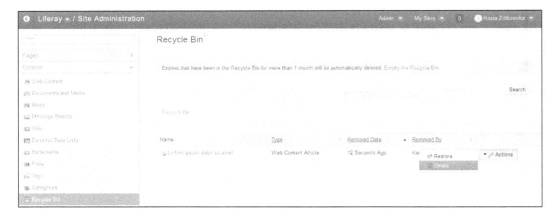

3. Click on the **Delete** action and confirm your choice by clicking on **OK**.

 Note that when you remove a folder, its entire content is also removed. By default, the trash is enabled and keeps removed items for 30 days. The trash availability for the particular site and the maximum age of trash entries can be changed by going to **Admin | Site Administration | Configurations | Site Settings | Recycle Bin**.

It is also possible to restore the web content or web content folder using the **Restore** action available in the **Actions** menu.

How it works...

The **Web Content** section allows us to create a tree-like folder structure to organize web contents stored within a site. It is possible to create or move a web content to a default folder (`Home`) or to one of the folders defined by users. It is also possible to merge one folder (and its content) with another. While creating or editing a web content, the user has a choice to save it as a draft or publish it. Draft versions of web content can be accessed by going to **Admin | Site Administration | Content | Web Content** for authorized users only. Published versions can be seen by end users. Each time a web content is published, its version increases. All versions are available in the web content history, which can be accessed from the web content editing form.

If there is a need to hide the previously published web content from end users but keep it within the system, the expire action should be used. As was shown previously, it is possible to schedule a time of publication and expiration of the web content.

Each web content has a unique ID, title, status, and version number. There are three available statuses:

- **Approved**: This is dedicated for published web contents, which can be placed in a portlet on a page and is available for end users
- **Drafts**: They are reserved for web content where the newest version has not been published yet
- **Expired**: This marks all the web contents that have been expired and are not available for end users

Permissions

Each folder and web content has its own permissions set, which defines the list of actions that can be performed on it by users assigned to different roles. For example, it is possible to set such permissions so that users with a specific role will be able to provide commentaries on one particular web content, but won't be permitted to do the same with some other web content.

Categorization

The **Categorization** tab in the web content adding and editing forms allows us to define the type, categories, and tags of the web content. Categories and tags provide an additional mechanism to mark, list, and search web content and allow their subsequent selection with the help of dedicated portlets such as Category Navigation, Asset Publisher, or Tag Cloud. Categories can create a tree-like structure. Each category is placed in the dictionary and can have subcategories. Tags, on the contrary, are not stored in dictionaries and create a flat structure. It is possible to assign a web content to one or more categories and tags. Types are used to search the web content within the **Web Content** section.

Related assets

In Liferay, an asset is a piece of content that can be shown on a page, such as a document, web content, blog entry, and so on. Each web content can be connected to another web content, document, or different types of assets, such as commentaries, blog entries, and so on. These web contents will be listed by portlets such as Asset Publisher.

Placing web content on a page

As was shown previously, the web content section allows us to organize web contents in a structure of folders that help us manage web contents within the site. However, this structure doesn't have any influence on the information architecture of the site. In order to place a web content on a page, it is required that you use dedicated portlets, such as the Web Content Display or Asset Publisher portlet. The Web Content Display portlet allows us to show the full content of exactly one web content at a time. The Asset Publisher portlet (described in the following chapter) is much more complex and enables us to create a different list of contents. It also allows us to display the web content in full-content view.

Display page

The Display page parameter allows us to decide on which page a particular web content will be shown in full-content view within the Asset Publisher portlet.

See also

- For more information on how to present web content on a page, refer to the *Tagging and categorizing content* and *Asset Publisher as a search-based tool for content presentation* recipes from *Chapter 8, Search and Content Presentation Tools*

- For more information about permissions, refer to the following recipes:

    - *Creating and configuring roles* from *Chapter 5, Roles and Permissions*

    - *Kaleo Web installation* and *The Single Approver workflow for the user creation process* from *Chapter 9, Liferay Workflow Capability*

- For more information on Web Content, refer to the *Creating a new structure* and the *Creating a new template* recipes from this chapter

Creating a new structure

Liferay gives users interesting features: structures and templates. Structures provide information about possible fields in our content, and templates are responsible for rendering these fields as an article in a frontend (for instance, in the Asset Publisher or Web Content Display portlet).

Let's assume that our goal is to define a new structure and template called *Internal publication*. This structure consists of the following fields:

Name	Type	Required	Repeatable
Author	Text	Yes	No
Department	Select	Yes	No
Project	Text Box	No	No
Client	Text	Yes	No
Content	HTML	No	No
Attachment	Documents and Media	No	Yes

How to do it...

In order to define a new structure, it is required that you log in as a user with the **Add Structure** permission in the **Web Content** section. To achieve this goal, go through the following steps:

1. Log in as an administrator.
2. Go to **Admin | Site Administration | Content | Web Content**.
3. Click on the **Manage** option and choose **Structures**.
4. Click on the **Add** button.
5. Type the name of the structure, which is `Internal publication`.
6. It is possible to choose the default language and add some description. We will leave it as default.
7. Go to the section where there is a drag-and-drop functionality to define fields.
8. Choose the **Text** field and drag and drop this field into the gray section.
9. Click on the added element, go to the **Settings** tab, and set the following properties:

   - **Field** label as **Author**
   - **Required** as **Yes**
   - **Indexable** as **Indexable – keywords**
   - **Repeatable** as **No**

10. Click on the **Close** button to save information and go back to the **Fields** tab.

11. Repeat steps 8 and 9 to define all the necessary fields that were described in our assumptions. The result should look like this:

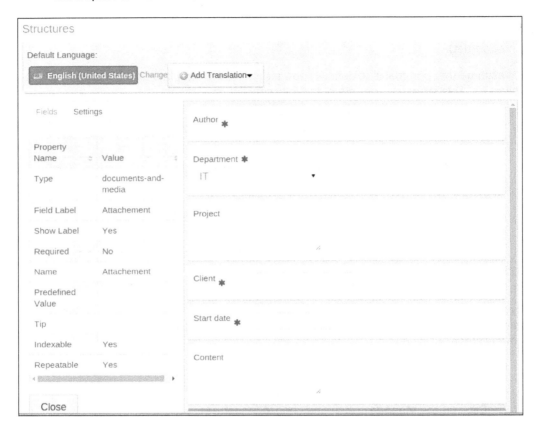

12. Click on the **Save** button.

13. To check out the newly created structure, go to **Web Content | Add | Internal publication**.

How it works...

The structure is an XML definition of the web content form. It gives users the following thirteen predefined types:

▶ **Boolean**: This adds a checkbox onto our structure with true/false values

▶ **Date**: Adds an input text with a calendar (date picker)

▶ **Decimal**: Adds an input that accepts only numbers and decimal point

▶ **Documents and Media**: Adds an existing uploaded document to attach to the structure

▶ **HTML**: Adds a WYSIWYG editor

▶ **Image**: Adds a browse-image application

▶ **Integer**: Adds an input that accepts only numbers

▶ **Link to page**: Adds a select list to select links to another page

▶ **Number**: Similar to Integer and allows only numbers

▶ **Radio**: Adds a radio button

▶ **Select**: Add a select list with options

▶ **Text**: Adds an input text

▶ **Text Box**: Adds a text area component

In the background, each definition is stored as an XML node called `<dynamic-element>`. It is possible to look at how the definition is built by clicking on the **Source** tab from the edit mode of the structure. Here is an example of our `Author` definition:

```
<dynamic-element dataType="string" indexType="keyword" name="Author"
readOnly="false" repeatable="false" required="true" showLabel="true"
type="text" width="small">
  <meta-data locale="en_US">
    <entry name="label">
      <![CDATA[Author]]>
    </entry>
    <entry name="predefinedValue">
      <![CDATA[]]>
    </entry>
    <entry name="tip">
      <![CDATA[]]>
    </entry>
  </meta-data>
</dynamic-element>
```

This definition describes all the fields that we set, such as `dataType: string`, `indexType: keyword`, `name: Author`, and so on.

Each row has many attributes, such as `predefinedValue`, `tip`, `required`, and so on. The following table shows the most important attributes:

Property name	Value	Description
Type	Predefined field type	Type of the field definition
Field label	String	Label of the field
Show label	Yes/No	Determines label visibility
Required	Yes/No	Sets field as required field
Name	String	Name of the field, usually the same as label
Predefined value	String	Sets the default value
Tip	String	A tip (description) of the field
Indexable	Not indexable / Indexable—Keyword / Indexable—Text	Defines an indexer type and indicates which type of search indexer will be used
Repeatable	Yes/No	Allows us to set the field as repeatable
Width	Small/Medium/Large	Allows us to define the width of the field

There is more...

The journal structure provides interesting functionalities to set default values for articles that will be created from this structure. One of the possibilities is to set a predefined value on the edit structure screen. However, Liferay also gives us an option called **Edit Default Values**. This setting is really interesting when our requirement is that every article that will be generated from this structure should have a predefined specific category, tag, display page, and so on. In the background, this is an article that has a specific setting in the database in order to prevent it from it being chosen or found by Asset Publisher, Web Content Display, or even searches.

To set the default values, follows these steps:

1. Log in as an administrator.
2. Go to **Admin | Site Administration | Content**.
3. Click on the **Manage** option and choose **Structures**.
4. In the selected structure, such as **Internal Publication**, go to **Actions | Edit default values**.
5. Fill in the default values and click on the **Save** button.

Creating a new template

This recipe requires basic programming skills. In general, a template is a pattern to render values from an article with a specific structure. In accordance with this fact, a template is relative to the structure, so a structure and template are a pair of definitions that can't exist alone. Structures define how the form looks; templates determine how the journal article will be rendered and arranged.

Getting ready...

Prepare a structure called **Internal publication**. To see how to achieve this, refer to the previous recipe.

Let's assume that our template is divided into four parts:

▸ Metadata definition that contains *Author* and *Department*

▸ Metric definition with *Client* and *Project* information

▸ Description part with *Content*

▸ *Attachments* section

How to do it...

Liferay gives users three languages to write a template: Velocity (.vm), FreeMarker (.ftl), and Extensible Stylesheet Language (.xsl). Regardless of the language definition, the process of creating a new template consists of the same rules. In order to create a new template, follow these steps:

1. Log in as an administrator.

2. Go to **Admin | Site Administration | Content | Web Content**.

3. Click on the **Manage** option and choose **Templates**.

4. Click on the **Add** button.

5. Fill in the form with the following values:

    ❑ **Name**: Type `Internal Publication`

    ❑ **Structure**: Choose **Internal Publication**

    ❑ **Language**: Choose **Velocity (.vm)**

6. Write a script that renders our assumptions as follows:

```
<div class="article-container">
  <div class="article-metadata">
    <span>Create Date: $dateTool.format( 'medium_date',
    $dateTool.toDate( "EEE, dd MMM yyyy hh:mm:ss Z" ,
    $reserved-article-display-date.getData(),
    $localeUtil.getDefault()) , $locale), Author:
    $Author.getData(), Department:
    $Department.getData()</span>
  </div>
  <hr />
  <div class="article-metric">
    <table>
      <tr>
        <td>Client:</td>
        <td>$Client.getData()</td>
      </tr>
      <tr>
        <td>Project:</td>
        <td>$Project.getData()</td>
      </tr>
    </table>
  </div>


#if($Content.getData().length() > 0)
  <hr />
    <div class="article-content">
      $Content.getData()
    </div>
  #end

  #if($Attachment.size() > 0)
  <hr />
    <div class="article-attachment">
      <div>Attachments:</div>
      #foreach($file in $Attachment.getSiblings())
      <a href="$file.getData()">Attachment #
      $velocityCount</a><br />
      #end
    </div>
  #end
  </div>
```

7. Click on the **Save** button.

How it works...

As we mentioned at the beginning, Liferay gives users three ways (languages) to write an article's template: Velocity (.vm), FreeMarker (.ftl), and Extensible Stylesheet Language (.xls). In this recipe, we chose Velocity macro, which allows us to mix logic (macros) with HTML and CSS. If we open an editor, we can see that on the left-hand side, there is a menu with **General Variables**, **Fields**, and **Util**, as shown in the following screenshot:

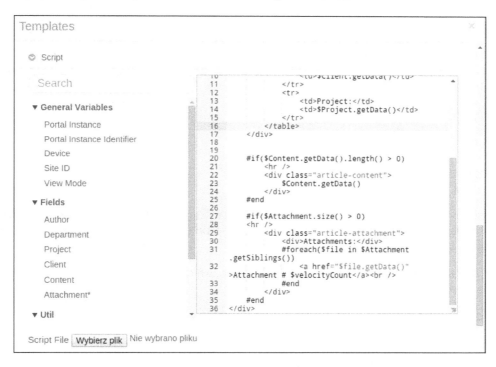

Variables

The **General Variables** section contains variables that can be used in the script. As a matter of fact, these definitions are used rarely and only in sophisticated VM or FTL scripts. The following variables are available:

Name	Variable	Liferay Class	Description
Portal instance	$company	Company	Object that represents the current portal instance
Portal instance identifier	$companyId	Long	Identifier of the current portal instance

Name	Variable	Liferay Class	Description
Device	`$device`	Device	Object that represents the device currently used to access the site
Site ID	`$groupId`	Long	The identifier of the current site
View mode	`$viewMode`	String	The desired view mode for the content; the value will be `print` for print mode

Fields

These objects can be used in our scripts. For instance, the `$Content.getData()` invocation prints a value from the `Content` field of the structure. As shown in the preceding code, we used this invocation for the following fields:

```
$Author.getData()
$Department.getData()
$Client.getData()
$Project.getData()
$Content.getData()
$file.getData()
```

The next useful invocation is `$Attachment.getSiblings()`. This method is used when our field is repeatable and contains many values. In our example, the `Attachment` field has two siblings.

To iterate over siblings, we used the `foreach` macro, which is very similar to the well-known `foreach` construction from the Java language.

Considering the preceding code, fields have other methods, such as the following ones:

- ▶ `$field.getName()`: This prints the field's name
- ▶ `$field.getType()`: This returns field's type, which is defined in the structure
- ▶ `$field.getChildren()`: This is used when a field has nested fields

Utils

The most powerful tools that are available in the script are utils. In fact, there are real Java-based classes that offer a huge range of functionalities. In our example, we used one to print a display date of the article:

```
$dateTool.format( 'medium_date', $dateTool.toDate( "EEE, dd MMM yyyy
hh:mm:ss Z" , $reserved-article-display-date.getData(), $localeUtil.
getDefault())
```

The full list of available services is placed in the following Java classes:

- ▶ com.liferay.portal.template.TemplateContextHelper
- ▶ com.liferay.portal.velocity.VelocityTemplateContextHelper (for Velocity)
- ▶ com.liferay.portal.freemarker.FreeMarkerTemplateContextHelper (for FreeMarker)

Reserved variables

The preceding code has a special invocation: $reserved-article-display-date. getData(). This is a reserved variable that is globally available in every template. In our example, it displays display date for the article. Liferay offers many reserved variables, such as reserved-article-title, reserved-article-type, reserved-article-version, and so on.

The full list of these variables is defined in the com.liferay.portlet.journal.model. JournalStructureConstants class.

8

Search and Content Presentation Tools

In this chapter, we will cover the following topics:

- ▸ Tagging and categorizing content
- ▸ Asset Publisher as a search-based tool for content presentation
- ▸ Defining application display templates for Asset Publisher
- ▸ Search portlet – basic configuration
- ▸ Solr installation and configuration

Introduction

Liferay provides a powerful built-in tool that allows us to search for content. This is one of the most important functionalities in Liferay. Why? The answer is simple: searching is needed everywhere. It is not possible to find or locate an article, wiki, or document in the tangle of content without a good search engine. Liferay architecture provides a useful tool to index, search, and display such documents as faceted results. Faceted means grouped by a specific thematic category, grouped by a specific entity type, or other such criteria.

In fact, there is a whole bunch of search functionalities in Liferay. It is possible to find entities using SQL queries as well as using a dedicated search engine called Apache Lucene (`http://lucene.apache.org`). In many places (especially in the configuration or in the control panel), Liferay finds entities using SQL queries. On the other hand, Portal provides a dedicated portlet called Search Portlet, which allows us to search using the Lucene engine.

Tagging and categorizing content

Categories and tags provide a powerful mechanism to mark, list, and search different assets and allow their subsequent selection with the help of dedicated portlets such as Category Navigation, Asset Publisher, or Tag Cloud. The mechanism is very simple: tags and categories are assigned to web contents, documents, or other types of assets. Then, it is possible to set portlets to present only those assets with a specific category and/or tags. It is possible to assign one or more categories and/or tags to an asset.

How to do it...

Categories and tags can be assigned to any asset while adding or editing this asset. For instance, as was shown in the previous chapters (*Chapter 6, Documents and Media in Liferay* and *Chapter 7, Working with Content*), a new (and edited) web content or a new (and edited) document form provides a categorization section. This section allows us to choose the set of categories and define the list of tags that will be assigned to a document or web content after submitting the form. However, what is important to know is that the process of assigning is different for categories and tags. Tags can be defined directly in the content adding form, while categories must be created in site administration to make it available for assigning.

Categories are stored in vocabularies. In order to create a category, you have to first create a vocabulary using the following steps:

1. Log in as an administrator and go to **Admin | Site Administration | Content | Categories**.
2. Click on the **Add Vocabulary** button.

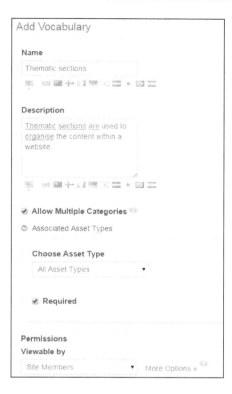

3. Provide a **Name** and **Description** for a new vocabulary.

4. Enable the **Allow Multiple Categories** option.

5. Set **All Asset Types** in the **Choose Asset Type** drop-down list.

6. Enable the **Required** option.

7. Determine **Permissions** for the vocabulary by setting all actions that may be performed by specific roles (you can find more permissions after clicking on the **More Options** link).

8. Click on the **Save** button.

When **Vocabulary** is ready, it is possible to fill it with **Categories**. To add a category, follow these steps:

1. Log in as an administrator and go to **Admin | Site Administration | Content | Categories**.

2. Click on the **Add Category** button.

3. Provide a **Name** and **Description** for the new category.

4. From the **To Vocabulary** drop-down list, choose the vocabulary you want to create a category in.

5. Determine **Permissions** for the category by setting all actions that may be performed by specific roles (you can find more permissions after clicking on the **More Options** link).

6. Click on the **Save** button.

After creating a category, it is possible to assign it to the asset. Let's assign the previously created category to an existing web content using the following steps:

1. Log in as an administrator and go to **Admin | Site Administration | Content | Web Content**.

2. Click on the name of one already existing web content.

3. Navigate to the **Categorization** tab.

4. Click on the **Select** button located near the name of the vocabulary you want to assign a category from.

5. Mark the category or categories you want to choose and close the window.

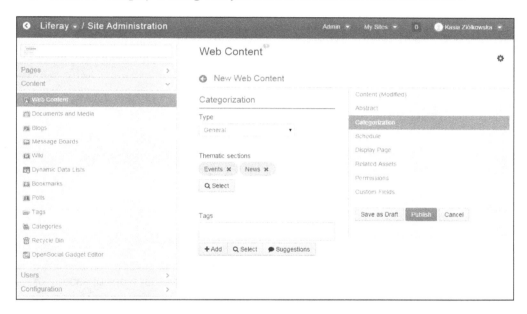

6. Click on the **Publish** button to save the changes of the web content.

Unlike categories, tags do not require to be created before entering the **Categorization** section of the add/edit asset form. You can create a tag and assign it in one task using the following steps:

1. Log in as an administrator and go to **Admin | Site Administration | Content | Web Content**.

2. Click on the name of one already existing web content.

3. Navigate to the **Categorization** tab.

4. Type a tag in the **Tags** field.

5. Click on the **+Add** button or press the *Enter* button.

 You can add more than one tag by typing the whole list of tags in the **Tags** field and separating them by commas.

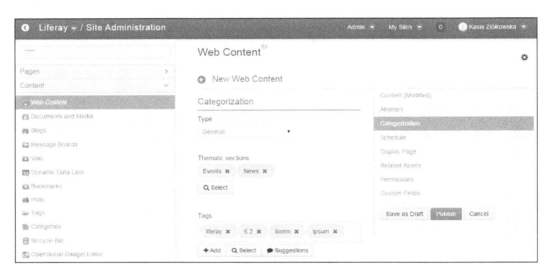

6. Click on the **Publish** button to save the changes of the web content.

It is also possible to define a list of tags in the **Site Administration** section to make it available for later use to users who create web contents, documents, and other types of assets. To define a tag, follow these steps:

1. Log in as an administrator and go to **Admin | Site Administration | Content | Tags**.

2. Click on the **Add Tag** button.

3. Provide a **Name** for the tag.

4. Click on the **Save** button.

To assign an already existing tag, follow these steps:

1. Log in as an administrator and go to **Admin | Site Administration | Content | Web Content**.

2. Click on the name of one already existing web content.

3. Navigate to the **Categorization** tab.

4. Click on the **Select** button located under the **Tags** field.

5. Mark the tag or tags you want to choose.

 You can also choose an existing tag by typing its name (the autocomplete function will help find existing tags) and pressing the *Enter* button.

6. Click on the **Publish** button to save the changes of the web content.

How it works...

Both categories and tags are managed using tools available in the **Site Administration** section and assigned to assets using assets add/edit forms (a new web content form, an edit web content form, a new document form, edit document form, and so on). When provided with categories and/or tags, each asset can be chosen by a specific portlet (such as Asset Publisher) and displayed on a page.

Categories

Categories are stored in vocabularies, and they form a tree-like structure—each category can have subcategories. All the categories available within the site can be managed by going to **Admin | Site Administration | Content | Categories**. This section allows us to create, edit, and delete vocabularies and categories.

Each vocabulary is identified by its name, and it can be provided with a description. Vocabularies can be set to work with all or just one specific asset (choose the **Asset Type** option). For instance, it is possible to create a vocabulary where categories can be assigned to web content only. Such vocabulary will not be available in other assets adding and editing forms.

While creating vocabulary, we can decide whether, while assigning categories to an asset, users have to assign at least one of its categories (the **Required** option) or whether they may use more than one category from this particular vocabulary (the **Allow Multiple Categories** option).

Categories are identified by their names, and they can be provided with descriptions. It is also possible to set permissions for both vocabularies and categories.

Tags

Tags, on the contrary, are not stored in vocabularies, but they build a flat structure. All the tags assigned to assets within the site can be accessed by going to **Admin | Site Administration | Content | Tags**. The **Tags** section allows us to add, edit, delete, or merge tags. Unlike categories, tags can be created while assigning them to the asset.

See also

For information about managing web content and files, refer to the following recipes:

- ▶ The *Managing files in Liferay using Documents and Media portlet* recipe in *Chapter 6, Documents and Media in Liferay*
- ▶ The *Managing and displaying web content* recipe in *Chapter 7, Working with Content*

Asset Publisher as a search-based tool for content presentation

Asset Publisher is a very complex and highly configurable portlet that allows us to present web content folders, web contents, document folders, documents, message board messages, bookmark folders, bookmark entries, blog entries, calendar events, and wiki pages on the page. Assets that are presented by a specific Asset Publisher may be chosen manually by authorized users or automatically based on the configured rules.

In this recipe, we will show you how to configure Asset Publisher to present web content using both manual and dynamic asset selection variants.

Getting ready

To step through this recipe, you will have to add a vocabulary containing News category and create a web content.

How to do it...

Let's assume that each week, on the main page of our intranet, we have to publish up to five of the most important news items chosen by employees responsible for news publishing. Such news can be displayed by the Asset Publisher portlet that is configured to list manually chosen web content articles. To configure such an Asset Publisher portlet, follow these steps:

1. Log in as an administrator and go to the page on which you want to configure a new **Asset Publisher**.
2. Click on the add icon (this is a **+** sign on the left side).
3. Click on the **Applications** tab.
4. Find the **Asset Publisher** portlet using the search feature or by browsing the list of available portlets.
5. Click on the **Add** link located next to the Asset Publisher (the link appears when you hover over the portlet name).
6. Click on the options icon of the newly added portlet (this will be a gear icon in the top-right corner of the portlet).

7. Choose the **Configuration** option.

8. Choose the **Manual** option from the **Asset Selection** section.

9. Click on the **Select** button in the **Asset Entries** section.

10. Choose the **Web Content Article** option.

11. Click on the **Choose** button next to the web content you want to choose.

 Repeat steps 9–11 as many times as needed to create the desired list of news.

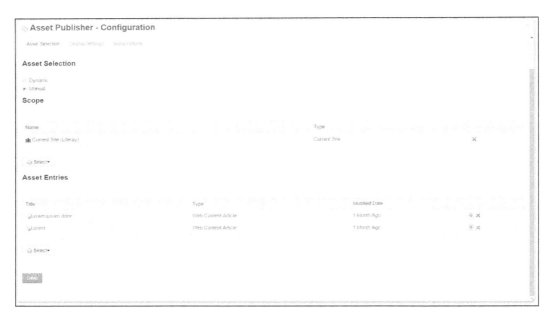

12. Click on the **Save** button.

13. Close the pop-up window by clicking on the **x** button. The Asset Publisher portlet you have just configured will present only the list of chosen web contents.

It is also possible to set Asset Publisher to automatically choose news articles based on a specified category (in our example, we will use the **News** category).

In order to change the Asset Publisher configuration to present only web content articles with the **News** category, follow these steps:

1. Click on the options icon of the previously added portlet.

2. Choose the **Configuration** option.

3. Choose the **Dynamic** option from the **Asset Selection** section.

4. Choose the **Web Content Article** option from the **Asset Type** list.

5. Set the **Contain any of the following categories** rule in the **Filters** section.

6. Click on the **Select** button.

7. Mark the **News** category and close the window.

8. Set **Order by fields** to **Publish Date** and **Descending**.

9. Click on the **Save** button. Close the pop-up window by clicking on the **x** button. The Asset Publisher portlet you have just configured will present only a list of web contents that contain the **News** category.

How it works...

Assets that are displayed by the portlet can be chosen manually by the user (**Manual Asset Selection**) or automatically, based on the set of rules (**Dynamic Asset Selection**). As was shown in the first part of the recipe, **Manual Asset Selection** allows us to select any assets corresponding to the type set in the **Asset Type** field and available within the scope that the Asset Publisher is working in (defined in the **Scope** field).

The scope is a very important parameter, because it defines the place of origin of the asset that is displayed by Asset Publisher. Asset Publisher can present assets created within **Current Site**, **Global** scope, or any other site chosen from the **Other Site** list.

The second part of the recipe provides an example of **Dynamic Asset Selection**, where Asset Publisher chooses, from a defined **Scope**, all the assets that comply with the defined **Asset Type** and are assigned to categories or tags specified in the **Filter** section. It is possible to specify that Asset Publisher should list only these assets with an assigned (or without an assigned) category, a set of categories, a tag, or set of tags. Additionally, the **Filter** section allows us to specify whether the asset must be assigned to all the categories from the set (the **All** option) or whether it is enough if at least one category from the set is assigned (the **Any** option). For instance, if we would like the Asset Publisher portlet to present only the assets that have both News and Sport categories, we have to set the **Contains All Categories** rule and choose both News and Sport categories from the list. If we would like to list all the assets, except these with News category assigned, we have to use the **Does not Contain Any Categories** rule and choose the News category from the list.

The Asset Publisher portlet provides many configuration options that allow us to customize its appearance and available functions. The configuration options can be accessed by going to **Asset Publisher | Configuration | Setup | Display Settings**. Here is a description of the most important options:

▶ The **Display Template** option allows us to choose how the asset should be displayed (as a Title List, Full Content, Abstract, and so on).

▶ **Abstract Length** allows defining the number of characters of text that will be displayed as an abstract.

▶ The **Asset Link Behaviour** defines whether, after clicking the title presented on the list, the full content should be displayed.

▶ The **Number of Items to Display** option defines how many assets will be displayed by the Asset Publisher portlet.

▶ **Pagination Type** allows us to choose whether, and what type of, pagination should be displayed to organize a long lists of assets.

▶ The **Set as the Default Asset Publisher for This Page** option allows us to set this particular Asset Publisher as the one that will be used to present content associated to this page. The page with Asset Publisher set as default will be available to choose as a display page while adding a new web content.

▶ The **Enable Print** option enables the print version of the web content.

▶ The **Enable Flags** option enables the flags functionality, which provides a contact form that notifies any irregularities.

▶ The **Enable Related Assets** option enables the related assets functionality, which lists all the assets defined as related in the adding/editing asset form.

▶ The **Enable Ratings** option enables the functionality that allows us to rate the content shown by Asset Publisher.

▶ The **Enable Comments** option allows us to comment on the assets shown by Asset Publisher.

- The **Enable Social Bookmarks** option displays the Google+, Facebook, and Twitter sharing buttons.

- The **Choose metadata** option allows us to choose the metadata information shown for each asset displayed by the Asset Publisher portlet.

See also

For information about managing web content and files, refer to the following recipes:

- The *Managing files in Liferay using Documents and Media portlet* recipe in *Chapter 6, Documents and Media in Liferay*

- The *Managing and displaying web contents* recipe in *Chapter 7, Working with Content*

Defining application display templates for Asset Publisher

Since Liferay Version 6.2 is the available option, it allows us to set a new display template for Asset Publisher. In real-world applications, it is quite a useful and powerful tool that helps define custom display templates for assets, such as journal article, blog entry, message board, and so on. For example, you may want to display only an asset's descriptions or add selected categories and tags.

Let's assume that we have a use case that describes Asset Publisher view requirements as follows:

- Display title
- Display description
- Display selected tags and categories
- Display asset links
- Display Read more link

How to do it...

In order to define a new display template, log in as an administrator and follow these steps:

1. Log in as an administrator. Go to **Admin | Configuration** and choose **Application Display Templates** from the left menu.
2. Click on the **Add** button and choose **Asset Publisher Template**.
3. Fill in the form by typing **Name** with the **Intranet template** value and choose the **Velocity (.vm)** language.

4. In the script area, write the following code:

```
#if (!$entries.isEmpty())
  #foreach ($curEntry in $entries)
     <div>$curEntry.getTitle($locale)</div>
     <div>$curEntry.getDescription($locale)</div>
     <div>
        $taglibLiferay.assetTagsSummary(
           $curEntry.getClassName(), $curEntry.getClassPK(),
           null, null, $renderResponse.createRenderURL()
           )
     </div>
     <div>
        $taglibLiferay.assetCategoriesSummary(
           $curEntry.getClassName(),
           $curEntry.getClassPK(), null,
           $renderResponse.createRenderURL()
           )
     </div>
     <div>
        $taglibLiferay.assetLinks(
           $curEntry.getEntryId(),
           $curEntry.getClassName(), $curEntry.getClassPK()
           )
     </div>

     <div>
        <a href="$assetPublisherHelper.getAssetViewURL(
           $renderRequest, $renderResponse, $curEntry)">
        Read more</a>
     </div>
     <hr />
  #end
#end
```

5. Click on the **Save** button.

6. Create a new page and put the Asset Publisher portlet (see the *Asset Publisher as a search-based tool for content presentation* recipe from this chapter).

7. Go to Asset Publisher configuration and choose the **Display Setting** tab.

8. In the **Display Template** field, choose the **Intranet** template and click on the **Save** button.

9. Close the configuration popup. In Asset Publisher view, you should see the new template.

How it works...

In previous Liferay versions, it was not possible to add a new display template for Asset Publisher from Control Panel. The only way was to add a new Java Server Pages file in the hook plugin. In Liferay 6.2 it is possible to define views as a Velocity or Freemarker script under Control Panel. Liferay developers implement a powerful editor that helps in creating new templates. Editor specifies the possible fields, displays hints, and provides an excellent autocomplete option.

Let's try to understand our script. The first line checks whether there are any elements in the entries collection. The `$entries` object is a collection of Asset Entry elements, which are selected by a specific criteria from the portlet configuration.

The next line iterates over the entries collection and assigns elements to the `$curEntry` variable.

The next section displays the title and description. The next three sections display tags, categories, and related assets. The last one renders the **Read more** option.

The most difficult thing in this process is understanding how each helper and util works, which parameters are required, and which ones are not required. Unfortunately, there is no easy way to understand it. The only way is to search for help in Liferay sources or examples.

See also

In order to learn more about templates, refer to the _Creating a new template_ recipe in _Chapter 7, Working with Content_

Search portlet – basic configuration

Let's assume that our intranet contains only articles and files that are distributed between many folders. Our goal is to configure the Search portlet in order to find only this content. However, our search should display the following facets:

- Asset type facet
- Asset tag and asset category facet
- User facet
- Time facet

Getting ready...

To start our journey with searching, our Liferay instance should have some content, such as journal articles, files and folders, users, and so on.

How to do it...

In order to properly configure the Search portlet using a basic configuration, follow these steps:

1. Log in as an administrator.
2. Create the search page with one column template.
3. Go to the **Search** page.
4. Click on the **Applications** tab on the left site.
5. Find the **Search** portlet by scrolling or writing inside the text search field.
6. Click on the **Add** button or drag and drop the portlet in the correct place on the layout.
7. Go to the **Configuration** mode of the portlet.
8. Make sure the following options are selected:
   - **Basic Display Settings**
   - **Display Asset Type facet**
   - **Display Asset Tags facet**
   - **Display Asset Categories facet**
   - **Display folder facet**
   - **View in context** in the **Other Settings** section
9. Leave the **Spell check** settings as the default configuration.
10. Click on the **Save** button and close the popup.
11. Try typing your keyword in the search form and press *Enter*. Liferay should display the following results:

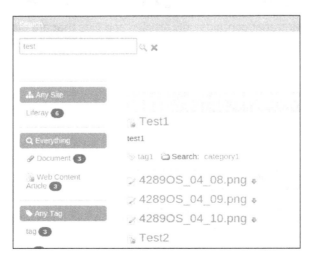

How it works...

Liferay provides a built-in search system based on Lucene. Every entity in Liferay (for instance, web content, document library file entry, blog, message board, and so on) has its own `Indexer` class. This class is responsible for parsing contents and putting them into the search index. When a user uses the search portlet and types a specific keyword, the search engine looks for results in the index.

The Lucene engine has its own query syntax to query its indexes. Accordingly, the Lucene index looks like a map with keys and values. If users ask about a specific keyword, a query is generated in the background. To browse the Lucene index, there is a tool called Luke (`https://code.google.com/p/luke`).

There's more...

When we analyze results that the Search Portlet displays, we notice that there are many unnecessary entries, such as users, message boards, and so on. Our assumption was to present web content and document library entities only. Furthermore, we want to disable unused facets such as folder facets. To achieve this result, it is required that you change the faceting configuration. Follow these steps to modify the faceted search:

1. Go to the configuration mode of the search portlet.
2. Check on the **Advanced** option in the **Display Settings** section.
3. Modify the JSON search configuration. Change the value node using the following lines:

```
"data": {
  "values": [
  "com.liferay.portlet.documentlibrary.model.DLFileEntry",
    "com.liferay.portlet.journal.model.JournalArticle"
    ],
  "frequencyThreshold": 1
}
```

4. Remove any unnecessary facets:

```
{
  "displayStyle": "folders",
  "weight": 1.2,
  "static": false,
  "order": "OrderHitsDesc",
  "data": {
    "maxTerms": 10,
    "frequencyThreshold": 1,
    "showAssetCount": true
  },
```

```
    "label": "folder",
    "className":
    "com.liferay.portal.kernel.search.facet.MultiValueFacet",
    "fieldName": "folderId"
}
```

5. Click on the **Save** button.

6. Close the popup, perform the same search you did earlier, and look out for the differences.

See also

For information about managing web content and files, refer to the following recipes:

▶ The *Managing files in Liferay using Documents and Media portlet* recipe in *Chapter 6, Documents and Media in Liferay*

▶ The *Managing and displaying web contents* recipe in *Chapter 7, Working with Content*

For information about tagging and categorizing, refer to the *Tagging and categorizing content* recipe in this chapter

Solr installation and configuration

Apache Solr (http://lucene.apache.org/solr) is a powerful search engine built on Apache Lucene. In fact, Apache Solr is a standalone enterprise search server with a REST API. The main advantage of this solution is that it can be easily installed as a cloud. Apache Solr has many other advantages, such as high traffic volume optimization, administration interfaces, easy monitoring, high scalability and fault tolerance, and more. Refer to the official site at http://lucene.apache.org/solr/features.html to read about these features.

Apache Solr supports both a schema mode as well as a schema-free one. The schema is a place where you build an index and define fields that consist of it. The schema-free mode allows users to rapidly construct an effective schema by simply indexing sample data, without having to manually edit the schema. The Liferay plugin called solr4-web provides schema and Solr configuration. Thus, we will use this configuration to run Solr in a defined schema mode.

How to do it...

In this recipe, we will show you the simplest way to install and run the Solr server with Liferay.

First, we need to install Apache Solr 4. The newest Solr 4 version is 4.10.4. Follow these steps to run Solr with the Liferay schema and configuration:

1. Download the Apache Solr 4 version (4.10.4) bundled with Jetty from the official site at `http://archive.apache.org/dist/lucene/solr/`.

2. Unpack `solr-4.10.4.tgz` on your local machine:

    `tar -xzvf solr-4.10.4.tgz`

3. Download `solrconfig.xml` and `schema.xml` from the official Liferay repository at `https://github.com/liferay/liferay-plugins/tree/6.2.x/webs/solr4-web/docroot/WEB-INF/conf`.

4. Copy `solrconfig.xml` and `schema xml` to `solr-4.10.3/example/solr/collection1/conf`.

5. Run Apache Solr:

    `solr-4.10.3/bin/solr start`

    Solr should print the following message:

    `Waiting to see Solr listening on port 8983 [/]`

    `Started Solr server on port 8983 (pid=2821). Happy searching!`

6. In the Liferay instance, install the `solr4-web` plugin from the marketplace.

7. Edit the `tomcat-7.0.42/webapps/solr4-web/WEB-INF/classes/META-INF/solr-spring.xml` file and change the `url` property in the `com.liferay.portal.search.solr.server.BasicAuthSolrServer` bean:

    `<property name="url" value="http://localhost:8983/solr" />`

8. Restart the Liferay instance.

9. Log in as administrator to the Liferay Portal.

10. Go to **Admin | Control Panel | Server Administration** and click on the **Execute** button in the **Reindex all search indexes** section.

11. In the frontend, add the **Search** page with the **Search** portlet.

12. Find your data by typing keywords in the **Search** portlet.

How it works...

Apache Solr is a powerful search engine with many configuration files. In order to run Apache Solr and Liferay, we need to override two files: `schema.xml` and `solrconfig.xml`.

The first file defines fields and field types that are available in Liferay. The `schema.xml` file has two sections: `types` and `fields`.

The `Types` section defines all the possible field types, for instance, Boolean, integer, float, double, and so on. The most important field is text, which is defined as follows:

```
<fieldType class="solr.TextField" name="text"
positionIncrementGap="100">
  <analyzer type="index">
    <tokenizer class="solr.WhitespaceTokenizerFactory" />
    <filter class="solr.LowerCaseFilterFactory" />
    <filter class="solr.RemoveDuplicatesTokenFilterFactory" />
    <filter class="solr.StopFilterFactory"
    enablePositionIncrements="true" ignoreCase="true"
    words="stopwords.txt" />
    <filter catenateAll="0" catenateNumbers="1" catenateWords="1"
    class="solr.WordDelimiterFilterFactory"
    generateNumberParts="1" generateWordParts="1" />
  </analyzer>
  <analyzer type="query">
    <tokenizer class="solr.WhitespaceTokenizerFactory" />
    <filter class="solr.LowerCaseFilterFactory" />
    <filter class="solr.RemoveDuplicatesTokenFilterFactory" />
    <filter class="solr.StopFilterFactory"
    enablePositionIncrements="true" ignoreCase="true"
    words="stopwords.txt" />
    <filter class="solr.SynonymFilterFactory" expand="true"
    ignoreCase="true" synonyms="synonyms.txt" />
    <filter catenateAll="0" catenateNumbers="0"
    catenateWords="0"
    class="solr.WordDelimiterFilterFactory"
    generateNumberParts="1" generateWordParts="1" />
  </analyzer>
</fieldType>
```

Let's try analyzing this definition:

▶ The first line of this definition contains the name of the field type called `text` with the `solr.TextField` implementing class. The `solr.` prefix is shorthand for `org.apache.solr.schema` in this case. The `PositionIncrementGap` attribute specifies the distance between multiple values, which prevents spurious phrase matches.

▶ The next couple of lines are `index analyzer` and `query analyzer` definitions. The `index` type means that data is analyzed when it is added to the index. The `query` type specifies analyzers in the query time (searching).

Now, let's try and look at the other terms used in the code:

- `solr.WhitespaceTokenizerFactory`: This splits the text stream on whitespace. Here is an example:

  Input: `This is an example`

  Output: `"This", "is", "an", "example"`

- `solr.LowerCaseFilterFactory`: This converts any uppercase letters in a token to the equivalent lowercase token. Here is an example:

  Input: `"This", "is", "an", "example"`

  Output: `"this", "is", "an", "example"`

- `solr.RemoveDuplicatesTokenFilterFactory`: This removes duplicate tokens in the stream. Here is an example:

  Input: `"one", "two", "two", "three"`

  Output: `"one", "two", "three"`

- `solr.StopFilterFactory`: This removes tokens that are on the given stopwords list.

  - `stopwords.txt` has words such as `hate`, `love`. Here is an example:

  Input: `"I", "hate", "my", "job"`

  Output: `"I", "my", "job"`

- `solr.WordDelimiterFilterFactory`: This splits tokens with specific rules. Refer to the official Solr documentation at `https://wiki.apache.org/solr/Analyze rsTokenizersTokenFilters#solr.WordDelimiterFilterFactory` to learn about the possible configuration.

- The next part of `schema.xml` is the fields section. It contains all field definitions. In general, Apache Solr provides three types of fields:

  - `defining fields`: This is a typical, declarative field definition. Every definition has the following attributes:

    ```
    <field indexed="true" name="content" stored="true"
    termPositions="true" termVectors="true" type="text" />
    ```

  - `copying fields`: This is the mechanism for making copies of fields with different analyzers or filters. It is not used in our `schema.xml` file.

  - `dynamic fields`: This allows us to define fields without any explicit definition. In our `schema.xml`, it is used for multilanguage fields:

    ```
    <dynamicField indexed="true" multiValued="true" name="*_
    en" stored="true" termPositions="true" termOffsets="true"
    termVectors="true" type="text_en" />
    ```

Every field definition can contain the following attributes:

- `name`: The name of the field
- `type`: A reference for the field types that are defined in a `<types>` section
- `default`: A default value that will be added automatically to any document that does not have a value

Other attributes are optional. The full list of optional attributes is available in the official Apache Solr documentation at `https://cwiki.apache.org/confluence/display/solr/Defining+Fields`.

The next file called `solrconfig.xml` is the most important configuration file in the Solr search engine.

The more commonly used elements in `solrconfig.xml` are:

- Data directory location specifying a location for index data with the `<datadir>` parameter
- Query and cache settings configured in child elements of the `<query>` tag
- Request handler `<requestHandle>` sections that process requests coming to Solr
- Search component `<searchComponent>` sections define the logic that is used by `SearchHandler` to perform queries for users

All documentation is available on the official Apache Solr site: `https://cwiki.apache.org/confluence/display/solr/Configuring+solrconfig.xml`.

9

Liferay Workflow Capability

In this chapter, we will cover the following topics:

- ▸ The Kaleo Web installation
- ▸ The Single Approver workflow for the user creation process
- ▸ The web content creation and the fork-join workflow
- ▸ Kaleo conditions in a message board example
- ▸ Kaleo timers

Introduction

A workflow is a series of activities necessary to complete a task. In other words, a workflow consists of a sequence of states connected by transition. Each state has a specific step before it and a specific step after it. In general, it's a linear-defined process, which describes the flow between states. The term workflow indicates how people do their work and how they handle information. To understand workflow definitions, let's define its specific vocabulary:

- ▸ **State**: This term describes a unique state that will execute a specific action (or many actions) on a work item. For instance, new, approved, commit, done, remove, and so on.
- ▸ **Task**: This defines an activity to be done on a work item between states.
- ▸ **Transition**: This defines how a transition rules from one state to another. It means that transition describes a list of tasks, which have to be done to transform items from one state to another.

Liferay Portal includes a workflow engine called Kaleo. This engine provides functionalities to define and deploy workflow definitions. Kaleo is an external web plugin, which needs to be deployed like other plugins. The current version of Kaleo is available on the Liferay marketplace.

The Kaleo Web Installation

The workflow engine called Kaleo is defined as a web plugin. Briefly, a web plugin is a normal web application, which also provides the ability to use the Liferay service layer that is built on Service Builder and other Liferay plugins, such as hooks, portlets, and so on. In general, it's a hybrid between a typical servlet application and Liferay-specific plugins.

Getting ready

To correctly install Liferay plugins, it's required to create an account on the official Liferay site. This account allows you to download plugins on the marketplace, discuss on a message board, creates blogs, and so on.

How to do it...

In the Liferay 6.1.1 GA2 version, Liferay provides a marketplace portlet to install all its available plugins. In Liferay 6.2 marketplace portlet is already installed, so the installation of the Kaleo plugin is really simple. In order to install the Kaleo workflow, go through the following set of steps:

1. Log in as an administrator on the intranet.
2. Navigate to **Admin | Control Panel**.
3. Select the **Store** option in the **Apps** section.
4. Authenticate yourself by entering the Liferay login and password.

 If Liferay provides a new marketplace portlet, there will be a wizard that updates a portlet and downloads the newest one.

5. On the marketplace search form, type `Kaleo Workflow CE` and select the proper result.
6. Click on the **Free** button.
7. Select or create a new project for the purchase; read and accept the terms of use. Fill **Legal Entity Name** and click on the **Purchase** button.

8. The system should display the following message:

    Thank You!

    Your receipt ID number is <RECEIPT_ID>

    A confirmation email for this order was sent to your inbox.

    Click on "See Purchased" to view and manage your purchases online, or you may go to the Marketplace through your Liferay Portal instance and manage your purchases from there.

9. Navigate to **See Purchased Apps** and click on the **Install** button.

10. Verify that a **Workflow** tab is in the **Control Panel | Configuration** section.

How it works...

Liferay uses its own product for the workflow implementation. All Kaleo entities are generated by the service-builder mechanism.

It means that `service.xml` defines a set of entities: Kaleo Action, Kaleo Condition, Kaleo Definition, Kaleo Instance, Kaleo Instance Token, Kaleo Log, Kaleo Node, Kaleo Notification, Kaleo Notification Recipient, Kaleo Task, Kaleo Task Assignment, KaleoTask Assignment Instance, Kaleo Task Instance Token, Kaleo Timer, Kaleo Timer Instance Token, and Kaleo Transition. It's not necessary to know the meaning of all these entities and their relations.

After successful installation, there are a couple of new options in the Liferay environment:

- The **Workflow** option in the **Control Panel | Configuration** section: This is a global workflow configuration, which allows you to define newer workflow definitions and manage default workflows between assets (for instance, web content articles, users, blogs, and so on)

- **Workflow configuration** in the **Admin | Site Administration | Configuration**: This defines workflows for the current site

- The **My Workflow tasks** tab in the **{USERNAME} | My account** section: This functionality lists all pending and complete workflows tasks assigned to a specific user

- **My Submission** in the **{USERNAME} | My account** section: This provides the list of assets submitted for the review process

Furthermore, Kaleo added specific roles, which can be used in workflow definitions:

- The organization content reviewer
- The portal content reviewer
- The site content reviewer

See also

For more information on how to manage files or web contents, refer to

- ▶ *Managing files in Liferay using Documents and Media portlet* recipe in *Chapter 6, Documents and Media in Liferay*
- ▶ The *Managing and displaying web contents* recipe in *Chapter 7, Working with Content*

The Single Approver workflow for the user creation process

By default, Kaleo Workflow provides a Single Approver definition. This workflow requires one approval state before any asset is published.

We will show you how to use this workflow for the user creation process.

How to do it...

Enabling the Single Approver definition is an easy process. To activate workflow for the user creation, perform these steps:

1. Navigate to the **Admin | Control Panel | Configuration | Workflow** tab.
2. Select the **Default Configuration** tab
3. Find the **User** resource and select the **Single Approver (version 1)** definition.
4. Click on the **Save** button.

 To check how Single Approver works, try to create a new account in the Sign In portlet.

5. Open the Sign In portlet page. By default, it is on the main page.
6. Select the **Create Account** option and fill in the form.
7. After submitting the form, the system should display the following message:

Thank you for creating an account. You will be notified via email at your-mail@ example.com when your account has been approved.

The last thing in this process is to approve a new user. In order to achieve this, run through the following steps:

1. Log in as an administrator.
2. Navigate to **My Account | My Workflow** tasks.
3. Find a pending task with the review status and edit it by clicking on the hyperlink in the table.
4. Select the **Assigned to Me** option next to **Assign to** field.
5. **Approve** the user (in the dialog box, it's possible to write a comment).

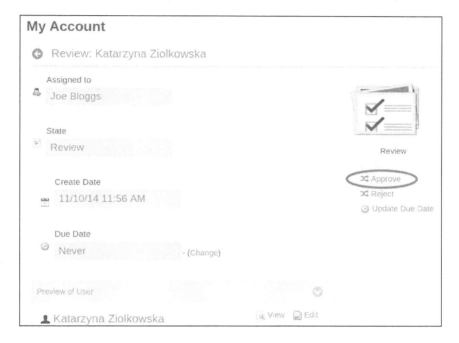

6. Go to the **Completed** tab and check the result. The approved user should be on the list.

 Only a user with an assigned task can transfer it to the next task or state.

How it works...

To understand this process, let's examine the Single Approver definition (`single-approver-definition.xml` located in `webapps/kaleo-web/WEB-INF/classes/META-INF/definitions`). This definition can be drawn as follows:

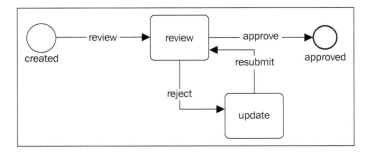

State

The starting point of this flow is a state called created. The definition of this state is present at the beginning of the `single-approver-definition.xml` file:

```
<state>
  <name>created</name>
  [..]
  <initial>true</initial>
  <transitions>
    <transition>
      <name>review</name>
      <target>review</target>
    </transition>
  </transitions>
</state>
```

The state node contains:

- ▸ `name`: This is the name of a state
- ▸ `initial`: This flag represents the initial state
- ▸ List of `transitions`: In this example, there is only one transition called review

The transition node can define:

- ▸ `name`: This is the name of a transition
- ▸ `target`: This is the name of the target state or task
- ▸ `default`: This is a flag which marks transition as default

Task

The next step of our flow is a `review` task, which is defined by a transition called `review`. Tasks are the most complex structures in a flow definition. The task review is the place where users can decide whether to approve an asset or reject it. The definition of this task is as follows:

```
<task>
  <name>review</name>
  <actions>
    <notification>
      <name>Review Notification</name>
      <template>${userName} sent you a ${entryType} for review in
      the workflow.</template>
      <template-language>freemarker</template-language>
      <notification-type>email</notification-type>
      <notification-type>user-notification</notification-type>
      <execution-type>onAssignment</execution-type>
    </notification>
    [...]
  </actions>
  <assignments>
    <roles>
      [...]
    </roles>
  </assignments>
  <transitions>
    [...]
  </transitions>
</task>
```

The main attributes of task are:

- `name`: This is the name of the task, for instance, review.
- `actions`: This specifies the list of action elements or notification elements. In this example, actions contain only e-mail notifications.
- `assignments`: This specifies the list of roles or users to whom the specific task is assigned.
- `transitions`: This specifies the list of transition elements, which describe all possible ways to change the state or task. In this example, it's approved or rejected.

Notification

Let's look deeper into the actions definition. As we mentioned earlier, actions can contain notification elements and/or action elements:

```
<notification>
  <name>Review Notification</name>
  <template>${userName} sent you a ${entryType} for review in the
  workflow.</template>
  <template-language>freemarker</template-language>
  <notification-type>email</notification-type>
  <notification-type>user-notification</notification-type>
  <execution-type>onAssignment</execution-type>
</notification>
```

The notification node has the following options:

- `name`: This is the name of the notification

- `template`: This defines the notification's message

- `template-language`: This is one of the three options: freemarker, velocity, and text

- `notification-type`: This specifies the e-mail, IM, private-message, or user-notification

- `execution-type`: This specifies one of the three options: `onAssignment` (a notification is sent when a specific user is assigned to a specific asset), `onExit` (a notification is sent when a specific asset leaves a state or task), and `onEntry` (a notification is sent when a specific asset enters the state)

 The IM type and the private-message type are placeholders for now. This means that the Kaleo Web doesn't support these types.

Action

The second possibility is to define an action, as shown in the following code:

```
<action>
  <name>approve</name>
  <script>
    <![CDATA[ {script here} ]]>
  </script>
  <script-language>groovy</script-language>
  <execution-type>onEntry</execution-type>
</action>
```

An action element has a simple structure, but it's a powerful tool to invoke every piece of code from Liferay. Action contains:

- `name`: This specifies the name of the action.
- `script`: This specifies the script definition. In this section, it's possible to write a code, which will be invoked on defining the execution type.
- `script-language`: This defines the language which will be used in the script, for instance, Groovy, BeanShell, DRL, JavaScript, Python, Ruby. The most commonly used is the BeanShell one.
- `execution-type`: This specifies one of the three options: `onAssignment` (a notification is sent when a specific user is assigned to a specific asset), `onExit` (a notification is sent when a specific asset leaves a state or task), and `onEntry` (a notification is sent when a specific asset enters some state).

The web content creation and the fork-join workflow

Let's assume that our goal is to create a Kaleo definition in order to publish articles with the following requirements. Everyone can write an article and submit it to reviewers. The review stage has two independent (parallel) steps:

- UI quality reviewing
- Content quality reviewing

Only after these steps, it's possible to publish an article. In this recipe, we will show how to use the fork and join functionality in order to create the Kaleo definition. Forks and joins are used for parallel processing purposes. Thus, they will be a good solution to our problem.

How to do it...

First of all, let's visualize workflow and define states, tasks, and transitions. This diagram will help us understand the whole process:

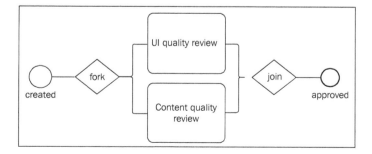

As shown in the preceding diagram, in our workflow there are following components:

- The **created** and **approved** state
- The **UI quality review** and **content quality review** tasks
- The fork and join functionality.

The second step is to write a prototype, which defines states, tasks, and transitions listed previously:

 This is only a draft of the real definition. You will find the working definition in the code files for this chapter along with this book.

```xml
<?xml version="1.0"?>
<workflow-definition>
  <name>Fork-Join Example</name>
  <state>
    <name>created</name>
    <transitions>
      <transition>
        <name>review-process</name>
        <target>review-process</target>
      </transition>
    </transitions>
  </state>
  <fork>
    <name>review-process</name>
    <transitions>
      <transition>
        <name>UI Quality Review</name>
      </transition>
      <transition>
        <name>Content Quality Review</name>
      </transition>
    </transitions>
  </fork>
  <task>
    <name>UI Quality Review</name>
    <transitions>
      <transition>
        <name>Submit</name>
        <target>join-tasks</target>
```

```
        </transition>
      </transitions>
    </task>
    <task>
      <name>Content Quality Review</name>
      <transitions>
        <transition>
          <name>Submit</name>
          <target>join-tasks</target>
        </transition>
      </transitions>
    </task>
    <join>
      <name>join-tasks</name>
      <transitions>
        <transition><name>approved</name></transition>
      </transitions>
    </join>
    <state><name>approved</name></state>
</workflow-definition>
```

The third step is to complete the preceding definition by specifying each node. It can be done by copying parts from the Single Approver definition.

The next step is to upload this definition in the Kaleo workflow configuration, which is placed in the **Admin | Control Panel | Configuration | Workflow** section. After uploading the Kaleo definition, there should be a successful message. Now, the new definition will be visible in the **Definitions** tab.

The final step is to enable a new workflow definition for the web content article. This step was described in the previous recipe.

How it works...

This definition uses the fork and join functionality for web content articles. In general, when the author adds a new web content and submits it for publication, Kaleo workflow creates two tasks: UI Quality Review and Content Quality Review. Only after acceptance of these two tasks, the article status changes to approved. When the reviewing process is in progress, an article has a pending status.

Let's look deeply into fork and join definitions.

The fork element

Fork has a similar structure as a state element. The main function of fork is to create a list of tasks in a parallel way. The main elements are:

- ▶ `name`: This specifies the name of the fork used in a transition definition
- ▶ `transitions`: This specifies the list of transitions (tasks or states)to be created

The fork element has many other functionalities and elements, such as scripts, timers, actions, and so on. It can have a really complex structure with a huge number of functionalities. In this recipe, we described only the basic function of this element.

The join element

Join is an eternal partner of fork. This pair is always together. The main responsibility of this element is waiting unless all parallel tasks are performed and accepted. The join element has the following structure:

- ▶ `name`: This specifies the name of the join, which is used in a transition definition
- ▶ `transitions`: This specifies the list of transitions. It's usually one transition, which describes a state or task after the joining process.

Join has exactly the same structure as fork. It can have a very complex structure with a whole bunch of functionalities.

There's more...

Instead of the `join` element, it's possible to use the `join-xor` element. The main difference between join and `join-xor` is that join waits for the completion of all parallel tasks, but `join-xor` waits only for the first complete task.

Join-xor element

The `join-xor` element has the same definition as join:

- ▶ `name`: This specifies the name of the join used in a transition definition.
- ▶ `transitions`: This specifies the list of transitions. It's usually one transition, which describes a state or task after the joining process.

See also

For more information on managing the web content, refer to *Managing and displaying web contents* recipe in *Chapter 7, Working with Content*.

Kaleo conditions in a message board example

Kaleo workflow contains conditions. It's possible to use conditions to branch workflows and execute different tasks. Let's assume that we are message board moderators. In our company, there is a user who must accept new threads and many users who accept replies in threads. It's possible to achieve this functionality that allows message boards to work this way using Kaleo workflow conditions.

How to do it...

This definition is similar to the fork and join workflow, but there is a great difference. There is no parallel workflow task. Instead, there is a condition, which moves an entity to a different state. Obviously, workflow is the same: the user creates a new entity and the moderator accepts it. There is little difference seen between roles, which are defined for a particular task.

As shown in the previous example, let's visualize workflow and define states, tasks, and transitions. The following diagram will help you understand the whole process in a better way:

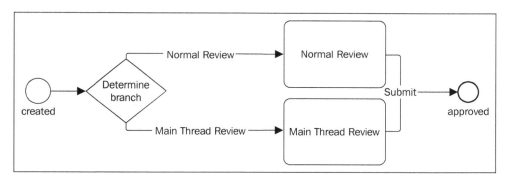

The preceding diagram contains following components:

- ▸ The **created** and **approved** state
- ▸ **Normal Review** and **Main Thread Review** tasks
- ▸ The condition statement.

Let's define these definitions:

```xml
<?xml version="1.0"?>
<workflow-definition>
  <name>Condition Example</name>
  <state>
```

```
    <name>created</name>
    <transitions>
      <transition>
        <name>determine-branch</name>
        <target>determine-branch</target>
      </transition>
    </transitions>
  </state>
  <condition>
    <name>determine-branch</name>
    <script>
      <![CDATA[SCRIPT DEFINITION]]>
    </script>
    <script-language>groovy</script-language>
    <transitions>
      <transition>
        <name>Normal Review</name>
        <target>Normal Review</target>
        <default>false</default>
      </transition>
      <transition>
        <name>Main Thread Review</name>
        <target>Main Thread Review</target>
        <default>false</default>
      </transition>
    </transitions>
  </condition>

  <task>
    <name>Normal Review</name>
    <transitions>
      <transition>
        <name>Submit</name>
        <target>approved</target>
      </transition>
    </transitions>
  </task>
  <task>
    <name>Main Thread Review</name>
    <transitions>
      <transition>
        <name>Submit</name>
        <target>approved</target>
```

```
    </transition>
  </transitions>
 </task>

 <state><name>approved</name></state>
</workflow-definition>
```

After defining Kaleo, let's write a conditional script which represents our Kaleo condition. In this example, we will use the Groovy script, which will be placed in the `<script>` tag in the `<condition>` definition. So, let's define it:

```
import com.liferay.portal.kernel.util.GetterUtil;
import com.liferay.portal.kernel.workflow.WorkflowConstants;
import com.liferay.portlet.messageboards.service.
MBMessageLocalServiceUtil;
import com.liferay.portlet.messageboards.model.MBMessage;

String className = (String)workflowContext.get(
WorkflowConstants.CONTEXT_ENTRY_CLASS_NAME);
boolean isMBMessage = false;
if (className.equals(MBMessage.class.getName())) {
  isMBMessage = true;
}
returnValue = "Answers Review";
long classPK = GetterUtil.getLong(
(String)workflowContext.get(WorkflowConstants.CONTEXT_ENTRY_CLASS_
PK));
if (isMBMessage) {
  MBMessage mbMessage =
  MBMessageLocalServiceUtil.getMBMessage(classPK);
  if (mbMessage.isRoot()) {
    returnValue = "Main Thread Review";
  }
}
```

How it works...

In the preceding example, we explained the workflow definition, which can be applied for all types of asset (for instance, user, web content article, message board, and so on). In every type, there is a typical flow: **Created | Normal Review Task | Approved**. However, if we apply this workflow for a message board entity, it will have a different flow: **Created | Main Thread Review | Approved**.

Why does this happen? Groovy script defines a condition and determines the complete flow.

The first line gets a `className` definition. Next, the if statement checks whether this is a `MBMessage` entity.

The next couple of lines get the specific `mbMessage` object and check whether this object is a root of `MBMessage`. It's worth noting that there are predefined values:

- ▶ `returnValue`: This contains the transition's target
- ▶ `workflowContext`: This object implements the `WorflowContext` interface

Condition statement

The `<condition>` tag has the following structure:

- ▶ `name`: This is the name of the condition.
- ▶ `script`: This defines a condition.
- ▶ `script-language`: This defines the language which will be used in the script, for instance: Groovy, BeanShell, DRL, JavaScript, Python, Ruby. The most common use is the BeanShell one.
- ▶ `transitions`: This specifies the list of transitions.

Kaleo timers

This last recipe concerns timers. This functionality allows users to define specific actions, which should be performed after a certain period of time. Let's modify our previous recipe a little with the condition example and add a timer definition. Our assumption is that the task called Main Thread Review shouldn't wait more than one hour for assignment to any user. After one hour, this task should be assigned to a user with the `test@liferay.com` e-mail.

How to do it...

First of all, open the previous definition and find the Main Thread Review task. Between the assignments tag and the transitions tag, enter the following code:

```
<?xml version="1.0" encoding="UTF-8"?>
<task-timers>
  <task-timer>
    <name>default-assignment</name>
    <delay>
      <duration>1</duration>
      <scale>hour</scale>
    </delay>
    <blocking>true</blocking>
    <timer-actions>
```

```
<timer-notification>
  <name />
  <template />
  <template-language>text</template-language>
  <notification-type>im</notification-type>
</timer-notification>
<reassignments>
  <user>
    <email-address>test@liferay.com</email-address>
  </user>
</reassignments>
        </timer-actions>
      </task-timer>
    </task-timers>
```

How it works...

The Kaleo web plugin gives users the possibility to react to the user's action after a specific time period. It allows you to assign tasks to specific users, send notifications, and so on.

The `<task-timers>` tag has the following structure:

- ▸ `task-timer`: This specifies complex type with the timer's definition.

- ▸ `name`: This specifies the timer's name.

- ▸ `delay`: This specifies the delay definition and defines how much time the timer will wait until its actions are executed. For instance 1 hour, 5 minutes, and so on.

- ▸ `recurrence` (not used in this example): This triggers the action several times depending on the argument specified. For instance, for every 1 hour, definition invokes a specific action.

- ▸ `blocking`: If this is true, stop the workflow engine execution until the timer is executed.

- ▸ `timer actions`: This specifies the list of actions to be done after the delay definition.

10
Collaboration Tools

In this chapter, we will cover the following topics:

- ▶ Setting up a blog for the intranet
- ▶ Setting up a wiki portlet
- ▶ Setting up a forum for an intranet
- ▶ Banning a user for an inappropriate post
- ▶ Setting up the calendar as a personal tasks management tool
- ▶ Using bookmarks to store favorite links
- ▶ Tracking social activities of site members
- ▶ Using the announcements portlet for group messaging

Introduction

Liferay provides a wide range of collaboration tools that can effectively improve communication between employees by encouraging them to produce and share information within their project teams, departments, or the entire company. Intranet users may create blogs, take part in forums, build a corporate knowledge base as a set of Wiki pages, gather useful links, receive or publish important messages, and plan their work in calendars. They can also track activities of other employees.

Setting up a blog for the intranet

Each site in Liferay has its own separate blog, which can be accessed by going to **Admin | Site Administration | Content | Blogs**. In addition, it is also possible to place the Blogs portlet on one of the pages, where it can be shared between users who do not have access to the admin functionalities.

The Blogs portlet presents blog entries created by members of the site. A blog entry can consist of text, graphics, tables, lists, and links to other assets. Additionally, each blog entry can be tagged and categorized or provided with the list of assets related to it, which will be listed in the related assets section under the main content of the blog entry. It is also possible to define permissions that specify which actions can be performed on it by users assigned to different roles.

In this recipe, we will show you how to create a shared blog for members of the site by placing the Blogs portlet on the page within this site. We will also show you how to configure this Blogs portlet to best fit users' purposes.

How to do it...

Let's imagine that our company's public relations department wants to launch a blog written by employees from different departments, informing other employees about interesting corporate initiatives. They would like to show on the page the list of 10 newest blog entries (each blog entry on the list should be presented in a form of abstract user clicks and is redirected to its full content), but do not want to allow users to comment or rate other users' entries. The blog should also provide some e-mail notifications and RSS functionality to help people stay updated.

In the first step, we will add the Blogs portlet to the page. In order to do this, follow these steps:

1. Log in as an administrator and go to the page on which the Blogs portlet should be placed.
2. Click on the add button (this is a **+** sign on the left side).
3. Click on the **Applications** tab.
4. Find the Blogs portlet using search mechanism or by browsing the list of available portlets (the Blogs portlet can be found in the **Collaboration** section).
5. Click on the **Add** link next to the portlet name. The Blogs portlet with basic configuration will be added to the page.

After adding the Blogs portlet to the page, we can change its default configuration. To configure the Blogs portlet, follow these steps:

1. Click on the options icon of the newly added portlet (this will be a gear icon in the portlet's top-right corner).
2. Choose the **Configuration** option.

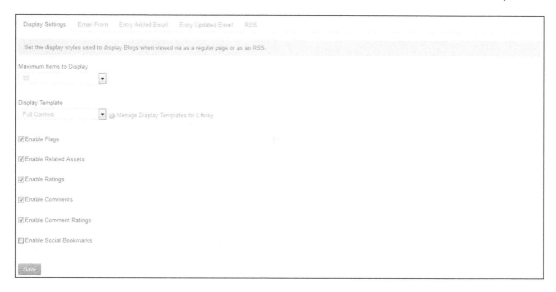

3. Set **Maximum Items to Display** to **10**.

4. Set **Display Template** to **Abstract**.

5. Disable the **Enable Flags** option.

6. Disable the **Enable Related Assets** option.

7. Disable **Enable Ratings** option.

8. Disable the **Enable Comments** option.

9. Disable the **Enable Comment Ratings** option.

10. Disable the **Enable Social Bookmarks** option.

11. Click on the **Save** button.

12. Click on the **Email From** tab.

13. Provide the sender's **Name** and **Address**.

14. Click on the **Save** button.

15. Click on the **Entry Added Email** or **Entry Updated Email** tab.

16. Set the **Enabled** option.

17. Provide **Subject** and **Body**.

18. Click on the **Save** button.

19. Click on the **RSS** tab.

20. Leave **Enable RSS Subscription** option enabled.

21. Set **Maximum Items to Display** to **10**.

22. Choose the **Abstract** option from the **Display Style** list.

23. Leave the **Format** option set as it is.

24. Click on the **Save** button.

How it works...

The Blogs portlet configuration allows us to set the following options:

- **Maximum Items to Display**: This option defines how many blog entries will be displayed on a single page of the Blogs portlet

- **Display Template**: This option allows us to choose how the asset should be displayed (as a title list, full content, abstract, and so on)

- **Enable Flags**: This option enables the flags functionality, which provides a contact form for notification of irregularities

- **Enable Social Bookmarks**: This option displays the Google+, Facebook, and Twitter sharing buttons

- **Enable Related Assets**: This option enables the related asset section of blogs entry, which presents a list of related assets defined for each Wiki page

- **Enable Ratings**: This option enables the rating functionality that allows us to rate each blog entry and presents the average rating for each entry

- **Enable Comments**: This option enables the comments functionality that allows you to comment on each blog entry

- **Enable Comment Ratings**: This option enables the comments rating functionality that allows you to vote for each comment on the blogs and presents the number of votes for each comment

- **Display Template**: This option allows you to choose the template to display the Wiki page

- **Email From**: This tab allows you to provide the sender's name and e-mail address

- **Entry Added Email** and **Entry Updated Email**: These tabs allow you to enable the e-mail messaging functionality and set subject and message content using the available variables

- **Enable RSS Subscription**: This option allows users to track activities using RSS

- **Display Style**: This option allows you to decide whether full content, abstract, or title should be shown

- **Maximum Items to Display**: This option allows us to set the maximum amount of items displayed by the RSS channel

- **Format**: This option allows us to decide whether RSS should be served in Atom 1.0, RSS 1.0, or RSS 2.0 format

See also

For information on how to configure SMTP servers, refer to the *Configuring Liferay with the SMTP server* recipe from *Chapter 11, Quick Tricks and Advanced Knowledge*.

Setting up a wiki portlet

Liferay provides the Wiki functionality that allows us to create a corporate database developed collaboratively by a community of employees similar to the commonly known Wikipedia. The Wiki functionality can be accessed by going to **Admin | Site Administration | Content | Wiki** or using the Wiki portlet, which allows users to manage and present Wiki pages on a site page on which it is located.

Each Wiki page presented by the Wiki portlet may contain text, headers, lists, pictures, tables, and links that can be defined using simple creole, media Wiki, or HTML languages. Additionally, Wiki includes a link-tracking mechanism, which provides information about incoming and outgoing links and allows us to create new pages by defining links to them. While editing a Wiki page, a user can provide an additional description of what has been done. This allows the user to track the changes made by different users.

In this recipe, we will show you how to configure the Wiki portlet to best fit users' purposes.

How to do it...

Let's assume that the Wiki functionality in our company's intranet (except all the management functions) should provide the possibility to comment on and rate Wiki pages. Additionally, users should receive e-mail notifications when a page is added or modified. However, the RSS functionality is not required.

To add a Wiki portlet to the page, perform these steps:

1. Log in as an administrator and go to the page on which the Wiki portlet should be placed.
2. Click on the add button (this is a **+** sign on the left side).
3. Click on the **Applications** tab.
4. Find the Wiki portlet using the search feature or by browsing the list of available portlets (the Blogs portlet can be found in the **Collaboration** and **Wiki** sections).
5. Click on the **Add** link next to the portlet name. The Wiki portlet with basic configuration will be added to the page.

After adding the Wiki portlet to the page, it is possible to change its default configuration. To configure the Wiki portlet, follow these steps:

1. Click on the options icon of the newly added portlet (this will be a gear icon in the top-right corner of the portlet).

2. Choose the **Configuration** option.

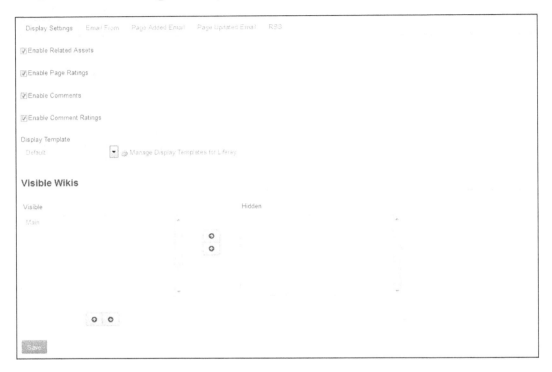

3. Make sure you are on the **Display Settings** tab.

4. Unmark the **Enable Related Assets** option.

5. Leave the **Enable Page Ratings** option enabled.

6. Leave the **Enable Comments** option enabled.

7. Unmark **Enable Comment Ratings** option.

8. Leave the **Display Template** and **Visible Wikis** options as they are.

9. Click on the **Save** button.

10. Click on the **Email From** tab.

11. Provide the sender's **Name** and **Address**.

12. Click on the **Save** button.

13. Click on the **Page Added Email** or **Page Updated Email** tab.

14. Set the **Enabled** option.

15. Provide a **Subject, Body** and **Signature**.

16. Click on the **Save** button.

17. Click on the **RSS** tab.

18. Unmark **Enable RSS Subscription** option.

19. Click on the **Save** button.

How it works...

The Wiki portlet configuration allows us to set the following options:

► **Enable Related Assets**: This option enables the related asset section of the Wiki page, which presents a list of related assets defined for each Wiki page

► **Enable Page Ratings**: This option enables the rating functionality that allows you to rate each Wiki page and presents its average rating for each page

► **Enable Comments**: This option enables the comments functionality that allows us to comment on each Wiki page

► **Enable Comment Ratings**: This option enables the comments rating functionality that allows you to vote for each comment on the Wiki page and presents the number of votes for each comment

► **Display Template**: This option allows you to choose the template to display the Wiki page

► **Visible Wikis**: This option allows you to define which available Wikis should be visible in this particular Wiki portlet

► **Email From**: This option allows you to provide the sender's name and e-mail address

► **Page Added Email** and **Page Updated Email**: These tabs allow you to enable the e-mail messaging functionality and set the subject and message content using the available variables

► **Enable RSS Subscription**: This option allows users to track activities using RSS

► **Display Style**: This option allows you to decide whether full content, abstract, or title should be shown

► **Maximum Items to Display**: This option allows you to set the maximum amount of items displayed by the RSS channel

► **Format**: This options allows you to decide whether RSS should be served in the Atom 1.0, RSS 1.0, or RSS 2.0 format

See also

For information on how to configure SMTP servers, refer to the *Configuring Liferay with the SMTP server* recipe from *Chapter 11, Quick Tricks and Advanced Knowledge*.

Setting up a forum for an intranet

Forum is a very powerful collaboration and social tool that allows multiple user communication. Liferay Portal CMS provides basic ready-to-use forum functionality called message boards. Message boards can be accessed by going to **Admin | Site Administration | Content | Message Boards** using the Message Boards portlet. This portlet can be used by end users of our intranet.

How to do it...

In this recipe, we will show you how to add a Message Boards portlet to the page and how to set it to best fit our purpose.

Let's start by adding the Message Boards portlet to the page. To do this, follow these steps:

1. Log in as an administrator and go to the page on which the message boards should be placed.
2. Click on the add button (this is a **+** sign on the left side).
3. Click on the **Applications** tab.
4. Find the **Message Boards** portlet using the search feature or by browsing the list of available portlets (the message boards portlet can be found in the **Collaboration** section).
5. Click on the **Add** link next to the portlet name. The message board with basic configuration will be added to the page.

To configure the message board portlet, follow these steps:

1. Click on the options icon of the newly added portlet (this will be a gear icon in the top-right corner of the portlet).
2. Choose the **Configuration** option.

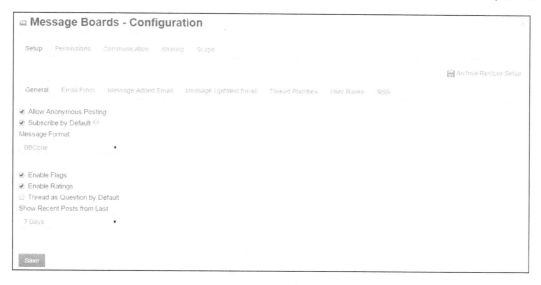

3. Make sure that you are on the **General** tab.

4. Disable the **Allow Anonymous Posting** option.

5. Leave the **Subscribe by Default** option enabled.

6. Choose HTML from the **Message Format** dropdown list.

7. Leave the **Enable Flags** and **Enable Ratings** options enabled.

8. Leave the **Thread as Question by Default** option disabled.

9. Set the **30 days** option on the **Show Recent Posts from Last** list.

10. Click on the **Save** button.

11. Click on the **Email From** tab.

12. Provide the sender's **Name** and **Address**.

13. Click on the **Message Added Email** or **Message Updated Email** tab.

14. Set the **Enabled** option.

15. Provide a **Subject**, **Body** and **Signature**.

16. Click on the **Save** button.

17. Click on the **Thread Priorities** tab.

18. Enter the name, image, and priority level for each level in descending order.

19. Click on the **Save** button.

20. Click on **User Rank** tab.

21. Provide rank names by entering ranks and minimum post pairs (for example, Yoda = 1000).

22. Click on the **Save** button.

23. Click on the **RSS** tab.

24. Make sure that the **Enable RSS Subscription** option is enabled.

25. Set **Maximum Items to Display** to **10**.

26. Choose the **Abstract** option form the **Display Style** list.

27. Leave the **Format** option as it is.

28. Click on the **Save** button.

How it works...

Message boards provide typical forum mechanisms that allow us to create a folder-similar structure built with categories and subcategories. Both categories and subcategories can contain other subcategories or threads, and each thread consists of at least one post. Threads in a message board can be split (as a result of splitting, we create two threads from one) or moved (by moving, we create one thread from two already existing threads). It is possible to lock the thread in order to block users from adding more posts and make it available for users in read-only mode. What's more, message board provides a banning mechanism for the message board user management. The banning mechanism will be described in the next recipe.

Message boards portlet configuration allows us to set the following options:

- **General**:
    - **Allow Anonymous Posting**: This allows you to decide whether it is possible for anonymous users to create posts or not
    - **Subscribe by Default**: This enables you to subscribe users by default to the threads they participate in
    - **Message Format**: This option allows you to choose the format of the messages added
    - **Enable Flags**: This option enables the flags functionality, which provides a contact form for notification of irregularities
    - **Enable Ratings**: This option enables the post rating functionality that allows us to rate each post and presents its rating for each post
    - **Thread as Question by Default**: After enabling this option, all new threads are marked as question by default (the **Mark As Question** option in the new thread form is marked). Threads marked as questions on the thread list are marked by "waiting for an answer" flag.

□ **Show Recent Posts from Last**: This option allows us to set the period for the recent Posts tab.

▶ **E-mail notifications**:

Message boards provide two types of e-mail notifications: Message Added Email and Message Updated Email. Here are the following configuration options for message boards e-mail notifications:

□ **Email From**: This tab allows us to provide the sender's name and e-mail address

□ **Message Added Email** and **Message Updated Email**: These tabs allow us to enable the e-mail messaging functionality and set the subject, signature and message content using the available variables.

▶ **Thread Priorities**:

It is possible to set priorities for threads. Threads with a higher priority are displayed before threads with a lower priority. The **Thread Priority** tab allows us to define multiple priorities by providing the following information for each of them:

□ **Name**: This option displays name of the priority

□ **Image**: This option displays image of the priority (URL or a path relative to the theme)

▶ **User Ranks**: The **User Ranks** tab allows us to define the ranks that the user will acquire to create the specified amount of posts.

▶ **RSS**: The message boards portlet also allows users to track activities using RSS. As was indicated in the preceding recipe, portlet configuration allows us to choose:

□ The amount of items displayed by the RSS channel

□ Whether full content, abstract, or title should be shown

□ Whether RSS should be served in the Atom 1.0, RSS 1.0 or RSS 2.0 format

See also

▶ For information on how to configure SMTP servers, refer to the *Configuring Liferay with the SMTP server* recipe from *Chapter 11, Quick Tricks and Advanced Knowledge*

▶ For information on how to ban and unban users, refer to the *Banning a user for inappropriate post* recipe from this chapter

Banning a user for an inappropriate post

The message boards portlet provides a built-in banning mechanism, which allows us to block a use from viewing and participating in forums.

How to do it...

To ban a user, perform these steps:

1. Log in as an administrator and go to the page on which the message board should be placed.

2. Go to the post added by the user you want to ban.

3. Click on the **Ban This User** link located under the screen name (or name and surname) of the user.

4. Click on the **Banned Users** tab in the **message boards** menu. The user you have just banned will be on the list.

To unban a user, perform these steps:

1. Click on the **Banned Users** tab in the **message boards** menu.

2. Click on the **Unban This User** link, located near the screen name of the user you want to unban. The user will disappear from the list and will not be blocked from using message boards any more.

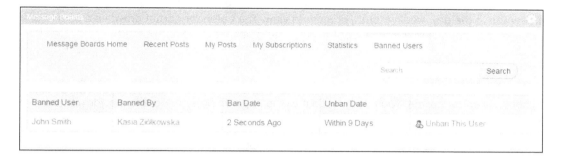

How it works...

As was shown in the preceding recipe, each user who added any post on the message board can be banned and unbanned by the site owner and administrator (or other users that have any custom role that permits it).

The banned user is not able to view the content of message boards or add a new category, thread, or post. If not unbanned by the message boards administrator (or other user who has permission to ban and unban other users), the banned user will be unbanned automatically in 10 days time. This default value can be changed in the `message.boards.expire.ban.interval` property (set to 0 to disable autoexpire). In order to override each property, you can put the specific property in the `${liferay.home}/portal-ext.properties` file.

Note that there is also the `message.boards.expire.ban.job.interval` property, which allows us to enter the time in minutes for how often the unbanning user job is run. This can affect the real time of unbanning a user. If a ban is expected to expire at 12:05 P.M. and the job runs at 2 P.M., the expiry will take place during the 2 P.M. run.

See also

For information on how to configure the message boards portlet, refer to the *Setting up a forum for intranet* recipe from this chapter.

Setting up the calendar as a personal tasks management tool

Liferay Calendar helps users manage their tasks, time, and resources. The Calendar portlet allows us to create events, invite other users to participate in them, set reminders, and manage resources (such as car or conference room) that can be reserved by other users. Events may be presented in the day, week, month, or agenda view. The Calendar portlet provides a couple of configuration options that help adapt the calendar functionality to our needs.

How to do it...

To set a Calendar portlet, you have to add it to the page. In order to do this, perform these steps:

1. Go to the page on which the Calendar portlet should be placed.
2. Click on the add button (this is a **+** sign on the left side).
3. Click on the **Applications** tab.
4. Find the **Calendar** portlet using the search feature or by browsing the list of available portlets (the Calendar portlet can be found in the **Collaboration** section).
5. Click on the **Add** link next to the portlet name. The Calendar portlet with basic configuration will be added to the page.

To configure the Calendar portlet, follow these steps:

1. Click on the options icon of the newly added portlet (this will be a gear icon in the top-right corner of the portlet).
2. Choose the **Configuration** option.

3. Make sure that you are on the **User Settings** tab.

4. Set **Time Format** to **24 hour**.

5. Set **Default Duration** to **60 minutes**.

6. Set **Default View** to **Day**.

7. Set the **Week Starts On** option to **Monday**.

8. Disable the **Use Global Time Zone** option.

9. Set **Time Zone** to **UTC**.

10. Click on the **Save** button.

11. Click on the **RSS** tab.

12. Leave the **Enable RSS Subscription** option enabled.

13. Set **Maximum Items to Display** to **10**.

14. Choose the **Abstract** option from the **Display Style** list.

15. Leave the **Format** option set as it is.

16. Click on the **Save** button.

How it works...

When configuring the Calendar portlet, you can set the following properties:

- ▶ **Time format**: This option allows you to decide whether the calendar will present hours in A.M./P.M. or in the 24-hour format

- ▶ **Default Duration**: The option allows you to set the default duration of an event (it works for fast-event creation only)

- ▶ **Default View**: This option allows you to set which view of the calendar will be present as default

- ▶ **Week Starts On**: This option allows you to choose the day presented as the first day of the week

- ▶ **Use Global Time Zone**: This option allows you to decide whether the calendar will work according to global time zone settings or the time zone specified in the **Time Zone** field in the calendar portlet configuration

- ▶ **Enable RSS Subscription**: This option allows users to track activities using RSS

- ▶ **Display Style**: This option allows you to decide whether full content, abstract, or title should be shown

- ▶ **Maximum Items to Display**: This option allows you to set the maximum amount of items displayed by the RSS channel

- ▶ **Format**: This option allows you to decide whether RSS should be served in the Atom 1.0, RSS 1.0, or RSS 2.0 format

Using bookmarks as good container to store favorite links

The Bookmarks functionality allows users to gather, organize, and share useful or favorite links. Each site in Liferay has its own separate bookmarks repository, which can be accessed by going to **Admin** | **Site Administration** | **Content** | **Bookmarks**. In addition, it is also possible to place the Bookmarks portlet on one of the pages where it can be shared between users who do not have access to the admin functionalities.

The Bookmarks portlet provides tools to create, edit, and delete bookmark folders and bookmarks. In this recipe, we will show you how to configure the Bookmarks portlet to adapt it to our users' needs.

How to do it...

First, let's add a new Bookmarks portlet. In order to do this, perform these steps:

1. Go to the page on which the Bookmarks portlet should be placed.
2. Click on the **Add** button.
3. Click on the **Applications** tab.
4. Find the Bookmarks portlet using the search feature or by browsing the list of available portlets (the Bookmarks portlet can be found in the **Community** section).
5. Click on the **Add** link next to the portlet name. The Bookmarks portlet with basic configuration will be added to the page.

After adding the Bookmarks portlet to the page, we can change its default configuration. To configure Bookmarks portlet, perform the following steps:

1. Click on the options icon of the newly added portlet (this will be a gear icon in the top-right corner of the portlet).
2. Choose the **Configuration** option.
3. Choose **Root Folder** by clicking on the **Select** button and then on the **Choose** button next to the name of the folder you want to set as root.
4. Enable the **Show Search** option.
5. Enable the **Show Subfolders** option.
6. Type **10** in the **Folders per Page** field.
7. Leave the selected columns in the **Show Columns** filed.
8. Click on the **Save** button.
9. Click on the **Email From** tab.
10. Provide the sender's **Name** and **Address**.
11. Click on the **Save** button.
12. Click on the **Entry Added Email** or **Entry Updated Email** tab.
13. Set the **Enabled** option.
14. Provide the **Subject** and **Body**.
15. Click on the **Save** button.

How it works...

The Bookmarks portlet configuration allows us to set folders listing, bookmarks listing, and e-mail notification messages.

Here are the following options to list folders:

- ▶ **Root Folder**: This option allows us to choose the folder that will be the highest (root) folder presented by the Bookmarks portlet
- ▶ **Show Search**: This option enables the search functionality within the Bookmarks portlet
- ▶ **Show Subfolders**: This option allows us to define the number of announcements presented on one list page
- ▶ **Folders per Page**: This option allows us to decide the number of folders shown on a single page of listing
- ▶ **Show Columns**: This option allows us to choose the set of columns presented on folders listing screen

Here are the following bookmarks listing options:

- ▶ **Enable Related Assets**: This option enables the related assets functionality, which lists all the assets defined as related in the adding/editing asset form
- ▶ **Documents per Page**: This option allows us to decide the number of folders shown on a single page of listing
- ▶ **Show Columns**: This option allows us to choose the set of columns presented on the folders listing screen
- ▶ **Email From**: This tab allows us to provide the sender's name and e-mail address
- ▶ **Page Added Email** and **Page Updated Email**: These tabs allow us to enable the e-mail messaging functionality and set the subject and message content using the available variables

See also

For information on how to configure SMTP servers, refer to the *Configuring Liferay with the SMTP server* recipe from *Chapter 11, Quick Tricks and Advanced Knowledge*.

Tracking social activities of site members

The Activities portlet shows social activities of members of the site within which it is located and allows us to track products of such activities by showing where they can be found. The portlet informs us who performed certain activities on a site and when these activities have been performed, and presents URL addresses to these products.

How to do it...

To configure the Activities portlet on a page, perform these steps:

1. Go to the page on which the Activities portlet should be placed.
2. Click on the add button (this is a **+** sign on the left side).
3. Click on the **Applications** tab.
4. Find the **Activities** portlet using the search feature or by browsing the list of available portlets (the Activities portlet can be found in the **Social** section).
5. Click on the **Add** link next to the portlet name. The Activities portlet with basic configuration will be added to the page.
6. Click on the options icon of the newly added portlet (this will be a gear icon in the top-right corner of the portlet).
7. Choose the **Configuration** option.

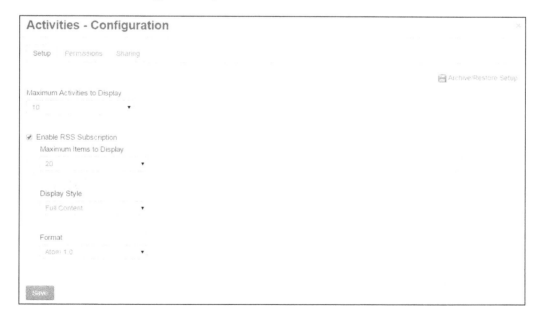

8. Make sure that you are on the **Setup** tab.

9. Choose **10** from the **Maximum Activities to Display** list.

10. Leave **Enable RSS Subscription** option enabled.

11. Set **Maximum Items to Display** to **10**.

12. Choose the **Abstract** option from the **Display Style** list.

13. Leave the **Format** option as it is.

14. Click on the **Save** button.

How it works...

The Activities portlet lists activities performed by users, such as adding or editing web content, Wiki pages, message boards categories, posts and threads, documents, shortcuts, blog entries, bookmarks, and calendar events. The portlet also informs us that the user rated some content.

The portlet lists as many activities as indicated in the portlet configuration by the amount set in the **Maximum Activities to Display** option. It also allows users to track activities by using RSS. As was indicated in the preceding recipe, portlet configuration allows us to choose the following:

▶ The amount of items displayed by the RSS channel

▶ Whether full content, abstract, or title should be shown

▶ Whether RSS should be served in the Atom 1.0, RSS 1.0 or RSS 2.0 format

There's more

It is also possible to use the Activities portlet on the user profile page. If the portlet is located within a user's profile page, it shows only this user's activities. To configure the Activities portlet on the user's profile page, click on the **My Profile** link located in the user's menu and follow all the steps indicated earlier.

Using the announcements portlet for group messaging

The Announcements portlet allows us to present and manage group messages called announcements. The Announcements functionality allows us to provide employees with some reminders or important organizational information. In the Announcements portlet, each user can see only messages that are dedicated to a group they belong to. Users will be notified via e-mails of new announcements.

How to do it...

To configure the Announcements portlet, perform these steps:

1. Go to the page on which the Announcements portlet should be placed.
2. Click on the add button (this is a **+** sign on the left side).
3. Click on the **Applications** tab.
4. Find the **Announcements** portlet using the search feature or by browsing the list of available portlets (the Announcements portlet can be found in the **Social** section).
5. Click on the **Add** link next to the portlet name. The Announcements portlet with basic configuration will be added to the page.
6. Click on the options icon of the newly added portlet (this will be a gear icon the top-right corner of the portlet).
7. Make sure you are on the **Setup** tab.
8. Choose the **Configuration** option.
9. Choose **10** from the **Maximum Items to Display** list.

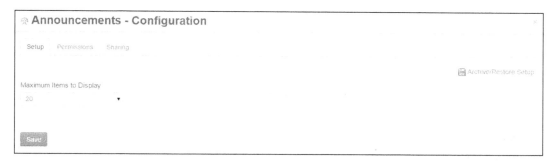

10. Click on the **Save** button.

To create a new announcement, perform these steps:

1. Go to the page on which the Announcements portlet is placed.
2. Click on the **Manage Entries** tab.

3. Choose the **Site Member** role from the **Distribution Scope** list. The **Add Entry** button will appear:

4. Click on the **Add Entry** button.

5. Provide **Title** for the announcement (obligatory).

6. Provide **URL** for the page to which the user will be redirected after clicking on the title of the announcement.

7. Provide **Content** for the announcement.

8. Choose **Type**, for example, **News**.

9. Set **Priority** to **Important**.

10. Leave **Display Date** as it is.

11. Leave the **Display Immediately** option enabled.

12. Set **Expiration Date**.

13. Click on **Save** button.

To edit an announcement, perform these steps:

1. Go to the page on which the Announcements portlet is placed.

2. Click on the **Edit** link, located next to the title of the announcement you want to edit.

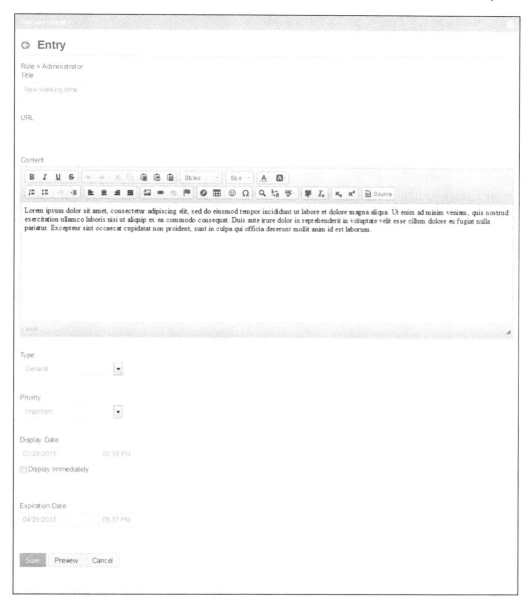

3. Modify the title, content, priority, and type of the announcement.

4. Set **Display Date** or enable the **Display Immediately** option.

5. Set **Expiration Date**.

6. Click on the **Save** button.

To remove an announcement, perform these steps:

1. Go to the page on which the Announcements portlet is placed.

2. Go to the **Entries** tab.

3. Click on the **Delete** link located next to the title of the announcement you want to remove.

4. Click on the **Ok** button. The announcement will be removed permanently.

How it works...

Announcements can be created by the site administrator or another user who has a role that contains permissions to create announcements. Such a user can distribute announcements to a specific group of users. However, a user who receives an announcement is not able to answer it or send it to other users (one-way communication). It is possible to distribute an announcement to all users from a specific organization, site, group, or to users having a particular role. The Announcement portlet consists of two tabs: the Entries and Manage Entries tabs. The Entries tab is available for all users and lists all the announcements dedicated to each user. The manage tab is visible for users having permissions to manage announcements and allows us to create, edit, and remove announcements.

Announcement management

While creating a new announcement, a user has to define the following properties:

▶ **Distribution scope**: This allows you to choose a group of users who will receive a message. Providing the distribution scope is obligatory.

▶ **Title**: The title text that will represent an announcement on the list. Defining the title is obligatory.

▶ **URL**: The page that will be shown after clicking on the title of the announcement.

▶ **Content**: The content of an announcement. Providing the content is obligatory.

▶ **Type**: The type of the announcement. The type is shown as a parameter on the list of entries on the **Manage Entries** tab.

▶ **Priority**: This allows you to define the priority of an announcement. Priority determines the position of an announcement on the list. Announcements with "Important" priority are listed before the "Normal" ones.

▶ **Display Date**: This allows you to define the day and hour of displaying an announcement.

▶ **Display Immediately**: This announcement will be displayed immediately after saving it.

▶ **Expiration Date**: This allows you to define the day and hour of the expiry of an announcement. Expired announcements are not listed on the **Entries** tab.

It is very important to choose the distribution group wisely while adding a new announcement. This is because the distribution group is the only parameter that cannot be changed by editing an announcement.

Unlike other types of content, such as web content or documents (which are always moved to the trash at first), deleting an announcement causes the permanent removal of an announcement.

Portlet configuration

Liferay allows us to customize this portlet setting. In order to change the settings, put the specific property in `${liferay.home}/portal-ext.properties`.

The Announcement portlet configuration allows us to define the number of announcements presented on one list page. To set the available values for the number of announcements to display per page, use the `announcements.entry.page.delta.values=5,10,20,30,50,75` property.

To set the list of announcement types, use the `announcements.entry.types=general,news,test` property.

You can also set the interval in minutes for how often `CheckEntryMessageListener` will run to check for new announcements and then inform users of new announcements via e-mail. To set this interval, use the `announcements.entry.check.interval` property.

11
Quick Tricks and Advanced Knowledge

In this chapter, we will cover the following topics:

- ▶ The language properties hook
- ▶ Setting up the portal session time and session policy
- ▶ Configuring Liferay with the SMTP server
- ▶ Intranet protection by the antisamy-hook plugin
- ▶ Migrating content from one database to another database
- ▶ Using the Liferay Service Bus for communication between portlets
- ▶ Clustering Liferay Portal

Introduction

This chapter covers various topics that are not connected to each other. Recipes cover some standard scenarios that a Liferay administrator will face and provide solutions. It will help you perform those specific tasks for your intranet sites. Almost everyone should know how to configure SMTP in order to send e-mails and receive notifications. The next important aspect is security. Administrators and developers should know how to install the antisamy-hook plugin or how to set session time and session policy. This is extremely important regardless of what type of portal Liferay will be used for. Also, this chapter will introduce important knowledge about advanced tricks in Liferay. It will describe the Liferay Service Bus and show how a user can use it. Furthermore, it will provide a detailed description of how clustering works in Liferay and how to migrate content from one database to another.

The language properties hook

Liferay has a multilanguage architecture and enables users to add content with many translations. Moreover, it gives users out-of-the-box functionality to change languages. Apart from this, the content portal also contains many labels that also have their own translation. It means that the Liferay design has a functionality in which it is possible to translate labels or fields. If we look into the sources (`portal-impl/src/content`), there are a lot of files with the following names: `Language_en.properties`, `Language_de.properties`, `Language_pl.properties`, and so on. The ISO 639-1 standard defines a set of possible codes for every language, such as **en** for English, **de** for German, and so on. The Liferay Portal supports up to 47 languages, which are defined in the `portal-impl/src/portal.properties` file called **locales**. Default translations do not always meet our expectations. Thus, in this recipe, we will show you how to change the existing labels using the hook plugin.

How to do it...

One of the functionalities of the hook plugin is to override messages in existing translations. Our goal is to change the **Sign in** label to **Intranet login**. The first step is generating a new hook called `language-hook`. To achieve it, use the Liferay Plugins SDK (`${SDK_HOME}/hook/create.sh language "Language hook"`) or Maven archetype generator (`mvn archetype:generate -Dfilter=liferay-hook`). If you encounter a problem with generating the language hook, go back and study the *Creating a custom portlet* recipe from *Chapter 1, Installation and Basic Configuration*. We assume that the user generates this plugin as a Maven project. Next, import the project to your favorite IDE, such as Eclipse, IntelliJ IDEA, or NetBeans, and follow these steps:

1. Open the `src/main/webapp/WEB-INF/liferay-hook.xml` file.

2. Define a new language property file:

   ```
   <language-properties>
     i18n/Language_en.properties
   </language-properties>
   ```

3. Create the `i18n` folder in `src/main/resources` and create the `Language_en.properties` file.

4. In `Language_en.properties`, add the following line:

   ```
   sign-in=Intranet login
   ```

5. Compile the plugin and deploy it by invoking the `mvn clean install liferay:deploy` command.

How it works...

As we said at the beginning, Liferay supports many languages and translations. Every translation is kept in the `Language.properties` file with a specific suffix, such as `_pl`, `_en`, `_de`, and so on. All the available locales are defined in the portal properties as follows:

```
locales=ar_SA,eu_ES,bg_BG,ca_AD,ca_ES,zh_CN,zh_TW,hr_HR,cs_CZ,da_
DK,nl_NL,nl_BE,en_US,en_GB,en_AU,et_EE,fi_FI,fr_FR,fr_CA,gl_ES,de_
DE,el_GR,iw_IL,hi_IN,hu_HU,in_ID,it_IT,ja_JP,ko_KR,lo_LA,lt_LT,nb_
NO,fa_IR,pl_PL,pt_BR,pt_PT,ro_RO,ru_RU,sr_RS,sr_RS_latin,sl_SI,sk_
SK,es_ES,sv_SE,tr_TR,uk_UA,vi_VN

locales.beta=ar_SA,eu_ES,bg_BG,ca_AD,zh_TW,hr_HR,cs_CZ,da_DK,nl_NL,nl_
BE,en_GB,en_AU,et_EE,gl_ES,el_GR,hi_IN,in_ID,it_IT,ko_KR,lo_LA,lt_
LT,nb_NO,fa_IR,pl_PL,pt_PT,ro_RO,ru_RU,sr_RS,sr_RS_latin,sl_SI,sk_
SK,sv_SE,tr_TR,uk_UA,vi_VN

locales.enabled=ca_ES,zh_CN,en_US,fi_FI,fr_FR,de_DE,iw_IL,hu_HU,ja_
JP,pt_BR,es_ES
```

The first property specifies all the available locales in the Liferay Portal. The second one lists languages that are in beta. A set of beta properties means that the translation is not finished, and Liferay can contain some errors or mistakes.

 It is possible to join the community that works with translations and participate with them. All the necessary information is available at `http://translate.liferay.com`.

The last property lists languages that Liferay supports by default. It is necessary to change it if we create a new project and fit it to our requirements. It can be changed later. This operation is available in the Control Panel section.

In this recipe, we showed you how to override the existing property. Overriding works for every single property defined in `portal-impl/src/content/Language.properties`. Additionally, in our `i18n/Language_en.properties`, it is possible to add a new property that can be used in our new functionalities.

In the Liferay language properties, there is a `portal-impl/src/content/Language.properties` file (without a language suffix). This set of properties is used when the system cannot find a property for the specific country/language.

There's more...

Apart from customizing language properties, Liferay lets you choose how your internationalization works. To understand this feature, you should know how to change the Liferay language first. By default, Liferay provides a unique URL for a specific language. The following are some of the examples:

- `http://localhost:8080/pl/web/guest/home`
- `http://localhost:8080/en_US/web/guest/home`

This context (`/pl`, `/en_US`) is handled by `I18nServlet`, which is defined in the `web.xml` file. This servlet changes the language and renders a page with dedicated translation.

In detail, there is a property called `locale.prepend.friendly.url.style` located in `portal-impl/src/portal.properties`. It has four possible values that are defined in the following table:

Value	Description
0	The locale is not automatically prepended to a URL. This means that each URL could potentially point to many different languages. For example, if a user sets the German language in their account settings, the Portal displays sites in English by default.
	If this property is set as 0, page `http://localhost:8080/web/guest` is displayed in English. However, when users log in, it is automatically translated to German. URI has the same value, `/web/guest`, without language context.
1	The locale is automatically prepended to a URL when the requested locale is not the default locale. This means that each URL points to just one language. Let's analyze the situation from the first example where a user sets a language different from the default one. The first visit to the `http://localhost:8080` portal displays content in the default language (English). After the login action, the user is redirected to the `http://localhost:8080/de` URL. On every page, there is the `/de/web/guest/{PAGE}` URI. After logout, the portal remembers the language and displays German translations.
2	The locale is automatically prepended to every URL. This means that each URL points to just one language.
3	The locale is automatically prepended to a URL when the requested locale is not the default user locale. In the case of guest users, the behavior is the same as having a value of 1. However, in the our case (the user has a different locale than the portal), there is the following situation:
	By default, the portal displays content in English, and there is no language context. The URL looks like `http://localhost:8080/`.
	When a user logs in, the language is German, but the URL is the same, `http://localhost:8080` (without language context).
	After the logout action, the URL is the same, but the language is still German. To change the language, it is necessary to invoke the `http://localhost:8080/en` URL.

The last thing connected with language settings, is the default language definition. It is placed in `portal-impl/src/system.properties` and can be overridden by `system-ext.properties`. To set the default language, override the following properties:

```
user.country=PL
user.language=pl
```

See also

In order to learn about creating plugins (especially portlets), refer to the *Creating a custom portlet* recipe in *Chapter 1, Installation and Basic Configuration*

Setting up the portal session time and session policy

In every project, especially the intranet one, the main functionality is authentication and authorization in order to provide correct permissions and serve dedicated content for an authenticated user. Every logged-in user has their own session; the expiry time can be set specifically. You can also set the session using any other settings, such as auto-extend session or redirection when a session expires. All the settings concerning the session can be found in `portal.properties`.

Let's assume that our goal is to configure the following session policy:

- ▸ The session expires after 10 minutes
- ▸ The system redirects the user to the default page after session expiration (if all pages don't have guest permission to display for unauthenticated users, the system should display the login page)
- ▸ Two minutes before session ending, the system should display a warning with a counter
- ▸ The session identifier shouldn't be visible in the URL

How to do it...

As we said at the beginning, Liferay overrides session-specific properties via `portal-ext.properties`. To achieve our goal, open `portal-impl/src/portal-ext.properties` and set the following definitions:

```
session.timeout=10
session.timeout.redirect.on.expire=true
session.timeout.auto.extend=false
session.timeout.warning=2
session.enable.url.with.session.id=false
```

Except for the `session.timeout` setting, it is required that you set the same value in `web.xml`. To complete this task, open the main `web.xml` file, which is located in the `{$TOMCAT_HOME}/webapps/ROOT/WEB-INF` folder. Find an XML tag called `session-config` and change it as follows:

```
<session-config>
  <session-timeout>10</session-timeout>
</session-config>
```

Finally, save this file and restart your application server.

How it works...

Our first goal was to change a default session timeout, which was 30 minutes. We decreased it to 10 minutes. It is important to know that changing the `session.timeout` property is not sufficient because the `web.xml` configuration overrides this setting. To finish our configuration, we also had to change this value into the `web.xml` descriptor.

Next, the assumption was connected with user redirection after timeout. In order to achieve our goal, we needed to change two properties:

- `session.timeout.redirect.on.expire`: This is set to `true` and redirects the user to the default page when the session expires
- `session.timeout.auto.extend`: This is set to `false` to deny the autoextend session

The `session.timeout.warning` property specifies the number of minutes before a warning, informing the user of the session expiration. We set this value to 2 minutes.

The last assumption was connected with security requirements. Of course, it is disabled by default, but we decided to show how it can be configured. Thus, the last property called `session.enable.url.with.session.id` was set to `false`.

Configuring Liferay with the SMTP server

Liferay sends e-mails in many cases, such as when adding calendar events and posts on the message board or when a user creates an account. In order to enable this function, it is required that you correctly configure the SMTP server and set the appropriate properties. In this recipe, we will explain how to configure the SMTP server in the easiest way.

How to do it...

There are three ways to configure the SMTP server correctly. The easiest way is to use Liferay's Control Panel and configure the SMTP settings using the GUI interface. To achieve it, go to **Admin | Control Panel | Server Administration** and choose the **Mail** tab. After that, enter your settings for your mail session under the **Outgoing SMTP Server** section and click on the **Save** button. This type of setting is a great choice when there is only one instance of the SMTP server or the SMTP is a third-party external server. In many cases this setting is insufficient. The best example is an application running in a clustered environment where each node (Liferay instance) has its own SMTP local server.

In many cases, for instance, in the clustered environment, it is a very common practice to install the SMTP server on the same node where the Liferay instance is. In this case, it is not possible to configure the SMTP server using the GUI interface, but this setting can be done in `portal-ext.properties`. In this file, we can put our settings that display the following listing:

```
mail.session.mail.pop3.host=localhost
mail.session.mail.pop3.password=
mail.session.mail.pop3.port=110
mail.session.mail.pop3.user=
mail.session.mail.smtp.auth=false
mail.session.mail.smtp.host=localhost
mail.session.mail.smtp.password=
mail.session.mail.smtp.port=25
mail.session.mail.smtp.user=
mail.session.mail.store.protocol=pop3
mail.session.mail.transport.protocol=smtp
```

The last possibility is to use the application server's mail session via **Java Naming and Directory Interface** (**JNDI**), which looks up the Java mail session. In order to enable the JNDI name, put the following configuration in the `portal-ext.properties` file:

```
mail.session.jndi.name=mail/MailSession
```

Make sure that, in your `{$TOMCAT_HOME}/conf/Catalina/localhost/ROOT.xml` file, there is defined a resource similar to the following tag:

```
<Resource name="mail/MailSession" auth="Container" type="javax.mail.
Session" mail.imap.host="localhost" mail.pop3.host="localhost" mail.
smtp.host="localhost" mail.store.protocol="imap" mail.transport.
protocol="smtp" />
```

The Liferay Portal recommends SMTP configuration over the GUI or by setting the properties as a unified configuration of Java mail, which doesn't depend on the application server.

How it works...

Liferay has its own message bus implementation. It is a service-level API used to exchange messages within Liferay. In this specific case, an e-mail sending mechanism uses *Liferay Message Bus*. As in every message bus implementation, there is a sender, that sends messages to the destination. This functionality is implemented in the `com.liferay.mail.service.impl.MailServiceImpl` class in the `sendEmail` method:

```
public void sendEmail(MailMessage mailMessage) {
    MessageBusUtil.sendMessage(DestinationNames.MAIL, mailMessage);
}
```

As we see in the preceding method, the sending action has quite a simple implementation that invokes only the `com.liferay.portal.kernel.messaging.MessageBusUtil.sendMessage` method, which gives with the type of destination and mail message arguments. `MailMessageListener` is responsible for sending e-mails to the specific address correctly.

At the opposite site, there is a listener that can recognize the message and consume it. For instance, it sends an e-mail message. This is the `com.liferay.mail.messaging.MailMessageListener` class, which receives the event (in this case, the mail event) and invokes an appropriate action to send the e-mail.

Intranet protection by the antisamy-hook plugin

Liferay 6.x exposes a new functionality called sanitizers. This is an implementation that protects content (HTML and JavaScript) against malicious code that users may pass to the journal article, wiki, message board, and so on. This can happen if a user copies and pastes the content from any Internet resources. In the Liferay core implementation, there are no sanitizers. One of the reasons is that Liferay allows users to implement their own policy and install it as a hook plugin. Fortunately, Liferay has a plugin called `antisamy-hook` in the official GitHub repository at `https://github.com/liferay/liferay-plugins/tree/master/hooks/antisamy-hook`.

In this recipe, we will show you how to install this plugin and also give you an idea about how it works.

How to do it...

The antisamy-hook plugin, like other plugins, is available on the official Liferay marketplace. Therefore, the installation process is really simple and unified. In order to achieve your goal, log in as an administrator, go to **Admin** | **Control Panel** | **Store**, find the **Antisamy CE** plugin, and purchase it by clicking on the **Free** button. This plugin is free if you have a valid marketplace account. After that, go to the **Purchased** tab and click on the **Install** button.

In the log file, you should find the following message:

```
INFO  [localhost-startStop-2][HookHotDeployListener:687] Registering
hook for antisamy-hook
Loading file:/home/piotr/clients/packt/project/tomcat-7.0.42/temp/6-
antisamy-hook/WEB-INF/classes/portal.properties
INFO  [localhost-startStop-2][HookHotDeployListener:814] Hook for
antisamy-hook is available for use
```

How it works...

The `antisamy-hook` plugin adds an *OWASP AntiSamy* implementation, which means that the plugin includes the OWASP `antisamy.jar` library, which is located in the `org.owasp.validator.html.AntiSamy` package. The OWASP AntiSamy project is an API that protects the content against malicious code.

 More details are available on the official OWASP site at `https://www.owasp.org/index.php/Category:OWASP_AntiSamy_Project`.

From a technical point of view, the `antisamy-hook` plugin is a very simple but powerful tool. It is simple, because it just overrides the `sanitizer.impl` property as follows:

```
sanitizer.impl=com.liferay.antisamy.hook.sanitizer.
AntiSamySanitizerImpl
```

It is powerful, because it uses an open source OWASP Antisamy project that filters our content.

The main implementation is in the `AntiSamySanitizerImpl` class (actually, there is only one class in this plugin) in the sanitize method:

```
public String sanitize([arguments])
  throws SanitizerException {

  if (Validator.isNull(contentType) ||
    !contentType.equals(ContentTypes.TEXT_HTML)) {
    return s;
  }
  try {
    AntiSamy antiSamy = new AntiSamy();
    CleanResults cleanResults = antiSamy.scan(s, _policy);
    return cleanResults.getCleanHTML();
  }
  catch (Exception e) {
    _log.error("Unable to sanitize input", e);
```

```
        throw new SanitizerException(e);
    }
}
```

This implementation checks whether `contentType` is HTML and the `AntiSamy` implementation filters the content and returns the clean results. The OWASP library is responsible for correctly filtering content.

Migrating content from one database to another database

The content migration tool is an interesting feature that Liferay provides as an out-of the-box core implementation. As you know, Liferay gives administrators a choice to select one of the database engines, such as MySQL, PostgreSQL, Oracle, and so on. It allows users to change the database engine without losing data.

Let's assume that our Liferay instance uses the PostgreSQL database, and we want to change it to MySQL engine.

Getting ready...

In order to migrate our content, we need to create a new MySQL database. To achieve it log in to your database:

```
mysql -u {USER} -p
```

Then, create a new database using the following command:

```
CREATE DATABASE lportal
DEFAULT CHARACTER SET utf8
DEFAULT COLLATE utf8_general_ci;
```

How to do it...

This functionality is available out-of-the-box. Moreover, it doesn't require developer support. All migration processes can be done with the help of the GUI. To migrate data, follows these steps:

1. Log in as an administrator.

2. Go to **Admin | Control Panel | Server Administration** and choose the **Data Migration** tab.

3. Fill in the form as follows:

- ❑ In **JDBC Driver Class Name**, enter `com.mysql.jdbc.Driver`
- ❑ In **JDBC URL**, enter `jdbc:mysql://localhost/lportal?useUnicode=true&characterEncoding=UTF-8&useFastDateParsing=false`
- ❑ In **JDBC User Name**, enter the database's user
- ❑ In **JDBC Password**, enter the database user's password

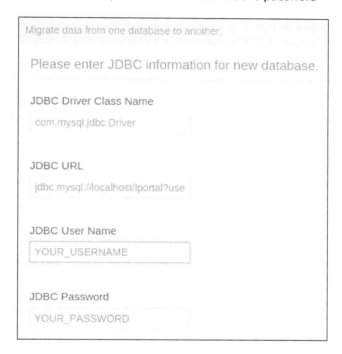

4. Click on the **Execute** button. All information about operation details will be available on the logfile. The following message will progressively appear on the screen:

> The system is currently undergoing maintenance. Please try again later.
>
> Sun, 22 Feb 2015 11:42:51 +0000 Executing com.liferay.portal.convert.ConvertDatabase
> Sun, 22 Feb 2015 11:42:51 +0000 Collecting information for database tables to migration
> Sun, 22 Feb 2015 11:42:57 +0000 24%
> Sun, 22 Feb 2015 11:43:08 +0000 49%
> Sun, 22 Feb 2015 11:43:11 +0000 73%
> Sun, 22 Feb 2015 11:43:14 +0000 98%

5. Make sure that the process is successfully finished. Inside the `catalina.out` logfile, you will find the following message:

   ```
   Finished conversion for com.liferay.portal.convert.ConvertDatabase
   in 18652 ms.
   ```

6. Next, shut down your application server, change the database properties to indicate a new database, and start an application server with a new configuration.

How it works...

The database migration process is supported by Liferay in order to retain compatibility with databases. This process uses Liferay Message Bus, which exposes listener to data migration. In this case, an event prepares and invokes the `com.liferay.portlet.admin.action.EditServerAction` class. The following listing shows how it was implemented:

```
protected String convertProcess([Arguments]) throws Exception {
    [..]
    MaintenanceUtil.maintain(portletSession.getId(), className);
    MessageBusUtil.sendMessage(DestinationNames.CONVERT_PROCESS,
    className);
}
```

This method is responsible for preparing specific data, showing a maintenance window, and sending an event to the message bus.

Listener is represented by `com.liferay.portal.convert.ConvertDatabase` with the `doConvert()` method. This method is responsible for preparing all database data and putting it into the new database. All details in this method are complex, but the main idea is to take every table, its data, and indexes and migrate them to the new database schema.

See also

If you want to migrate a storage data, refer to:

- ▶ The *Integration with the Amazon S3 cloud* recipe from *Chapter 6, Documents and Media in Liferay*
- ▶ The *Data migration between storage hooks* recipe from *Chapter 6, Documents and Media in Liferay*

Using Liferay Service Bus for communication between portlets

The message bus is a mechanism for sending messages to different components in Liferay. This approach is very common, because it prevents class-loading issues. It is very important, because Liferay is a portlet container, and each portlet doesn't have information about the others. For that reason, Liferay provides a message bus that allows communication between portlets. An application that sends an event/message is called a producer, and an application that receives messages is called a consumer.

The message bus architecture supports asynchronous and synchronous messaging. Synchronous messages wait for a response, and asynchronous messages send a message, forget it, or receive a callback. The main difference between synchronous and asynchronous messages is the fact that the first one block threads and wait for the response.

In this recipe, we will show you how to use a message bus in a real example. Let's assume that our goal is to write a search portlet with one input with the autocomplete feature. This will be a simple form with only one input that can autocomplete our query. After submitting the form, the search criteria should be sent to the existing out-of-the-box search portlet. The Liferay message bus will be used to communicate with the Lucene indexer.

It is not possible to show and explain all the implementations, so we will explain a piece of code with the message bus. In the following *How to do it...* section, we will show you the steps to compile, deploy, and install our portlet. In the *How it works...* section of this recipe, we will explain a message bus implementation.

How to do it...

In order to correctly compile, deploy, and install the portlet, follow these steps:

1. Download `quicksearch-portlet` from `http://www.liferay-guru.com/code/ch11/quicksearch-portlet.zip`.

2. Copy the portlet to the `workspace` folder.

3. Open `quicksearch-portlet/pom.xml` and set the appropriate paths in the `<properties>` section.

4. Invoke the `mvn clean install liferay:deploy` command.

5. Run your Liferay instance and check whether, in the logfile, there is a message to successfully deploy:

   ```
   INFO  [DispatcherPortlet:282] FrameworkPortlet
   'quicksearchportlet': initialization completed in 81 ms
   INFO  [DispatcherPortlet:119] Portlet 'quicksearchportlet'
   configured successfully
   INFO  [localhost-startStop-3] [PortletHotDeployListener:490] 1
   portlet for quicksearch-portlet is available for use
   ```

6. Log in as an administrator, create a page called **Search**, and put the **Search** portlet, which is available under the **Tools** category in the left menu called **Add**.

7. Create the second page, for example, `Quick Search`, and add the **QuickSearch** portlet.

8. Open a search portlet configuration window and set the layout to the Search portlet (in our case, it will be the **Search** page).

9. Click on the **Save** button and close the pop-up configuration window via the **X** button.

10. Try to write a word (with at least three letters) in the **QuickSearch** portlet and enjoy the autocomplete feature.

How it works...

In this portlet, Liferay Message Bus is used to ask the search engine about the autocomplete results. In our case, the producer is a class called `com.liferay.guru.portlet.quicksearch.util.QSMessageBusUtil`. Its code looks like this:

```
public class QSMessageBusUtil {

  public static JSONArray sendSynchronousMessage(SearchContext
  searchContext)
  throws MessageBusException {
    Message message = new Message();
    message.setDestinationName(QSDestinationNames.
    SEARCH_AUTOCOMPLETE);
    message.setPayload(searchContext);
    message.setResponseDestinationName(DestinationNames.
    MESSAGE_BUS_DEFAULT_RESPONSE);

    Object response = MessageBusUtil.sendSynchronousMessage(
      message.getDestinationName(), message,
      SearchConstants.AUTOCOMPLETE_TIMEOUT);


    if (response instanceof JSONArray) {
      return (JSONArray) response;
    } else {
      throw new MessageBusException("Invalid message response");
    }
  }
}
```

This class has only one method that returns a JSON array with search results. The first three lines are responsible for creating the `Message` object, which will be sent to the message bus. The `Message` object is an instance of the `com.liferay.portal.kernel.messaging.Message` class with the following fields:

- `String _destinationName`: This is the name of our destination. It is the place to which we address our message

- `Object _payload`: This field represents an object (payload) that will be sent to the consumer

- `Object _response`: This field contains an object that represents the response message

- `String _responseDestinationName`: The place where the consumer (listener) sends back the response. In our example, this is `DestinationNames.MESSAGE_BUS_DEFAULT_RESPONSE`, which defines the response back to the destination, the producer

- `String _responseId`: This value represents the response identifier

- `Map<String, Object> _values`: Additional maps of objects that will be sent to the consumer or producer

In our implementation, we set the payload as `SearchContext` (our Lucene query) and set `responseDestinationName` as a default response.

To send our message to the message bus, we invoked the following method:

```
Object response = MessageBusUtil.sendSynchronousMessage(
    message.getDestinationName(), message,
    SearchConstants.AUTOCOMPLETE_TIMEOUT);
```

There is a question: which class should receive our message? The answer and all of the configuration are in the `applicationContext-messaging.xml` file, which looks like this:

```
<util:constant id="destination.name.search.autocomplete"
  static-field="com.liferay.guru.portlet.quicksearch.util.
  QSDestinationNames.SEARCH_AUTOCOMPLETE" />
<bean id="messageListener.autocomplete.lucene"
  class="com.liferay.guru.search.lucene.AutocompleteListener" />
<bean id="destination.search.autocomplete"
  class="com.liferay.portal.kernel.messaging.
  SynchronousDestination">
  <property name="name" ref="destination.name.
    search.autocomplete" />
</bean>
<!-- Configurator -->
<bean id="messagingConfigurator"
```

```
      class="com.liferay.portal.kernel.messaging.config.
      PluginMessagingConfigurator">
      <property name="messageListeners">
        <map key-type="java.lang.String" value-
          type="java.util.List">
        <entry key-ref="destination.name.search.autocomplete">
          <list>
            <ref bean="messageListener.autocomplete.lucene" />
          </list>
        </entry>
      </map>
    </property>
    <property name="destinations">
      <list>
        <ref bean="destination.search.autocomplete" />
      </list>
    </property>
  </bean>
```

The preceding configuration specifies the following beans:

▶   The `listener` bean with the `messageListener.autocomplete.lucene` ID.

▶   The `destination` bean with the `destination.search.autocomplete` ID.

▶   The `configurator` bean that maps listeners to their destinations. In our
     case, it maps our `destination.search.autocomplete` destination to the
     `messageListener.autocomplete.lucene` bean. In other words, it links the
     destination with the listener.

Let's look at our listener implementation:

```
public class AutocompleteListener extends BaseMessageListener {
  @Override
  protected void doReceive(Message message) throws Exception {

    Message response = MessageBusUtil.createResponseMessage(
    message );

    Object payload = message.getPayload();
    if ( payload instanceof SearchContext ) {
      response.setPayload( getSuggestions( (SearchContext) payload
      ) );
    }
    else {
```

```
        _log.error( "Message payload is invalid: " +
        Objects.toString( payload ) );
        response.setPayload( JSONFactoryUtil.createJSONArray() );
    }

    MessageBusUtil.sendMessage( response.getDestinationName(),
    response );
    }
[...]
}
```

`AutocompleteListener` extends `BaseMessageListener` and overrides the `doReceive` method.

The body of this method is responsible for creating a new response and sending it back to our producer. An object that was received and that will be sent is put to the payload field. Therefore, our implementation gets an object from payload, checks whether it is `SearchContext`, looks for new suggestions, and sets suggestions as a new payload.

Summarizing this recipe, remember the following things:

▶ Liferay Message Bus implements a communication between producer and consumer

▶ The `Message` object is sent between the producer and consumer

▶ The producer creates a `Message` object with the following attributes:

    ❑ `payload`: This field represents the object (payload) that will be sent to the consumer

    ❑ `responseDestinationName`: This is the name that is provided for listeners to use in replying

    ❑ Optionally, `responseId` (the `setResponseId` method) and other objects that should be sent to the consumer as a key/value pair (put method)

▶ To send a synchronous message, you should use the `MessageBusUtil.sendSynchronousMessage` method

▶ The listener (consumer) must be registered in the XML definition

▶ The listener has a `doReceive` method that sends back a message

▶ The consumer extracts values from the message and prepares a response message

▶ `MessageBusUtil.createResponseMessage` should be used to create a response message

▶ Consumers send back a message to the producer via the `MessageBusUtil.sendMessage` method

There's more...

In this recipe, we discussed only synchronous communication that is a basic example of using a message bus. As a matter of fact, using synchronous messaging is not a good idea in many cases. Why? The answer is simple: this type of communication blocks waiting for a response from a recipient. Communication via messages was basically designed for asynchronous communication. There are two types of asynchronous messaging:

- **send and forget**: This means *push an event and forget about it*. This type of communication is useful in notification cases, for example, if a producer wants to notify listeners about some action.

- **call-back**: The producer defines a call back destination in `responseDestinationName` for the message. The listener can send the message back to the specific `responseDestinationName`. The important information is that the producer is free for further processing.

From a technical point of view, an asynchronous implementation is very similar to our example. The main difference is that it invokes a different method from `MessageBusUtil`. To send an asynchronous message, the following invocation should be used, as you can see in the listener code when you send the response:

```
MessageBusUtil.sendMessage(message.getDestinationName(), message);
```

The important information is that the `sendMessage` method does not return any values, because it is an asynchronous message, and we don't know whether there is call-back information or not. All of the configurations where call back should be sent are placed in the `messaging.xml` file. Here is an example:

```
<entry key="YOUR_RESPONSE_DESTINATION_NAME">
  <list value-
  type="com.liferay.portal.kernel.messaging.MessageListener">
    <ref bean="messageListener.listener1" />
    <ref bean="messageListener.listener2" />
    <ref bean="messageListener.listenerN" />
  </list>
</entry>
```

See also

In order to learn about creating plugins (especially portlets), refer to the *Creating a custom portlet* recipe from *Chapter 1, Installation and Basic Configuration*.

Clustering Liferay Portal

Liferay supports clustering out-of-the-box in the **Community Edition** (**CE**) version as well as the **Enterprise Edition** (**EE**) version. It is designed to build scalable systems that can be used by large companies with a huge amount of data, so it allows us to run several portal instances on parallel servers. In order to build Liferay clusters, you need to know which components are sensitive to clustering. The clustering process has a huge impact on the following components:

- ▸ Databases, where Liferay instances keep their data
- ▸ Documents and media as a folder on the hard drive
- ▸ Lucene search engine files
- ▸ Liferay caches

This recipe will go through each point and show you how to cluster Liferay correctly.

Getting ready...

This recipe is not a tutorial on how to correctly run clustered environments, such as Apache server, load balancers, and so on. Instead, our goal is to show you how to correctly configure Liferay so that it works with a parallel environment. Let's assume that you have properly configured all the components. The last step is configuring Liferay to work in a cluster properly.

How to do it...

As we said at the beginning, there are several points that should be checked before running Liferay on a cluster.

Check database configuration

The first thing, which is really simple, is checking database configuration. There should be one database instance shared between all Liferay nodes. To check configuration correctness, open the property file where database access configuration is present. Usually, it is `portal-ext.properties`. Make sure that, in every node, the configuration is the same. Here is an example:

```
jdbc.default.driverClassName=com.mysql.jdbc.Driver
jdbc.default.url=jdbc:mysql://localhost/lportal?useUnicode=true&characterEncoding=UTF-8&useFastDateParsing=false
jdbc.default.username=<USERNAME>
jdbc.default.password=<PASSWORD>
```

Documents and media clustering

In *Chapter 6, Documents and Media in Liferay*, we explained how the Documents and Media portlet works. It is also important to know that file metadata is stored in a database, but binary data (files) are stored on the hard drive. As you can guess, it will be a problem when Liferay works as a clustered environment, because each node can have its own repository and files are not shared between nodes. In order to resolve this problem, there are three ways:

▶ Sharing the repository between nodes via **Storage Area Network** (**SAN**), **Network Attached Storage** (**NAS**), GlusterFS and so on: Ask your system administrator which option is available on a specific machine and correctly install the clustered filesystem. In many solutions, we have seen a GlusterFS system, which shared a data folder between nodes. This solution guarantees that each node has the same repository of files. Make sure that the following property indicates a proper location for shared disk storage:

```
dl.store.file.system.root.dir=${liferay.home}/data/document_
library
```

▶ Using database storage: All data, including binary files, is stored in a database table. To enable this configuration, set the following property:

```
dl.store.impl=com.liferay.portlet.documentlibrary.store.DBStore
```

This setting automatically uses the database instead of filesystem. The database should support the BLOB's field.

▶ Using external storage systems, such as the following ones:

  ❑ **Amazon Cloud**: We showed you how to configure this storage in the *Integration with the Amazon S3 cloud* recipe in *Chapter 6, Documents and Media in Liferay*

  ❑ **Content Management Interoperability Services** (**CMIS**) Store such as Alfresco: After successful installation of Alfresco (or other CMIS Store system), set the following properties:

```
dl.store.impl=com.liferay.portlet.documentlibrary.store.CMISStore
dl.store.cmis.credentials.username=none
dl.store.cmis.credentials.password=none
dl.store.cmis.repository.url=http://localhost:8080/alfresco/
service/api/cmis
dl.store.cmis.system.root.dir=Liferay Home
```

▶ **A Java Content Repository** (**JCR**) store such as Jackrabbit: This is an Apache project implemented as a JSR-170 specification. Liferay supports it, but this configuration is deprecated because of performance issues and concurrency conflicts. In this solution, the Jackrabbit repository must be placed on the SAN shared storage (mounted on every node).

Search engine

We already mentioned the search engine topic in *Chapter 8, Search and Content Presentation Tools*. We showed two search engines: Apache Lucene and Apache Solr. If you use Solr or Solr Cloud as a search engine, everything will work perfectly because Solr is an external application with which Liferay establishes a connection. In the clustered environment, this is the best option because of performance and the quality of the search results.

As you know, Lucene keeps its data in a local storage filesystem. It is a problem to keep an up-to-date index on every Liferay node in the clustered environment. We cannot replicate the index file by GlusterFS, because Lucene sometimes locks data when it writes to an index or optimizes it. In order to resolve this conflict, Liferay gives a functionality that provides a replication mechanism between all Liferay's nodes. To enable this functionality, set the following properties:

```
cluster.link.enabled=true
lucene.replicate.write=true
```

These properties need to be set for all of Liferay's nodes. The `cluster.link.enabled` property turns on the whole mechanism of cache replication, which we will describe in the following section.

Cache replication

Liferay uses EhCache to cache some content, such as the result of SQL queries. In a clustered environment, cache distribution is a very important issue. Each node should know about the changes on the database and cache invalidations. Phil Karlton once quoted:

> *"There are only two hard things in Computer Science: cache invalidation and naming things."*

I completely agree with him.

Multicast

Cache distribution between nodes works perfectly with multicasting. Make sure that your servers support multicasting. Next, set the following property to enable replication:

```
cluster.link.enabled=true
```

This property turns on the clustered mode.

The following properties define five channels for distributing messages between nodes:

```
multicast.group.address["cluster-link-control"]=239.255.0.1
multicast.group.port["cluster-link-control"]=23301

multicast.group.address["cluster-link-udp"]=239.255.0.2
multicast.group.port["cluster-link-udp"]=23302
```

```
multicast.group.address["cluster-link-mping"]=239.255.0.3
multicast.group.port["cluster-link-mping"]=23303

multicast.group.address["hibernate"]=239.255.0.4
multicast.group.port["hibernate"]=23304

multicast.group.address["multi-vm"]=239.255.0.5
multicast.group.port["multi-vm"]=23305
```

Set a proper IP addresses and port number for the preceding properties (settings). In many environments, it works out of the box.

Unicast

In some servers, it might not be possible to send messages by multicasting. Fortunately, it is possible to force Liferay to use unicast protocols instead of multicast. Configuration is not very difficult, but it is hard to discover it. To reduce the time spent on Google, follow this part of the recipe and correctly set this type of communication.

First, turn on the clustering mode by setting the `cluster.link.enabled` property with the `true` value.

Next, you have to use the `JGroups` library to establish communication via TCP. To achieve this, set the following properties:

```
ehcache.bootstrap.cache.loader.factory=com.liferay.portal.cache.
ehcache.JGroupsBootstrapCacheLoaderFactory
ehcache.cache.event.listener.factory=net.sf.ehcache.distribution.
jgroups.JGroupsCacheReplicatorFactory
ehcache.cache.manager.peer.provider.factory=net.sf.ehcache.
distribution.jgroups.JGroupsCacheManagerPeerProviderFactory

ehcache.multi.vm.config.location.peerProviderProperties=file=unicast-
ehcache.xml
net.sf.ehcache.configurationResourceName.peerProviderProperties=file=u
nicast-ehcache.xml

cluster.link.channel.properties.control=unicast-ehcache.xml
cluster.link.channel.properties.transport.0=unicast-ehcache.xml
```

Analyze the highlighted part in the preceding section. All channels have references to the `unicast-ehcache.xml` file. Thus, create the `unicast-ehcache.xml` file on a classpath (`${TOMCAT_HOME}webapps/ROOT/WEB-INF/classes`). It is also possible to create it in the `ext` plugin at `ext-impl/src/main/resources/unicast-ehcache.xml`. The content of the file is as follows:

```
<config
  xmlns="urn:org:jgroups"
  xmlns:xsi="http://www.w3.org/2001/XMLSchema-instance"
  xsi:schemaLocation="urn:org:jgroups
  http://www.jgroups.org/schema/JGroups-2.8.xsd"
>
      <TCP singleton_name="liferay"
          bind_port="7800"
          loopback="true"
          recv_buf_size="${tcp.recv_buf_size:20M}"
          send_buf_size="${tcp.send_buf_size:640K}"
          discard_incompatible_packets="true"
          max_bundle_size="64K"
          max_bundle_timeout="30"
          enable_bundling="true"
          use_send_queues="true"
          sock_conn_timeout="300"
          timer.num_threads="4"
          thread_pool.enabled="true"
          thread_pool.min_threads="1"
          thread_pool.max_threads="10"
          thread_pool.keep_alive_time="5000"
          thread_pool.queue_enabled="false"
          thread_pool.queue_max_size="100"
          thread_pool.rejection_policy="discard"
          oob_thread_pool.enabled="true"
          oob_thread_pool.min_threads="1"
          oob_thread_pool.max_threads="8"
          oob_thread_pool.keep_alive_time="5000"
          oob_thread_pool.queue_enabled="false"
          oob_thread_pool.queue_max_size="100"
          oob_thread_pool.rejection_policy="discard"/>

    <TCPPING timeout="3000"
            initial_hosts="${jgroups.tcpping.initial_hosts:localhost[
7800],localhost[7801]}"
            port_range="1"
            num_initial_members="3"/>

    <MERGE2 min_interval="10000" max_interval="30000"/>
    <FD_SOCK/>
    <FD timeout="3000" max_tries="3" />
    <VERIFY_SUSPECT timeout="1500" />
    <BARRIER />
```

```
        <pbcast.NAKACK use_mcast_xmit="false" gc_lag="0"
        retransmit_timeout="300,600,1200,2400,4800"
        discard_delivered_msgs="true"/>
        <UNICAST timeout="300,600,1200" />
        <pbcast.STABLE stability_delay="1000"
        desired_avg_gossip="50000" max_bytes="400K"/>
        <pbcast.GMS print_local_addr="true" join_timeout="3000"
        view_bundling="true"/>
        <FC max_credits="2M" min_threshold="0.10"/>
        <FRAG2 frag_size="60K" />
        <pbcast.STREAMING_STATE_TRANSFER/>
        <!-- <pbcast.STATE_TRANSFER/> -->
    </config>
```

The last thing to enable communication is to tell `JGroups` about the available nodes (Liferay instances). Let's assume there are two nodes of Liferay with the following IP addresses:

- **node1** with 192.168.0.10 address
- **node2** with 192.168.0.11 address

In order to configure it, set the following `JAVA_OPTS` variable in your application server (for instance, at `${TOMCAT_HOME}/bin/setenv.sh`):

node1:

```
JAVA_OPTS="${JAVA_OPTS} -Djgroups.bind_addr=192.168.0.10"
JAVA_OPTS="${JAVA_OPTS} -Djgroups.tcpping.initial_hos
ts=192.168.0.10[7800],192.168.0.11[7800] "
```

node2:

```
JAVA_OPTS="${JAVA_OPTS} -Djgroups.bind_addr=192.168.0.11"
JAVA_OPTS="${JAVA_OPTS} -Djgroups.tcpping.initial_hos
ts=192.168.0.10[7800],192.168.0.11[7800] "
```

How it works...

In this recipe, we touched upon several subjects from database configuration to Ehcache replication. All of these steps are necessary to correctly run Liferay in a clustered environment. Liferay is a huge system with many dependencies, so it is quite difficult to install it in many server instances. We believe that our advice will help you configure and run Liferay CMS. Our intention was to introduce the possible ways of configuration. Every company has its own ideas and solutions to install Liferay. In our experience, here are some of the best configurations:

- Apache with the `mod_jk` module and load balancer as a reverse proxy
- Squid as a caching proxy
- GlusterFS as a shared filesystem where documents and media portlets keep their data
- The Solr server and Zookeeper as a search engine cloud
- The MySQL database with a master/slave configuration
- The EhCache replication via multicast (or unicast)

 If you need more detailed information, go to Liferay's official documentation at `https://dev.liferay.com/discover/deployment/-/knowledge_base/6-2/liferay-clustering`.

See also

In order to learn more about scalable infrastructure, refer to the following recipes:

- The *Scalable infrastructure* recipe from *Chapter 12, Basic Performance Tuning*
- The *Integration with the Amazon S3 cloud* and the *Data migration between storage hooks* recipes from *Chapter 6, Documents and Media in Liferay*

12
Basic Performance Tuning

In this chapter, we will cover the following topics:

- ▶ Scalable infrastructure
- ▶ Setting up database access for the master/slave configuration
- ▶ Enabling JS and CSS minification
- ▶ Turning on the CDN host
- ▶ Disabling unused Liferay features
- ▶ JVM tuning

Introduction

One of the most important aspects of successful project realization is system performance. Everybody knows that Web users often face a long wait when downloading web pages. What is the tolerable waiting time for web page download? In our opinion, a comfortable response time should be less than 2 seconds. If users have to wait more than 4 seconds, they usually go away. Performance issues is the most difficult subject in a big data portal or intranet. System architecture affects performance. Portals with a lot of images, movies, and audio should have a different architecture compared to intranets, as these portals have a lot of users who log in very often at the same time.

Fortunately, there are some general rules that help improve Liferay's performance:

▸ Scalable infrastructure with HTTP cache proxy

▸ Fast database

▸ Appropriate Java settings, such as garbage collector engine or memory settings

▸ Minimal number of included files, such as JS, CSS, images, and so on

▸ **Content distribution network** (**CDN**) for static resources

▸ Liferay Portal tuning, for instance, disabling unused filters, changing properties, and so on

Scalable infrastructure

Defining the architecture is the most important part of a successful installation. A good architecture should be fault-tolerant and have a high level of availability. To achieve this, it is necessary to cluster all the possible nodes, such as Tomcat nodes, search nodes, and so on. The second important thing is building a scalable infrastructure that lets us add new nodes.

How to do it...

In this recipe, we will try defining reference infrastructure, which can be used on production deployments. This type of infrastructure is used in our projects and works perfectly. The main parts of our environments are: squid cache, Apache servers with mod_jk module and software load balancers, Apache Tomcat Application Servers, Solr Cloud and Database server. The following image shows the most important parts:

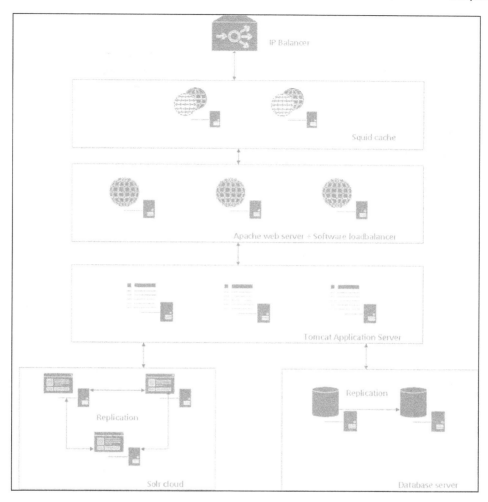

Squid cache

The first tier of our architecture is Squid cache (http://www.squid-cache.org/). It is a caching proxy for the Web. It supports HTTP, HTTPS, and other protocols. It reduces the number of requests, which go to another tier, especially to the Liferay instance. Squid cache reads HTTP headers and decides whether a specific request can be cached and how long they can be cached. This option can be used for content that doesn't change frequently, such as images, CSS, JS, and so on. This kind of solution gives a noticeable boost to our application.

Apache web server and software load balancer

The next tier has Apache web server instances with a load balancer software. Each instance of the Apache server is connected with all Liferay nodes. This connection is established by the `mod_jk Tomcat-Apache` plugin (`https://tomcat.apache.org/tomcat-3.3-doc/mod_jk-howto.html`). This plugin handles the communication between Tomcat and Apache using the AJP protocol. Every Apache server instance has a load balancer configuration. The most common load balancer configuration uses the `mod_jk` plugin. The configuration is placed in the `workers.properties` file in the `$APACHE_HOME/conf` directory. The following listing shows an example of the `mod_jk` and load balancer configuration:

```
worker.list=node1,node2,loadbalancer
worker.template.port=8009
worker.template.type=ajp13
worker.template.ping_mode=A
worker.template.reply_timeout=60000
worker.template.socket_connect_timeout=10000

worker.node1.reference=worker.template
worker.node1.host=<IP_ADDRESS>

worker.node2.reference=worker.template
worker.node2.host=<IP_ADDRESS>

worker.loadbalancer.type=lb
worker.loadbalancer.balance_workers=node1, node2
worker.loadbalancer.sticky_session=True
worker.loadbalancer.retries=1
```

The first line specifies a list of workers. In our example, there are three workers: `node1`, `node2`, and `loadbalancer`. Workers with names `node1` and `node2` describe connection with Liferay (host, port, and timeout definitions).

The bold definition describes the load balancer configuration. It contains a list of workers (the `worker.loadbalancer.balance_workers` property), and specifies the sticky session policy and the number of retries if a request fails. Load balancer can be configured with the following two modes:

▶ **Sticky session**: This distributes all the requests for a specific session to a specific Liferay Portal server node.

▶ **Session replication**: This provides a mechanism for session replication. From a business point of view, this is a great feature because it is failure-independent. If one of the nodes fail, load balancer decides to send the request to a different one. Users don't see any difference.

From the performance tuning point of view, the best option is sticky session, because it eliminates many requests compared to session replication. In other words, sticky session reduces traffic and saves resources.

Apache Tomcat Application Server

This tier is the heart of the application, because in this tier, the Tomcat container, with our Liferay Portal instance, is placed. In a clustered environment, it is important to properly configure Liferay Portal, because all the components must have a dedicated configuration, such as sharing documents and media files, configuring the same access to the database, and configuring cache and search index replication.

If we use the Apache `mod_jk` module, it is important to set the `jvmRoute` identifier in every Apache Tomcat instance. To do this, place the following configuration in `${TOMCAT_HOME}/conf/server.xml`:

```
<Engine name="Catalina" defaultHost="localhost" jvmRoute="node{X}">
```

To share documents and media files, we recommend that you use the glusterFS system (`http://www.gluster.org/`), which shares documents and files between nodes. There are different ways to configure documents and media working in a clustered environment, which we described in the previous chapter. We will describe other configurations in the upcoming recipes.

Database server

The database server tier is responsible for storing data on the database system. In a huge system, the database is usually one of the major bottlenecks, and database administrators often have a lot of problems with performance. In our projects, we generally use the MySQL database with master/slave configuration. The master database is responsible for writing, while the slave database is responsible for reading. Liferay provides out-of-the-box mechanisms that allow us to configure it. We will describe them in the upcoming recipes.

Solr search engine server

The last tier is an Apache Solr search engine server (`http://lucene.apache.org/solr/`). Solr is highly reliable, scalable, and fault-tolerant, providing distributed indexing, replication and load-balanced querying, automated failover and recovery, centralized configuration, and more. These things are possible to configure if we install Apache Zookeeper (`https://zookeeper.apache.org/`) and Apache Solr together. Zookeeper is a centralized service that maintains configuration information, naming, and provides distributed synchronization and group services, for instance, Apache Solr. Therefore, Apache Zookeeper can be installed as a cloud solution that can eliminate single point of failure. The Zookeeper server selects a Solr node, which is a master, and gives a token.

See also

For information on clustering and configuring the environment, refer to the following recipes:

- ▶ The *Integration with the Amazon S3 cloud* recipe from *Chapter 6, Documents and Media in Liferay*
- ▶ The *Solr installation and configuration* recipe from *Chapter 8, Search and Content Presentation Tools*
- ▶ The *Clustering Liferay Portal and the Configuring Liferay with the SMTP server* recipes from *Chapter 11, Quick Tricks and Advanced Knowledge*
- ▶ The *Setting up database access for the master/slave configuration* recipe from this chapter

Setting up database access for the master/slave configuration

Liferay allows us to configure two different data sources: first for writing and second for reading. This configuration, in an easy way, allows users to split writing and reading requests. This type of configuration lets us build scalable and high-performance infrastructure.

Getting ready...

As we mentioned at the beginning, we are focusing on Liferay configuration aspects. Our assumption is that you are ready to use database servers with master/slave replication. The MySql official documentation at `https://dev.mysql.com/doc/refman/5.1/en/replication-configuration.html` describes how to configure replication.

How to do it...

In order to achieve our goal, open `portal-ext.properties` and configure the following settings:

```
jdbc.write.driverClassName=com.mysql.jdbc.Driver
jdbc.write.url=jdbc:mysql://<DB_WRITE_ADDRESS>/lportal?useUnicode=true
&characterEncoding=UTF-8&useFastDateParsing=false
jdbc.write.username=<USERNAME>
jdbc.write.password=<PASSWORD>

jdbc.read.driverClassName=com.mysql.jdbc.Driver
jdbc.read.url=jdbc:mysql://<DB_READ_ADDRESS>/lportal?useUnicode=true&c
haracterEncoding=UTF-8&useFastDateParsing=false
jdbc.read.username=<USERNAME>
jdbc.read.password=<PASSWORD>
```

The next step is to enable the Spring configuration, which contains settings to read/write data sources. Add the following property into `portal-ext.properties`:

```
spring.configs=\
META-INF/base-spring.xml,\
META-INF/hibernate-spring.xml,\
META-INF/infrastructure-spring.xml,\
META-INF/management-spring.xml,\
META-INF/util-spring.xml,\
META-INF/editor-spring.xml,\
META-INF/jcr-spring.xml,\
META-INF/messaging-spring.xml,\
META-INF/scheduler-spring.xml,\
META-INF/search-spring.xml,\
META-INF/counter-spring.xml,\
META-INF/document-library-spring.xml,\
META-INF/lock-spring.xml,\
META-INF/mail-spring.xml,\
META-INF/portal-spring.xml,\
META-INF/portlet-container-spring.xml,\
META-INF/wsrp-spring.xml,\
META-INF/mirage-spring.xml,\
META-INF/dynamic-data-source-spring.xml,\
#META-INF/shard-data-source-spring.xml,\
META-INF/ext-spring.xml
```

At the end, restart your application server. Make sure that database replication works correctly.

How it works...

In our configuration, all write transactions will address the `jdbc.write.*` data source and read transactions will use the `jdbc.read.*` data source. In order to verify this configuration, follow these steps:

1. Shut down the master database instance (`jdbc.write`).
2. Run your Liferay instance.
3. Try to browse Liferay Portal and upload a new content, such as an article or file.
4. In the `catalina.out` log file, there should be an appropriate error message.

From a technical point of view, Liferay extends the `org.springframework.aop.TargetSource` Spring class, which can recognize whether the method contains a read or write operation. The rule is really simple: if a method on a service layer has the `@Transactional` annotation, then all queries go to the write data source. In other cases, queries go to the read data source.

There's more...

Some projects use Liferay with a lot of Portal instances. In this case, the term "Portal instances" means Liferay allows administrators to run more than one portal instance on a single server. Data for each portal instance can be kept separately from every other portal instance. This separation can be organized in the database tier. Each database node can store different types of data, depending on the portal instance. This separation is called database shard.

Portal instance configuration allows us to choose the shard in which data will be stored. A database shard is a horizontal partition of data in a database. Each shard is held on a separate database server instance to spread the load. To configure sharding in Liferay, follow this instruction:

1. In the `portal-ext.properties` file, specify an algorithm to select a new shard on portal instance creation. Use `ManualShardSelector` for shard selection via the web interface or round robin in other case. The round-robin algorithm evenly distributes the data between shards. A manual selector lets us assign each Liferay instance to the specific shard:

   ```
   shard.selector=com.liferay.portal.dao.shard.
   RoundRobinShardSelector
   #shard.selector=com.liferay.portal.dao.shard.ManualShardSelector
   ```

2. Next, set your shard data sources:

   ```
   jdbc.default.driverClassName=com.mysql.jdbc.Driver
   jdbc.default.url=jdbc:mysql://<SERVER1>/lportal?useUnicode=true&ch
   aracterEncoding=UTF-8&useFastDateParsing=false
   jdbc.default.username=<USERNAME>
   jdbc.default.password=<PASSWORD>

   jdbc.shard1.driverClassName=com.mysql.jdbc.Driver
   jdbc.shard1.url=jdbc:mysql://<SERVER2>/lportal1?useUnicode=true&ch
   aracterEncoding=UTF-8&useFastDateParsing=false
   jdbc.shard1.username=<USERNAME>
   jdbc.shard1.password=<PASSWORD>
   ```

```
jdbc.shard2.driverClassName=com.mysql.jdbc.Driver
jdbc.shard2.url=jdbc:mysql://<SERVER3>/lportal2?useUnicode=true&ch
aracterEncoding=UTF-8&useFastDateParsing=false
jdbc.shard2.username=<USERNAME>
jdbc.shard2.password=<PASSWORD>

shard.available.names=default,shard1,shard2
```

3. The last thing is the `spring.configs` configuration, which should look like this:

```
spring.configs=<DEFAULT_CONFIGURATION>,\
    META-INF/shard-data-source-spring.xml
```

The `<DEFAULT_CONFIGURATION>` placeholder keeps all the original `spring.configs` configurations, which are defined in the `portal.porperties` file.

Enabling JS and CSS minification

When your web page loads in a browser, the browser sends an HTTP request to the web server for the page in the URL. Then, as the HTML is delivered, the browser parses it and looks for additional requests for images, scripts, CSS, and so on. Every time it sees a request for a new element, it sends another HTTP request to the server. In order to decrease the number of additional requests, Liferay has the following ready-to-use mechanisms:

▸ Minifier (compressor) that allows you to compress and minify your JavaScript and CSS files

▸ Merging JavaScript files to reduce the number of HTTP requests using `barebone.jsp` and `everything.jsp`

▸ Merging CSS files and images for faster loading

▸ Enabling Gzip compression

How to do it...

To set Liferay's fast-load mechanisms, set the following properties in the `portal-ext.properties` file:

```
minifier.enabled=true
javascript.fast.load=true
theme.css.fast.load=true
theme.images.fast.load=true
layout.template.cache.enabled=true
```

Additionally, if you use custom scripts, add them to the `javascript.barebone.files` and `javascript.everything.files` properties in the `portal-ext.properties` file. The last step is enabling Gzip compression. It is possible to do this by turning on the following property:

```
com.liferay.portal.servlet.filters.gzip.GZipFilter=true
```

A better option is delegating this responsibility to Apache server, because it reduces the number of requests in the Apache Tomcat server. To enable Gzip compression on Apache server, open `${APACHE_HOME}/conf/httpd.conf` and add the following configuration:

```
SetOutputFilter DEFLATE
SetEnvIfNoCase Request_URI \.(?:exe|t?gz|zip|bz2|sit|rar)$ no-gzip
dont-vary
SetEnvIfNoCase Request_URI \.(?:gif|jpe?g|png)$ no-gzip dont-vary
```

Make sure that the `deflate` module is enabled. Look for the following line:

```
LoadModule deflate_module modules/mod_deflate.so
```

How it works...

In this recipe, we were concentrating on reducing the number of requests and decreasing the size of the response. Liferay combines JS files into one file and stores it in the application server's `temp` directory. On the page, the link to this file for unauthenticated users looks as follows:

```
<script src="/html/js/barebone.jsp?browserId=other&amp;themeId=cl
assic&amp;colorSchemeId=01&amp;minifierType=js&amp;minifierBundle
Id=javascript.barebone.files&amp;languageId=en_US&amp;b=6201&amp
;t=1414241572000" type="text/javascript"></script>
```

For authenticated users, it is very similar. Instead of `barebone.jsp`, there is the `everything.jsp` file.

If we dig deep inside the generated HTML source code, there are links to CSS files with the `minifierType=css` parameters. This parameter turns on file minification, which reduces the size of a file.

The last magic configuration is Gzip compression. If our browser sends a request with the `Accept-Encoding: gzip,deflate` header, our system returns Gzipped content. To test it, invoke the following command from your command line:

curl -I -H "Accept-Encoding: gzip,deflate" http://localhost:8080

In the response, there should be the `Content-Encoding: gzip` header.

Turning on the CDN host

In the previous recipe, you learned how to connect with minifying CSS and JS files and reduce the number of requests to the Liferay Portal. The next step in our configuration is reducing requests to the application server where Liferay is. The idea is that some static resources can be served by Apache server or, better, by Squid cache. Delivering static resources through the Apache server or Squid cache instead of the application server improves the response time.

Liferay supports CDN. Wikipedia defines this term as follows:

> *"A content delivery network or content distribution network (CDN) is a large distributed system of servers deployed in multiple data centers across the Internet. The goal of a CDN is to serve content to end-users with high availability and high performance."*

Getting ready...

Our idea is to use CDN domains to serve static resources and cache them in the Squid cache. The most difficult part is the Squid configuration, which caches all the static files coming from a CDN host. In this recipe, we will assume that this configuration is done, and we have a static domain for our resources, for example, `http://static.mysite.com`

How to do it...

CDN configuration is very simple in Liferay. There are only two properties, which should be set in the `portal-ext.properties`. These properties are as follows:

```
cdn.host.http=http://static.mysite.com
cdn.host.https=https://static.mysite.com
```

How it works...

After successful CDN configuration, all of the static resources are served from an external domain. When we look inside HTML sources, we see that all static resources, such as CSS files, JavaScript files, and images, come from a different domain that was defined in the `cdn.host.http` property.

In this recipe, we built our little CDN in which our Squid cache serves static resources.

In huge systems, when the intended users are spread across the globe, it is necessary to use real CDN hosts, which are large networks of servers deployed across the world. There are several companies that provide this type of service, such as Amazon, CloudFlare, Bootstrap CDN, CacheFly, OVH, and so on.

Disabling unused Liferay features

Everybody knows that Liferay is a big system with many functionalities. The main idea of this portal is: we give you all the features and you fit them to your needs. This topic can be divided into three parts: disabling unused servlet filters, disabling unused autologin hooks, and disabling unused features.

How to do it...

Disabling unused filters allows you to increase performance, but you have to know which filters can be disabled. It is a difficult subject for beginners. Unfortunately, we cannot give you a golden rule that covers your needs. We will only try to give some advice and information about filters that can be turned off in the `portal-ext.properties` files:

▶ If you don't use CAS authentication, disable the `com.liferay.portal.servlet.filters.sso.cas.CASFilter=false` filter

▶ If you use Gzip compression on Apache server, disable the `com.liferay.portal.servlet.filters.gzip.GZipFilter=false` filter

▶ If you don't use NTLM authentication, disable the: `com.liferay.portal.servlet.filters.sso.ntlm.NtlmFilter=false` and `com.liferay.portal.servlet.filters.sso.ntlm.NtlmPostFilter=false` filters

▶ If you don't use OpenSSO authentication, disable the `com.liferay.portal.servlet.filters.sso.opensso.OpenSSOFilter=false` filter

▶ If you don't use SharePoint, disable the `com.liferay.portal.sharepoint.SharepointFilter=false` filter

▶ If you use Tomcat server to remove blank lines and whitespaces from the outputted content, disable the `com.liferay.portal.servlet.filters.strip.StripFilter=false` filter

The next configuration is to connect with authentication systems. Liferay supports many single-sign-on systems, which are enabled by default. Remove unused `AutoLogin` hooks from the following property:

```
auto.login.hooks=com.liferay.portal.security.auth.CASAutoLogin, \
com.liferay.portal.security.auth.FacebookAutoLogin, \
com.liferay.portal.security.auth.NtlmAutoLogin, \
com.liferay.portal.security.auth.OpenIdAutoLogin, \
com.liferay.portal.security.auth.OpenSSOAutoLogin, \
com.liferay.portal.security.auth.RememberMeAutoLogin, \
com.liferay.portal.security.auth.SiteMinderAutoLogin
```

If you disable the `auto.login.hooks` definition, make sure that every autologin definition is also disabled under the properties with the `com.liferay.portal.servlet.filters.sso` prefix. For instance, if you disable `com.liferay.portal.security.auth.NtlmAutoLogin`, check whether `com.liferay.portal.servlet.filters.sso.ntlm.NtlmFilter` is set as `false`.

The last configuration disables some features that affect the performance:

- If you don't use user session tracker or this functionality is not required, disable the: `session.tracker.memory.enabled=false` property

- If you don't use the read count for document library files, disable the `dl.file.entry.read.count.enabled=false` property

- If you don't use file rank for document library files, disable the `dl.file.rank.enabled=false` property

- If you don't use the view counter for assets, disable the `asset.entry.increment.view.counter.enabled=false` property

- Disable pingbacks and trackbacks if you don't use them:

  ```
  blogs.pingback.enabled=false
  blogs.trackback.enabled=false
  message.boards.pingback.enabled=false
  ```

How it works...

Liferay gives users a file called `portal.properties` that can be overridden by the `portal-ext.properties` configuration file. The `portal.properties` file is located in the `portal-impl/src/` folder. This is the main tool to customize the Liferay Portal and disable unnecessary options. Every administrator and developer should study this file and try to fit portal to the project's requirements. It is hard work, because the configuration file has more than 10,000 lines. The good news is that every property has a comment.

JVM tuning

JVM tuning is an operation that should be done after performance tests or during production. JVM configuration affects the Java application's performance. There are two necessary configurations:

- Memory settings (such as heap configuration)
- Garbage collector settings

There are a lot of publications about JVM tuning. Thus, in this recipe, we will only mention the main aspects.

How to do it...

Every JVM setting can be set in `JAVA_OPTS` (Java Environment Options). A great place to do it is in the `${TOMCAT_HOME}/bin/setenv.sh` file.

First, let's set a proper garbage collector. The best option for portal systems is **Concurrent Collector** or **G1** (in Java 8). These garbage collectors perform most of their work concurrently with only a small period of stop-the-world time. These garbage collectors give the best performance. The typical setting is as follows:

```
JAVA_OPTS = "$JAVA_OPTS -XX:+UseParNewGC -XX:+UseConcMarkSweepGC
-XX+CMSParallelRemarkEnabled -XX:ParallelGCThreads=8
-XX:+CMSScavengeBeforeRemark
-XX:+CMSConcurrentMTEnabled -XX:ParallelCMSThreads=2"
```

The following settings are connected with memory allocation. It is very hard to estimate the correct configuration. Our experience shows that the best performance is when each node has equal to or more than 8 GB RAM. Our setting looks as follows:

```
JAVA_OPTS = "$JAVA_OPTS -server -d64 -XX:NewSize=1024m
-XX:MaxNewSize=1024m -Xms6144m -Xmx6144m -XX:PermSize=512m
-XX:MaxPermSize=512m -XX:SurvivorRatio=10"
```

 Every project has a different memory characteristic. The given JVM settings form the initial configuration and should be verified by your Java engineering team.

How it works...

We mentioned that the best garbage collector for portal solutions is Concurrent Collector or G1. Let's analyze each setting in our `JAVA_OPTS` variable:

- ► `+UseParNewGC`: This turns on the parallel young generation collector.

- ► `+UseConcMarkSweepGC`: This turns on concurrent mark-sweep collection for the old generation.

- ► `+CMSParallelRemarkEnabled`: This enables the garbage collector to use multiple threads during the CMS remark phase. This decreases the pauses during this phase.

- ► `ParallelGCThreads`: The number of threads used during parallel phases of the garbage collectors. It shouldn't be more than the number of cores (processors) on the server.

- ► `+CMSScavengeBeforeRemark`: This forces young space collection before CMS remark.

- ► `+CMSConcurrentMTEnabled`: This allows CMS to use multiple cores for concurrent phases.

- ► `ParallelCMSThreads`: This controls the number of threads used for the CMS (concurrent mark and sweep) garbage collector.

Index

E

Eclipse IDE
custom portlet, importing 18
sources, importing 12
e-mail notifications
setting 26-30
empty site
creating 83
Enterprise Content Management (ECM) 136

F

fields, template
$field.getChildren() 160
$field.getName() 160
$field.getType() 160
about 160
files
managing, Documents and Media portlet
used 120
fork-join workflow
fork element 196
join element 196
used, for web content creation 193-195
forum
setting up, for intranet 210-213

G

G1 268
garbage collector
setting 269
GitHub 11
GlusterFS
URL 259
using 259
group messaging
with announcements portlet 222-226
guests 81

I

inactive site 81
intranet
blog, setting up 204-207
forum, setting up 210-213

protecting, with antisamy-hook
plugin 236-238

J

Java Content Repository (JCR) 248
Java Development Kit (JDK) 12
**Java in Administration Special Interest
Group (JASIG) 38**
**Java Naming and Directory Interface
(JNDI) 235**
Java Portlet Specification 2.0 (JSR 286) 112
Java Specification Requests (JSRs) 1
JetS3t
URL 137
join-xor element
about 196
defining 196
journal structure 156
JS minification
enabling 263, 264
JVM
tuning 269

K

Kaleo workflow
about 186
conditions 197
installing 186-188
timers 200

L

language properties hook
about 230
implementing 230-233
possible values 232
LDAP
integrating, with Liferay 47-49
integrating, with Liferay and CAS 50-55
Liferay
about 1
additional information 128
autodeploy scanner, starting 6
categories 127
configuration descriptor, loading 4

SMTP server
  Liferay, configuring 234-236
social activities
  tracking, of site members 221, 222
software load balancer 258, 259
Solr search engine server
  about 259
  URL 259
sourceforge.net 11
Squid cache
  about 257
  URL 257
staging 99
standalone site
  creating 78-81
Storage Area Network (SAN) 248
storage hooks
  data, migrating between 139
storage implementation
  AdvancedFileSystemStore 136
  CMISStore 136
  DBStore 136
  FileSystemStore 136
  JCRStore 136
  S3Store 136
structure
  about 153
  creating 153-156
  default values, setting 156
  predefined types 154, 155

T

tags
  about 164
  assigning 169
  creating 167, 168
  defining 168
  managing 170
template
  about 157
  creating 157-159
  fields 160
  reserved variables 161
  utils 161
  variables 159

timers, Kaleo workflow
  about 200
  adding 200, 201
Tomcat bundle
  Liferay, running 3, 4
translations
  about
  URL 231

U

unused Liferay features
  disabling 266, 267
user
  activating 71
  adding 66-69
  adding, as member of organizations 69
  adding, as member of sites 69
  adding, as member of user groups 69
  assigning, to organization 72, 73
  assigning, to user group 74, 75
  attributes, setting 69, 70
  banning, for inappropriate post 214, 215
  customizing 70, 71
  deactivating 71
  exporting 75, 76
  impersonating 71
  roles, assigning 110, 111
  sites, managing 70
user group
  creating 64, 65
  modifying 65, 66
  user, assigning 74, 75
utils, template 161

V

variables, template
  $company 159
  $companyId 159
  $device 160
  $groupId 160
  $viewMode 160
  about 159, 160

W

Thank you for buying
Liferay 6.x Portal Enterprise Intranets Cookbook

About Packt Publishing

Packt, pronounced 'packed', published its first book, *Mastering phpMyAdmin for Effective MySQL Management*, in April 2004, and subsequently continued to specialize in publishing highly focused books on specific technologies and solutions.

Our books and publications share the experiences of your fellow IT professionals in adapting and customizing today's systems, applications, and frameworks. Our solution-based books give you the knowledge and power to customize the software and technologies you're using to get the job done. Packt books are more specific and less general than the IT books you have seen in the past. Our unique business model allows us to bring you more focused information, giving you more of what you need to know, and less of what you don't.

Packt is a modern yet unique publishing company that focuses on producing quality, cutting-edge books for communities of developers, administrators, and newbies alike. For more information, please visit our website at www.packtpub.com.

About Packt Open Source

In 2010, Packt launched two new brands, Packt Open Source and Packt Enterprise, in order to continue its focus on specialization. This book is part of the Packt open source brand, home to books published on software built around open source licenses, and offering information to anybody from advanced developers to budding web designers. The Open Source brand also runs Packt's open source Royalty Scheme, by which Packt gives a royalty to each open source project about whose software a book is sold.

Writing for Packt

We welcome all inquiries from people who are interested in authoring. Book proposals should be sent to author@packtpub.com. If your book idea is still at an early stage and you would like to discuss it first before writing a formal book proposal, then please contact us; one of our commissioning editors will get in touch with you.

We're not just looking for published authors; if you have strong technical skills but no writing experience, our experienced editors can help you develop a writing career, or simply get some additional reward for your expertise.

open source
community experience distilled

Liferay Portal Performance Best Practices

ISBN: 978-1-78216-368-8   Paperback: 150 pages

A practical tutorial to learn the best practices for building high performing Liferay-based solutions

1. Learn best practices for architecting high performing Liferay- based solutions.

2. Practices for configuring a load balancer and cluster of Liferay portal.

3. Find out how to perform load testing and performance tuning activity for Liferay- based solutions.

Liferay Portal Systems Development

ISBN: 978-1-84951-598-6   Paperback: 546 pages

Build dynamic, content-rich, and social systems on top of Liferay

1. Use Liferay tools (CMS, WCM, collaborative API and social API) to create your own Web sites and WAP sites with hands-on examples.

2. Customize Liferay portal using JSR-286 portlets, hooks, themes, layout templates, webs plugins, and diverse portlet bridges.

3. Build your own websites with kernel features such as indexing, workflow, staging, scheduling, messaging, polling, tracking, auditing, reporting and more.

Please check **www.PacktPub.com** for information on our titles

[PACKT] open source ✻
PUBLISHING   community experience distilled

Instant Liferay Portal 6 Starter

ISBN: 978-1-78216-966-6   Paperback: 54 pages

Create your portal with Liferay and learn its concepts on the go!

1. Learn something new in an Instant! A short, fast, focused guide delivering immediate results.

2. Get acquainted with Liferay's interface.

3. Learn the core concepts and terms of Liferay.

4. Create and manage content and learn to apply workflow to it.

Liferay 6.2 User Interface Development

ISBN: 978-1-78216-234-6   Paperback: 356 pages

A comprehensive guide to user interface development with Liferay Portal

1. Create eye-catching themes, develop responsive layouts, and write portlets with various technologies that ensure efficiency and performance.

2. Showcase the latest features in the user interface of Liferay 6.2 and provide solutions to real problems on recent projects.

3. Implement Alloy User Interface to achieve the best page appearance and generate reports.

Please check **www.PacktPub.com** for information on our titles

www.ingramcontent.com/pod-product-compliance
Lightning Source LLC
Chambersburg PA
CBHW060516060326
40690CB00017B/3301